Baseball at the Abyss

Baseball at the Abyss

The Scandals of 1926, Babe Ruth, and the Unlikely Savior Who Rescued a Tarnished Game

Dan Taylor

ROWMAN & LITTLEFIELD
Lanham · Boulder · New York · London

Published by Rowman & Littlefield
An imprint of The Rowman & Littlefield Publishing Group, Inc.
4501 Forbes Boulevard, Suite 200, Lanham, Maryland 20706
www.rowman.com

86-90 Paul Street, London EC2A 4NE, United Kingdom

British Library Cataloguing in Publication Information Available

Library of Congress Cataloging-in-Publication Data
Names: Taylor, Dan, 1957– author.
Title: Baseball at the abyss : the scandals of 1926, Babe Ruth, and the
    unlikely savior who rescued a tarnished game / Dan Taylor.
Description: Lanham, Maryland : Rowman & Littlefield, 2023. | Includes
    bibliographical references. | Summary: "Baseball at the Abyss is the
    story of one of baseball's darkest days and how innovative,
    behind-the-scenes work of the first-ever player agent pushed the game's
    greatest player to a history making season, one which rescued a
    tarnished game"— Provided by publisher.
Identifiers: LCCN 2022039756 (print) | LCCN 2022039757 (ebook) | ISBN
    9781538174005 (cloth) | ISBN 9781538174012 (epub)
Subjects: LCSH: Baseball—United States—History—20th century. |
    Baseball—Corrupt practices—United States—History—20th century. |
    Ruth, Babe, 1895–1948. | Walsh, Christy, 1891–1955.
Classification: LCC GV863.A1 T38 2023 (print) | LCC GV863.A1 (ebook) |
    DDC 796.3570973/0904—dc23/eng/20220922
LC record available at https://lccn.loc.gov/2022039756
LC ebook record available at https://lccn.loc.gov/2022039757

Contents

Acknowledgments

My sincere thanks to the team at Rowman & Littlefield, specifically, Christen Karniski, Samantha Delwarte, Susan Hershberg, and David Bailey for their assistance.

Resources utilized include Baseball-Reference.com, the National Baseball Hall of Fame Giamatti Research Center, *The Sporting News*, *Los Angeles Times*, Los Angeles Public Library, Margaret Herrick Library, *New York Daily News*, Newspapers.com, Society for American Baseball Research, Retrosheet.org, and *Variety*.

Every project is a product of inspiration, motivation, education, and perspiration. That came in big quantities from Artie Harris, Don Barone, Cassidy Lent, Gary Mintz, Genevieve Maxwell, John Van Ornum, Michelle Victoria Asci, Robert Walsh, Steve Menchinella, Terri Garst, and Woody Wilk, to whom I am grateful.

Most of all, my deepest thanks to my wife, Eve, for your steadfast support, meticulous assistance, and inspiring enthusiasm. Thank you.

Introduction

It began as a buzz rippling through the crowd of more than fifty-seven thousand, initiated mere seconds after Mark Koenig's mighty swing missed the pitch and "Red" Ormsby, the home-plate umpire, bellowed "strike three." As the large figure stepped away from the on-deck circle, the buzz of anticipation erupted into cheers of expectation. With each step the next batter made toward home plate, shouts of encouragement were barked from men in coats and ties, their heads topped by fedoras, Panamas, or bowlers. They hollered at the top of their lungs, regardless of whether they were five hundred feet away in the packed bleachers or within earshot in the three decks of chairback seats in Yankee Stadium.

Cloudy skies that dumped morning rain couldn't put a damper on the exuberance that permeated the large ballpark.[1] The anxiousness that rattled within fans from Pittsburgh paled against the animated behavior of confident, if not cocky, New Yorkers. The massive scoreboard that towered above the bleachers in right center field bared the reason for the conflicting emotions. In the score column were the numbers 1–1. This was not just a tie-ball game in the bottom of the fifth inning, nor could this be called an ordinary game. What made the moment all the more gripping was that baseball's ultimate prize was on the line. It was Game Four of the 1927 World Series. The heightened noise level throughout this massive venue was not sparked by just the situation in the game. Rather, it had much more to do with the batter about to step into the batter's box, the greatest hitter in the game, Babe Ruth.

High above, in front of the second deck of stands and in an overflow area nearby, more than four hundred members of the press sat poised to chronicle a moment of history. Of this horde, ten worked under the direction of Christy Walsh, a man whose newspaper syndication service helped to enhance Babe

Ruth's reputation as the most popular man in America. Walsh's management skills also harvested riches for the slugger and, in doing so, chiseled severe tarnish from the game of baseball.

Hope, the normal reaction of fans in such situations, had been replaced during the summer of 1927 by expectation. The heightened confidence came from an entirely different Babe Ruth, a rejuvenated Ruth. He had acceded the pleadings of his business manager, curtailed his usual vices, embraced fitness training like no ballplayer ever had before, and from it produced a season like none previously recorded in the annals of the game—60 home runs, a record, 165 runs batted in, and a batting average of .356, the fifth-highest figure in the American League.

Fueled in part by Ruth, the New York Yankees razed all rivals in a record-setting summer romp that saw them win 110 games, more than any American League team had before. So powerful was this Yankees team that they sucked the life out of the pennant race by the Fourth of July, much to the detriment of attendance around the league. That the Yankees won the pennant by a staggering 19 games over Connie Mack's star-studded cast of Philadelphia Athletics was shocking to many observers. The team's accomplishments and the ease with which the Yankees blitzed through the first three games of the World Series made sportswriters and many in the game boast that this was undeniably the greatest team in baseball history.

As the Yankee Stadium crowd stirred, Pittsburgh Pirates pitcher Carmen "Bunker" Hill wiped perspiration from his glasses, and Ruth groomed the dirt in the batter's box with the metal spikes of his jet-black baseball shoes. His dark-brown bat rested upon his left shoulder. Ruth swung a heavy bat, one of the heaviest in the game, a Louisville Slugger model that measured thirty-five and three-quarters inches in length and weighed thirty-eight ounces. Once he assumed his batting stance, Ruth positioned his body at a 120-degree angle. To the fans seated behind third base with a straight-on view, Ruth's feet appeared pigeon-toed. He twisted his torso ever so slightly toward the catcher while peering over his right shoulder toward a spot where he expected the baseball would emerge from the Pittsburgh pitcher's right hand.[2]

Earle Combs represented the potential go-ahead run on first base. He had dumped a single into short center field to open the Yankees' half of the inning prior to Koenig's strike out. As Hill prepared to pitch to Ruth, Combs took four and then five steps off the bag. The Yankee base runner could hear the encouraging chatter from his teammates in the dugout. From his crouch behind home plate, Earl Smith, the Pirates' catcher, extended his right index finger in the signal to his pitcher to throw a fastball. Every pitcher and catcher in the game knew Ruth went to the plate looking for the fastball. He feasted on the pitch. The harder thrown, the better, as men like Walter Johnson and

Lefty Grove, pitchers able to throw a fastball well over ninety miles an hour experienced in their career. Hill's was a good fastball; nothing, however, was comparable to Johnson's or Grove's. He wasn't about to challenge Ruth but hoped to tempt the slugger, to test his anxiousness by throwing a fastball an inch or so outside. When the baseball streaked toward home plate, then popped loudly into Smith's padded mitt, the pitcher's and catcher's strategy had failed. Ruth resisted and Ormsby called the pitch a ball.

The faces around Yankee Stadium reflected the intense interest in the game from all levels of society. Being a Saturday afternoon, working men flocked there. Laborers sat alongside executives. Celebrities dotted the box seats. The numbers who poured through the turnstiles were akin to the crowds that greeted the Yankees throughout the summer, be they in Detroit or St. Louis, Chicago, Philadelphia, Cleveland, Washington, DC, or Boston. So riveting was Ruth's pursuit of the single-season-home-run record that every American League club enjoyed its finest attendance whenever the Yankees came to town. Four of the biggest turnouts in all of baseball in 1927 were, in fact, recorded in the Yankees' own park—seventy-two thousand on Opening Day and again on the Fourth of July, and crowds that topped sixty thousand were tallied on two other occasions.

Large crowds, enthusiasm over the record pursuit, and accompanying favorable headlines in newspapers all across the country were a reassuring sight for the game's commissioner. From his front-row box, Kenesaw Mountain Landis was a mixture of emotions. Just as he could calmly enjoy the action one minute, the next, he would angrily wave photographers away, while later, a cigarette still hanging from the right side of his mouth would reveal the nervousness churning inside. Landis had seen baseball enter spring training smeared by scandal—two of its most popular players accused of fixing games and two managers charged with gambling on games. The scandal wrought damning off-season publicity. Baseball's integrity was roundly impugned. Columnists proclaimed the once-proud game now hovered about with professional wrestling and horse racing, its outcomes open to question and mired in suspicion. That was before a new Babe Ruth, a revived Babe Ruth—a Babe Ruth who, made by his business manager, Christy Walsh, to take the game more seriously than ever before, began a record-setting assault on American League pitching, one that riveted an entire nation.

Just as American League pitchers knew Babe Ruth loved to hit a fastball, the more experienced, more intelligent pitchers in the game knew full well slow pitches were his Achilles' heel. During the 1926 World Series, the Cardinals' Grover Cleveland Alexander boasted of facing Ruth: "He will get them only around the knees and he will get screwballs and slow curves."[3]

Carmen Hill possessed an excellent curveball and evoked loud groans from the large Yankee Stadium crowd when he induced Ruth to swing and miss one for strike one.

The Yankees' sensation assumed his batting stance once again. Buoyed by the success of his curveball, Hill decided he would tempt Ruth with another. Only this time, he would throw it with slightly less effort to decrease its speed. Once the pitch left Hill's hand, Ruth lifted his right heel off the ground. He recognized the spin as that of a curveball, slow at that. Ruth raised his bent right knee and synchronously twisted his hips ever so slightly to the left. As the pitch drew near, the slugger dipped the head of his bat four inches, flicked his wrists to bring the bat forward, then began a swift, violent swing.[4] The curveball broke inward toward the left-handed-batting Ruth. It traveled waist high and caught the bat two inches above his hands. On contact, frustration struck Hill, who would call the pitch "a real pooper."[5] Instantly, the ball shot high into the air, and a mighty roar went up from the crowd.[6]

Major J. Andrew White, describing the game over the CBS radio network, told of the ball's flight and its landing in the bleachers in right center field. The scoreboard operator was put to work and changed the numbers on the board to reflect a 3–1 Yankees lead.

Yankee Stadium became awash in delirium. Exaltation from the stands, as opposed to moisture from clouds overhead, rained on Ruth as he trotted from base to base.[7] At that moment in time, the record-setting slugger was not only the focal point of thousands in Yankee Stadium but also millions more who listened by radio or watched special game-tracking boards set up outside newspaper buildings, in garages, and restaurants in both the major metropolises and small burghs. At that very moment, nothing anywhere in America held more interest.

As he completed circling the bases and then touched home plate, Ruth's Bunyanesque power hitting had the Yankees on the threshold of a World Series title. But far more important was not just what it had done for the Yankees but the game of baseball. By captivating Americans throughout the summer of 1927, Babe Ruth wiped away the cynicism from the winter scandal. His astounding record chase engendered new fans and ignited passion anew among old. More importantly, Babe Ruth lifted baseball from the smoldering ashes of controversy and placed the game back onto its rightful throne as America's favored sport.

Ruth's unmatched achievements during the summer of 1927 were the product of a transformative journey, one that turned animus to awe and put to rest suggestions that he was washed up and his own worst enemy. He traversed an improbable path, prodded by an unlikely initiator, an unrelenting man who instigated with kick, cajole, and a bit of deception. The seeds for Ruth's remarkable productivity and, with it, the resuscitation of baseball were planted in the most implausible of settings—not in any ballpark nor any of the resort spas where ballplayers often prepared for a season. It was on the set of a Hollywood movie where baseball began its improbable recovery from a winter at the abyss.

Sour Grape Grower

The loud barks from a German shepherd resonated about the farm. It always did whenever a vehicle turned from Ventura Boulevard onto Leonard Road to enter one of the largest farms in Central California. Enormous in mass and situated sixteen miles east of Fresno, Leonard Brothers Farm featured seemingly endless rows of grapevines. A small army of men bustled to myriad tasks associated with the operation of what was not just the largest farm in the area but one with the region's biggest packing house, storage facility, and shipping operation. The vast farm's expanse and the concentration commanded by its associated duties made warning of an approaching visitor either by the sound of a dog's bark or sight of dust kicked up by vehicle tires invaluable.

As the Ford convertible sped past the workers, the passenger's head of shaggy white hair announced who had come to visit. The men now realized the guest their boss sped off to collect from the 11:30 a.m. train at the Sanger Railroad Depot was none other than the most powerful man in baseball, the game's commissioner, Kenesaw Mountain Landis.

Only a day earlier, Landis caused genuine surprise when he withdrew from a Los Angeles golf tournament after just one round of play. He satisfied inquisitive sportswriters with the explanation he was headed north to Fresno to "rest and see a whole lot of scenery."[1] To persistent questions, Landis added he was off to visit his "good friend, 'Dutch' Leonard."[2] However, his assertion that baseball business was not part of his itinerary was far from the truth. Actually, it had everything to do with the purpose of the commissioner's trip. Landis was fighting to keep under wraps the possibility baseball might be on the precipice of scandal—a damning one that involved some of the biggest names in the game. The key evidence, Landis had been told, was held by

Dutch Leonard. It was a piece of evidence Landis was keen to see with his own eyes.

Beneath a warm, late-October sun, Landis and his host toured the vast farming operation. Eighty-six-degree weather brought beads of sweat to the commissioner's brow, which he occasionally dabbed with a handkerchief. The men traversed the rows of grapevines, though not comfortably in Landis's case. His feet were badly blistered from wearing golf shoes that were the wrong size. His own had been stolen the night before the tournament teed off in Los Angeles.

The expansive agricultural holdings, palatial home, and significant wealth of Landis's host represented the spoils of a teenaged decision to diverge from family pursuits. Hubert Benjamin Leonard had been known to one and all as Dutch since childhood. He was pinned with the nickname not because he was, but because someone felt his appearance looked as one from the Netherlands would. Music permeated the Leonard household during the boy's youth. David Leonard, the patriarch, played clarinet and led a brass band. His wife, Ella, was melodious on the piano and played the organ in church. Each of David and Ella Leonard's six children took up an instrument and achieved different levels of proficiency. At one extreme was Cuyler, who received acclaim for the performances of his thirty-two-piece band and solos on the cornet. Then there was Dutch, who hammered away at the drums in amateurish fashion.

It was in 1910, while attending Fresno High School, that Dutch Leonard was made to realize he could pitch a baseball like nobody in these parts ever had before. From that point on, said his mother, "it was play all the time."[3]

Out of Dutch Leonard's left arm and hand shot lightning bolts. With a flick of the wrist and fingers, he could unleash a ball that would bend with devastating effect, a pitch that humiliated older, more experienced players and drove admiring fans to call it the "raisin wiggle."[4] Equally effective was a slow ball Leonard liked to call the "dipsey dew."

In 1913 Leonard joined the Boston Red Sox and one year later was, according to the *Boston Globe*, "the pitching sensation of the year."[5] During the summer of 1914, Dutch Leonard would compile one of the greatest seasons by a pitcher in the history of the game. In the 224 innings he pitched, Leonard allowed a paltry thirty-four runs. He pitched seven shutouts and his earned run average was a measly 0.96, the second lowest ever and would remain such for more than a century. He won nineteen games but would have likely won more had he not broken a bone in his wrist in a bout of locker-room horseplay. With his hand and wrist in a splint and his left arm in a sling, Leonard was unable to pitch for the final six weeks of the season.

In 1915 and again in 1916, Leonard teamed with Ernie Shore, Rube Foster, "Smoky" Joe Wood, and a fellow lefthander, Babe Ruth, to pitch the Red Sox to back-to-back World Series championships. Winning two World Series brought a handsome supplement to Leonard's baseball salary. Each championship saw the twenty-five Red Sox players divvy up $100,000. Back

Figure 1.1 During the seasons he spent with the Boston Red Sox, Dutch Leonard was among the premier pitchers in the American League. *Source: Courtesy of the author.*

home in Fresno, a banker advised Leonard to invest his earnings. Buying farmland was his recommendation. The land, the banker felt, would grow exponentially in value. Leonard identified an area of fertile land southeast of Fresno near a small town, Sanger. An initial purchase of 80 acres grew a year later by 200 more. Over time Leonard's land holdings swelled with regular purchases until his farm numbered 2,500 acres.

Leonard planted hundreds of acres of grapes and reaped a bounty from it. His first crop alone, from the initial 200 acres he planted, brought $8,000 and grew significantly in subsequent years. Leonard married a vaudeville showgirl, Muriel Worth. He built a lavish home on his property, one replete with a rarity for the day: a large swimming pool. The extravagance brought ballplayers and entertainers from miles around to visit the couple and enjoy their hospitality.

In his spare time, Leonard became an accomplished golfer. Without the benefit of formal lessons, he regularly carded scores in the 70s. He played recreational rounds with Walter Hagen, the PGA champion, and the celebrated sportswriter Grantland Rice. Leonard won tournaments and long-drive competitions up and down the state and was champion of his home course, Sunnyside Country Club in Fresno.

The accomplished and enterprising Dutch Leonard was also both prin-cipled and headstrong, mindful yet vengeful. He refused to be taken ad-vantage of and stood up to anybody who tried. Leonard was stubborn with an obstinate streak. He could threaten to stop picking his grapes unless he received a hike from $1.25 to $2 per lug or fly off the handle, punch an employee, and find himself in court on an assault charge.

Twice Leonard's obstinacy impacted his baseball career. The first was during the winter of 1919, when he demanded a pay raise. As happened in previous years with Tris Speaker, Carl Mays, "Smokey" Joe Wood, and later Babe Ruth, the Red Sox owner Harry Frazee refused such demands. As he had with the aforementioned, Frazee got rid of Leonard. At the urging of the team's player-manager Ty Cobb, Leonard wound up with the Detroit Tigers.

After his third season with the Tigers, Leonard again requested a raise. Frank Navin, the Tigers' owner, turned him down. Leonard retreated to his farm and vowed not to play until his demand was met. When sportswriters called it a holdout, Leonard corrected them, clarifying that "I simply quit."[6]

Reporters warned Navin in print that a spat with Leonard would not be a typical salary fight. A couple of missed paychecks would not make Leonard acquiesce as it might for most any other player. By the winter of 1921–1922, farming had made Dutch Leonard wealthy. In fact, most considered the pitcher and his team's manager, Ty Cobb, to be the wealthiest players in the game.

Navin, however, was shrewd. He first threatened to put Leonard on the retired list, to no avail. Then when he learned Leonard was pitching for semipro teams in the Fresno area, he appealed to the commissioner. Kenesaw Mountain Landis suspended Leonard from baseball for three years for violating the reserve clause of his contract, which bound the pitcher exclusively to the Tigers.

It was during the dog days of summer in 1924 when Ty Cobb's previously moribund Tigers awakened. Buoyed by an eight-game-win streak and eleven wins in thirteen games, the Tigers vaulted into the thick of the pennant race. With a win on July 22, they leapfrogged the mighty New York Yankees into first place in the American League.

Cobb knew the Tigers needed additional pitching if they were to win the pennant. The player-manager urged both Navin and Leonard to resolve their differences. Once they did and Leonard met face-to-face with Landis and Ban Johnson, president of the American League, he was reinstated to baseball and returned to the Tigers.

On August 24, Leonard pitched the Tigers to a 7–2 triumph over the Yankees. The only blemish to Leonard's performance was a two-run home run in the first inning, whacked by his old Boston teammate, Babe Ruth. Otherwise, Leonard held the Yankees scoreless the rest of the game. Upon rejoining the team, Leonard said he hoped to win five games and help the ball club reach the World Series. In the end he won three, but Detroit faded and wound up in third place.

During the first half of the 1925 season, Dutch Leonard looked like his old dominant self. He was the Tigers' Opening-Day pitcher, an assignment usually reserved for a team's best pitcher. By June, Leonard had won six of seven decisions and showed, in the words of one sportswriter, "much of his old time cunning."[7] He won his eleventh on July 9 and resumed his place among the best pitchers in the American League. But Dutch Leonard would never win another game in the major leagues.

A week later, in a loss to the Philadelphia Athletics, a sportswriter noted, "There was something radically wrong with Leonard."[8] Philadelphia scored nine runs in six of the first seven innings. "Outfielders could not have run more had they been training for a marathon," typed one sportswriter. From the press box, men were flummoxed, "Manager Cobb showed no symptoms of desiring to relieve him."[9] In all, Leonard surrendered a dozen runs. Detroit lost, 12–4.

In his next start, Leonard was removed by Cobb after five innings. He had given up seven hits and walked four. Worse, he told Cobb his arm had gone dead. While the team moved on to Washington, DC, for a series with the Senators, Leonard traveled back to Detroit. A specialist prescribed rest, and for two weeks, the pitcher did not so much as pick up a baseball. The two-week rest became a month and then six weeks. Sportswriters pressed for information. Leonard blamed it on the new, livelier baseball the game had adopted. "You pitch hard to every man every inning for a full nine innings. It's a strain," he explained.[10] Actually, his injury was much more than a strain. The specialist employed to treat Leonard told Cobb and Navin that Leonard would likely never pitch again.

With two weeks remaining in the 1925 season, the Tigers saw the chance to gain a better third baseman. The player they wanted was in the minor leagues, in the Pacific Coast League with the Vernon Tigers. Jack Warner, they learned, could be acquired in a trade. To get Warner, Detroit sent five players to Vernon. Among them was Dutch Leonard. When Leonard learned of the trade, he retired from baseball. His new team tried to convince him to continue pitching. Leonard, though, submitted the required paperwork to be placed on baseball's voluntary retired list.

In the year that followed his departure from baseball, many of Leonard's friends from the game as well as his wife's friends from the vaudeville circuit visited their Central California farm. Some came simply to visit and relax, others to enjoy their pool, while a few joined Dutch for a round of golf. It was in a conversation with one—Tigers outfielder Harry Heilmann—that Leonard made known he possessed potentially incendiary information. They were letters he had kept stuffed in a drawer for seven years. In them were damning revelations—tangible proof that two of the biggest names in baseball, Ty Cobb and Cleveland's player-manager, Tris Speaker, had fixed games, then bet on them.

Heilmann was stunned. "You are to bring that story before [Detroit Tigers owner] Frank Navin not later than ten o'clock tomorrow morning. I'd advise you to do this because I will be there at 10:10 and what he doesn't know at that time, he will know in five minutes."[11]

Muriel Leonard pleaded with her husband not to turn over the letters. She feared the consequences: retribution from Cobb and Speaker, being shunned by friends, and being made outcasts by baseball itself. Dutch Leonard was well aware of his predicament. Ty Cobb was an icon. He was as irascible as a person as he was both talented and tenacious as a ballplayer. For the first fifteen seasons of his career and before Babe Ruth erupted into a full-fledged home-run-bashing phenomenon, Ty Cobb was unquestionably the best and most popular player in the game.

From his rookie year in 1905 through the 1926 season, Cobb won the American League batting title twelve times. Nine of them were won consecutively. Tris Speaker beat him out in 1916, before Cobb won three more in a row. Three times—in 1911, 1912, and again in 1922—Cobb compiled a batting average higher than .400. Sportswriters opined that prior to the emergence of Ruth, the most popular players in the game were Cobb and Speaker. Now, Dutch Leonard was faced with revealing information that would impugn both men personally and professionally.

Within days of his conversation with Heilmann, Leonard traveled to Detroit, where he handed over the two letters in question to Frank Navin. The Tigers' owner, in turn, passed them on to Ban Johnson, president of the American League, who ultimately made Landis aware of them. Landis was keen to know more. He invited Leonard to come to his office in Chicago but was rebuffed. It was harvest season, and the farmer had grapes to pick. Then following the harvest, grapes intended as raisins had to be laid out to dry while the weather was still warm and before fall rain came. If Leonard wouldn't travel to Landis, the commissioner agreed he would travel to Leonard instead.

After their tour of the farm and midday meal, Landis and Leonard sat down to discuss what brought the baseball commissioner to this rural area of Central California. Leonard had copies of each of the letters he had turned over to Navin. He gave them to Landis. One was from Cobb, sent to Leonard on October 23, 1919. In it, Cobb wrote:

> Wood and myself were considerably disappointed in our business as we had $2,000 to put into it and the other side quoted us $1,400, and when we finally secured that much money it was about two o'clock and they refused to deal with us as they had men in Chicago to take up the matter with and they had no time so we completely fell down and of course we felt badly over it.[12]

Cobb's writing carefully avoided any reference to the outcome of a game or games and wagering that took place. Leonard, however, explained that what Cobb had referred to was a two-game series between Detroit and Cleveland in the final days of the 1919 season. In the first game of the series, Leonard pitched the Tigers to a 4–1 win over the Indians. The victory helped Detroit jump the New York Yankees into third place. After the game, Leonard, Cobb, Tris Speaker, and "Smokey" Joe Wood happened to meet under the stands. The Detroit players told of being keen to lock up third place and the extra money that came with it. According to Leonard, Speaker said, "Don't worry about tomorrow's game. We have got second place cinched and you will win tomorrow."[13] Leonard said Speaker (Cleveland's player-manager) added that he would go in and pitch himself if he had to. It was then the four agreed that since the outcome was prearranged, they ought to place bets on the game.

The second letter was from Wood, who had been Leonard's roommate with the Boston Red Sox before he joined Cleveland:

Dear Friend Dutch

Enclosed please find certified check for sixteen hundred and thirty dollars ($1,630.00).

The only bet West could get down was $600 against $420 (10 to 7). Cobb did not get up a cent. He told us that and I believed him. Could have put up some at 5 to 2 on Detroit but did not as that would make us put up $1,000 to win $400.

We won the $420. I gave West $30 leaving $390 or $130 for each of us. Would not have cashed your check at all, but West thought he could get it up at 10 to 7, and I was going to put it all up at those odds. We would have won $1,750 for the $2,500 if we could have placed it.

If we ever have another chance like this, we will know enough to try to get down early.

Let me hear from you Dutch. With all good wishes to Mrs. Leonard and yourself, I am,

Joe Wood.[14]

This letter, Leonard told Landis, had to do with wagers the four men decided to put down on the game once they agreed to arrange the outcome. The person identified as West in Wood's letter was Fred C. West, an employee of the Tigers whom Leonard asserted was recruited by Cobb to handle the money.

A check of the results of the game that took place on Thursday afternoon, September 25, gave credence to Leonard's claim. It was the Tigers' final home game of the 1919 season. Tris Speaker pitched Elmer Myers and left him in the entire game while Detroit hammered out eighteen hits and clobbered Cleveland, 9–5, in a game that took just one hour and fifteen minutes to complete. Wrote one Detroit sportswriter, "Cleveland didn't care much whether it won or lost and the Tigers catching the visitors in that mood, smashed their way to the top and held the advantage to the finish."[15] For his part, Speaker said he wanted to get the game over quickly so his players could catch a five-o'clock train for home rather than take a nighttime boat trip. The alleged scheme, however, went for naught. Though the Tigers did win their final five games, the Yankees, by virtue of a win over Philadelphia on the final day of the 1919 season, edged them out for third place.

As serious as the evidence was, there was unquestionably a case of sour grapes involved. Leonard conceded he, like many who played for Cobb, didn't particularly like the man. There were specific rubs. One in particular involved a rescinded invitation to spring training earlier in the year by the Pittsburgh Pirates. Leonard told the commissioner he suspected Cobb had something to do with the Pirates' change of heart.

While the commissioner had told reporters in Los Angeles his itinerary called for spending the weekend on Leonard's farm, he was deposited by his host at the train station in the late afternoon the same day he arrived. Questions were exhausted. Evidence was in hand. Once back in his office in Chicago, Kenesaw Mountain Landis would concede to an associate that he was about to tackle the hardest job he had ever faced.

2

Landing the Big One

A heightened level of energy surged through the house at 2190 Ponet Drive. Only the day before, Oscar and Margaret Souden's daughter and son-in-law had arrived for their annual Christmastime visit. A notice in the newspaper of the couple's arrival brought callers to the home, a stone's throw from the southwest corner of Los Angeles's Griffith Park. Margaret worked to put the finishing touches on a tea to appease friends who wanted to visit her daughter. Oscar—or O. M. Souden, as the door to the president's office at the United States National Bank read—organized a lunch at the toney Jonathon Club to bring friends together with his son-in-law. It was a lunch the men annually relished. They loved to hear Souden's son-in-law tell tales of his clients, especially his biggest: Babe Ruth.

To his in-laws and Los Angeles-area friends, Walter Walsh, known to everyone by his middle name, Christy, was a genuine success story. Born in Missouri, raised in San Francisco, Christy Walsh graduated from St. Vincent's College in downtown Los Angeles, teeming with ambition and filled with entrepreneurial verve. Not long after graduation, cartoons that featured his byline began to appear regularly in the *Los Angeles Express* newspaper. Shortly thereafter Walsh joined the newsroom staff of the *Los Angeles Herald.*

It was while with the *Herald* that the ardent baseball fan conjured his first scoop. Christy Mathewson, the greatest pitcher of the day, was to vacation in the area. Walsh staked out the bungalow Mathewson had rented, came away with comments from the New York Giants' star, and hurried back to the newsroom in an exuberant state. The young reporter's bubble was burst, though, when an editor ordered him to give his notes to one of the paper's star reporters, Adela Rogers St. John, who instead wrote the story under her byline. The slight left Walsh crestfallen. But it would rekindle nine years later in the form of inspiration during a time of near desperation in Walsh's life.

In 1914 Walsh left the newspaper business for advertising. He was hired by the Green-Robbins Advertising Agency in San Francisco and made manager for the Chalmers luxury-car account. For three years he traveled between California, New York, and the Chalmers' headquarters in Detroit. Then in 1917 a job offer from the Van Patten Advertising Agency lured Walsh and his new bride, Madeline, east to New York City. It was during his time in New York that life undertook a most fantastic change. It was one Christy Walsh would talk about time and again for decades.

For over three years (around an eight-month stint in the army), Walsh enjoyed success in the advertising world. Then, days into the 1921 calendar year, he was summoned to meet with his boss. The news was grim. The agency had lost two major accounts. Only days earlier, five employees were let go. Now, it was Walsh who was handed a check for two-weeks' severance pay and shown the door.

Every effort to land another job proved futile. It was then that Christy Walsh had a stroke of ingenuity. Actually, he remembered the stinging incident in the *Los Angeles Herald* newsroom nine years earlier. If someone could write a story for someone else in a newsroom setting, why couldn't it be done in the area of news syndication, he wondered. Ghostwriting, or work credited to someone else, was the name for it in the industry. The concept was hardly new. It was common in the literary world, where authors would write under a pseudonym. As for newspapers—in particular, the sports pages— as far back as 1911, Bell Syndicate was sending ghostwritten stories under the byline of pitching-great Christy Mathewson to its subscribers. Walsh knew he had to have an attention-grabbing subject, a person people would want to read about. He set his sights high—very high. After all, there was no target higher than the man he sought, Babe Ruth.

Only fourteen months earlier, Babe Ruth had joined the New York Yan- kees amid much fanfare. During his first season with the team, Ruth had erupted into a phenomenon. Not just a baseball phenomenon but as W. O. McGeehan suggested in the *New York Tribune*, he was "the idol of the American male."[1] To baseball fans, Ruth was a marvel, a unique combination of power hitter, acrobatic and strong-armed outfielder, and fleet base run- ner. To average Americans, Babe Ruth was a freak, akin to a carnival strong man, a man of superior strength able to not only send a baseball far greater distances than any player ever had before but to do it with greater frequency than any in the game's history.

Prior to his purchase by the Yankees, Ruth had spent six seasons with the Boston Red Sox. During that time, he was principally a pitcher—and a very good one. In 1916 Ruth won twenty-three games, the third best in the American League. A year later, he won twenty-four, the second best in the league. Ruth was part of what was arguably the best pitching staff in the American League. Three times during those six seasons, the Red Sox reached the World Series and won it each time.

During the 1918 season, the Red Sox saw their roster depleted by the manpower needs of World War I. With several players away to serve in the military or work in defense-industry jobs, Babe Ruth played the outfield in addition to pitching. Playing half the team's games in the field, Ruth hit eleven home runs, a tally that tied "Tillie" Walker of the Philadelphia Athletics for the American League lead. Going into the 1919 season, the Red Sox had glaring voids in the outfield. Attempts to trade for help fell through. Babe Ruth implored the Red Sox manager, Ed Barrow, to let him play in the field even more. Barrow acceded. On Opening Day, Ruth rewarded the manager by hitting a home run. In all that season, he hit twenty-nine. His total was more than triple what the runner-up, Frank "Homerun" Baker of the Yankees, hit. Bigger yet, Ruth's twenty-nine broke the single-season record of twenty-five, set by "Buck" Freeman in 1899.

For all of Babe Ruth's skill, there was a side to him that angered Harry Frazee, the man who owned the Red Sox. Ruth could be petulant, abrasive. He clashed with his manager. During a game in 1918, the two had to be held apart in the dugout, after which Ruth packed his bags, left the ball club, and returned to his home in Baltimore. After breaking the single-season home-run record, Ruth sought a pay raise. Though still under contract for two more seasons at a salary of $10,000 per year, Ruth demanded Frazee double his pay. To Frazee, the salary demand was the last straw.

On the afternoon of January 5, 1920, newsboys all around New York City waved newspapers with bold headlines akin to that in the *New York Times*, which read, "Yanks Buy Babe Ruth for $125,000."[2] The revelation sparked a gamut of emotions: revelry among Yankees fans and disconsolation among Red Sox faithful. "I figure the Red Sox club is now practically ruined," said Charlie Lavis, one of the team's oldest fans.[3] "The team's future looks gloomy," said another fan, Miah Murray.[4] For his part, Frazee explained, "Ruth has been insubordinate on occasions and has insisted on having his own way to such an extent that he endangered the discipline of the whole squad."[5]

Once with the Yankees, Ruth erupted into a full-fledged sensation. Except for a very rare occurrence, pitching would be a thing of the past. Ruth was made the team's right fielder. With his attention fully on hitting, he put together a season like no other, one which held a nation spellbound. Ironically, he hit his first home run as a Yankee against his old team to highlight an 8–0 win on

May 1. By the end of the month, he'd hit thirteen. Ruth slugged eleven more in June, one of which (his twenty-second) was hailed the longest ever hit in New York's Polo Grounds. In July, Ruth went on a tear. He hit four home runs during a span of five games to put him on the cusp of his own single-season record. On July 15, in the eleventh inning of a 10–10 game with the St. Louis Browns, Ruth came to bat against Bill Burwell. His uniform was muddy in spots and wet in more from diving for balls on outfield grass soaked by morning rain. There were two runners on base when Ruth's hard swing connected with Burwell's pitch. Impact left little doubt the ball would win the game and be a home run. All that was left was to marvel at how far it traveled. Sportswriters noted the ball missed hitting the grandstand roof by a mere three feet and rattled off seats six feet from the back of the stand. Babe Ruth had hit his twenty-ninth home run of the season.

Four days later against the White Sox, Ruth eclipsed his own record when he homered twice off Dickey Kerr. There were still sixty-six games to be played. Over that span Ruth hit twenty-three more home runs to obliterate his record. The last came on the next-to-last day of the 1920 season at Shibe Park in Philadelphia and gave Ruth fifty-four for the year.

Ruth's total was greater than that hit by each of the other seven teams in the American League during the 1920 season. It was thirty-five more than that of the runner-up in the American League home-run race, George Sisler, who hit nineteen. Rule changes helped. Prior to 1920, if a player hit a home run with runners on base in the final inning and one of the baserunners accounted for the winning run, the batter did not get credit for a home run. The rule cost Ruth two home runs in 1919. The rule was changed to give the batter credit for a home run in 1920. Prior to 1920, umpires kept a ball in play no matter how dirty and discolored it became. Beginning in the 1920 season, Kenesaw Mountain Landis instructed umpires to toss out discolored baseballs and only use balls that were new. Ruth acknowledged the whiter, more discernable ball was a big help to him and all hitters.

Throughout the summer Ruth's home-run spree sparked frenzy. "The Country Is Babe Ruth Mad," trumpeted *The Sporting News*.[6] When the Yankees played their first game of the season in St. Louis, fans filled Sportsman's Park like never before. Once seats ran out, people were packed five deep in front of the outfield fence. Hundreds of late arrivals were turned away, and gates were shut once game time arrived. Observed *The Sporting News*, "It was the greatest gathering of fans that has ever turned out to a ball game in St. Louis at least during the present generation."[7] When Ruth took the field in Detroit, "he was accorded the welcome due a conquering hero."[8] In Chicago, a throng of fans keen to shake Ruth's hand after a game at Comiskey Park was so large police had to be summoned to clear a path so the slugger could leave.

Ruth's exploits propelled attendance upward at American League parks. It grew to 5,084,300, which was a 74 percent increase over 1919. Nowhere was the mania greater than in New York, where the Yankees almost doubled their 1919 crowd count. They became the first team in American League history to top 1,000,000 fans, with 1,289,422 pouring through the entry gates. "There isn't any doubt that Ruth is the greatest drawing card of all time. He pulls them in. He really makes the turnstiles click," said Yankees manager Miller Huggins.[9]

Ruth was a phenomenon. He made the previously disinterested interested, people like John Heydler's family members who, according to the National League president, "never cared for baseball, but got the Babe Ruth fever and wouldn't be content until they had gone out to the Polo Grounds and seen him play."[10]

From the adoration came nicknames. As for "Babe," Ruth explained to the *New York Evening World* that it emanated from a bout of homesickness while in school. The name was softly uttered to soothe him by a Christian Brother, Brother Matthias. Years later while playing for the Baltimore Orioles, a coach called him Jack (Dunn)'s Babe, and the nickname stuck. Bambino came from New York City's Italian neighborhoods, the word in their language for a male baby or babe. Sportswriters used nicknames to proclaim Ruth's renown. W. O. McGeehan first tagged Ruth "Bambino" in print in the *New York Tribune*.[11] A *New York Daily News* columnist expanded it to "Battering Bambino." Marshall Hunt of the *Daily News* hailed Ruth, "The Great Bam."[12] In his syndicated column in August 1920, Grantland Rice called Ruth the "Sultan of Swat."[13] It was a label that soon caught on with other sportswriters. Advertisers, too, got into the act. Brill Brothers headlined their newspaper ads by hailing Ruth as the "Colossus of Swat" and sent the Yankee sensation a free pair of socks every time he hit a home run. Dozens more lesser-used monikers followed.

Being an avid baseball fan himself, Christy Walsh believed Ruth to be the ideal candidate to bring his business idea to fruition. On a chilly day in early February 1921, Christy Walsh, filled with chutzpah, set out for the Ansonia Hotel, the luxury apartment building where Ruth lived with his wife, Helen. On the first day he arrived, Walsh was surprised to find several others outside the building. It seemed everyone who had what they felt was a surefire, money-spinning scheme had staked out the building in hopes of pitching it to the New York Yankees' star. Each day for two weeks in weather that hovered between thirty-four and forty degrees, Walsh and the others paced Broadway near Seventy-Third Street. Unbeknownst to them, Ruth knew they were there and used a back exit to avoid them.

Walsh was near despair. He had just $8.96 left in the bank. Eviction was on the horizon. On Monday, February 21, his frustration turned to alarm.

Newspapers carried pictures of Ruth packing for a trip to Hot Springs, Arkansas. There, with Yankees teammates Waite Hoyt and Carl Mays, Ruth would prepare for spring training. The players would take daily hikes, receive deep-tissue massages, and soak in the renowned mineral baths before they traveled to Shreveport, Louisiana, where the Yankees would conduct spring training.

Anxiety grew the following morning as Walsh paced the perimeter of the Ansonia Hotel. Time was running out. Again, as in previous days, there was no sign of Ruth. It was then that good fortune smiled on Christy Walsh. After several hours of pacing, Walsh decided to take a break. He ducked into a corner delicatessen. Walsh engaged the owner in conversation, only to be interrupted by the telephone. Walsh heard the man take down an order, hang up the phone, then mutter, "Yoi, yoi, yoi." The customer, he moaned, wanted his order—a case of beer—right away, but the man's delivery boy was gone. In his frustration, the shop owner muttered the name of the customer, "Baby Root."[14] Christy Walsh pounced. He knew who the man meant and eagerly offered to make the delivery.

In less than ten minutes, the out-of-work adman was in Babe Ruth's kitchenette, counting bottles of beer with his intended target. For a moment Ruth thought he recognized Walsh but could not recall how. That's when the man with the idea and little else went for broke. Christy Walsh laid out what he had in mind, an idea that could add to Babe Ruth's wealth, if not his popularity. Newspapers sought content—sports content, to be specific. *Hearst, United Features,* and the *Chicago Tribune* were churning out news and feature articles for hundreds of newspapers around the country, but nobody was doing the same with sports. What better sports content could there be, Walsh explained, than insightful articles about baseball from the biggest name in the game. He told Ruth he wouldn't have to do anything but count his money. Walsh would procure a team of writers, skilled sportswriters, who would write the articles anonymously in Babe's name. Ruth liked the idea. The men discussed terms, and an agreement was made. Ruth excused himself to retrieve a fountain pen. That is when panic struck.

Christy Walsh had been carrying a contract in his coat pocket for days. Now, just when he needed it, just when he could get the signature of Babe Ruth to secure the deal that would change his fortunes, the contract was nowhere to be found. Pondering the dilemma, Walsh realized he had left the contract in the delicatessen. He went into a panic. Ruth was leaving the next day for Arkansas. Thinking quickly, Walsh told Ruth he would bring the contract to him at the train station. The Babe agreed and Walsh left the Ansonia, oblivious to the smack of cold air that hit him as he pushed open the door to the outside.

The next day a blizzard blanketed New York in snow. Sidewalks were piled high. Statues were painted white. Walsh navigated the biting wind to reach Pennsylvania Station at 4:30 in the afternoon, twenty minutes before Ruth's train was to depart. He had little trouble finding Ruth. The squeals and cackles of schoolboys led him to the platform where the St. Louisan would embark for Hot Springs. There, dozens of admiring youths had the man in a camel hair coat and flat cap surrounded as they pleaded for autographs. When Helen Ruth saw Walsh, she shooed the boys to make room for his meeting with her husband. Walsh was struck by the orange glow where the tip of Ruth's large cigar met the chilly air. Ruth reached for a fountain pen. In an instant, Christy Walsh was able to mentally, if not physically, breathe an enormous sigh of relief as Ruth's right hand scrawled his given name, George Herman Ruth, at the bottom of the rumpled letter of agreement.

With a $2,000 bank loan, Walsh created his own newspaper syndication service, The Christy Walsh Syndicate. It was the industry's first sports syndication service. Walsh rented space for a small office in the Hecksher Building, one of the most expensive office buildings in New York City. He hired a stenographer and paid her $18 per week. With Babe Ruth's signature on a crude contract, he set out to secure agreements with newspapers to run Ruth's articles. It wasn't easy. Bill Farnsworth, sports editor of the *New York American*, was the first to sign on. Harry Bitner, managing editor of *The Pittsburgh Press,* agreed soon after. Walsh mailed postcards to newspapers all across the country. "Advance Tip to Sporting Editors," it read. "Tell the Chief you Want BABE RUTH."[15] As editors realized this would be the best way to get quotes from Ruth exclusive to their city or town, interest grew.

On Opening Day of the 1921 season, when Ruth and the Yankees returned from spring training, Walsh surprised the slugger with a check for $1,000, an advance on expected earnings. Their agreement didn't call for Walsh to make his first payment to Ruth for ninety days. This was a show of good faith. Giving the Yankees' star an advance, he hoped, would separate him from the slick talkers and fast-buck seekers who regularly beseeched Ruth. It did.

When the season began, Westbrook Pegler, a sportswriter with *United News*, was in place as Ruth's ghostwriter. He would travel with Ruth throughout the season and confer with him about just what to write. On May 4, the first ghostwritten article under Babe Ruth's byline appeared in a handful of newspapers around the country. Seven days later, Ruth's second article regaled even more readers with what it was like to hit a home run off Washington Senators pitching star, Walter Johnson. Slowly, throughout the summer, subscribers to Walsh's syndication service grew.

Figure 2.1. From a failed cartoonist and fired adman, Christy Walsh changed the fortunes of Babe Ruth and rescued baseball. *Courtesy:* Herald Examiner *collection/Los Angeles Public Library photo collection*

Three months into Walsh's endeavor, baseball was hit with a staggering blow. It was a scandal the type of which the game had never before incurred. Seven members of the Chicago White Sox went on trial in Chicago. They were accused of consorting with gamblers to throw the outcome of the 1919

World Series to the Cincinnati Reds. The accused players were derisively labeled the "Black Sox." It was a matter first taken up by a grand jury, where newspapers reported that three of the accused players—Eddie Cicotte, Claude "Lefty" Williams, and "Shoeless" Joe Jackson—confessed. Based on the testimony, a twelve-count indictment was issued and a jury trial scheduled. All three players agreed to testify at the trial for the prosecution in exchange for immunity. Once the trial began in July of 1921, prosecutors made a startling admission. The confessions made by Cicotte, Williams, and Jackson, along with their immunity waivers, could not be found. Newspaper reports claimed that eastern gambling interests had offered a $10,000 bounty to anyone who could pilfer the confessions and spirit them out of the state. The three players immediately changed their pleas and, with their four teammates, fought for their innocence.

On August 3, 1921, after deliberating for two hours and forty-seven minutes, a jury acquitted the seven White Sox players. The very next morning, Commissioner Kenesaw Mountain Landis banned all seven players from baseball. Mistrust had been bred. Baseball was stained. Around the country debate over the players' guilt or innocence raged among fans. The correctness or error of Landis's decision was argued. Fans who wondered what the game's most popular player thought of it all could only find out in his articles distributed by Christy Walsh. In his piece that appeared four days after Landis's decision, Ruth threw his support behind the commissioner. "Crooked ball players ought to be barred forever," the article read.[16] The article excoriated the seven ballplayers. "They stand guilty in the eyes of the fans and ballplayers in America."[17]

The words in Ruth's column were a powerful salve to baseball's painful wound, almost as much as his play during the remaining days of the 1921 season. On the day the acquittal was announced in Chicago, Ruth had amassed thirty-eight home runs on the season. In the eight days that followed, he hit six more, and soon baseball fans would switch conversation from the scandal to the possibility of a new home-run record.

Ruth finished the month of August with forty-nine home runs, five short of his record. Twenty-nine games remained. Talk of a new record became both real and rampant. When the calendar turned to September, Ruth again went on a long-ball-hitting tear. He smacked six in eight games to equal his record of fifty-four. For six days, fans pined to see the Yankees' slugger belt a long ball, only to leave the park disappointed. Then on September 15, in the fifth inning of a game against the St. Louis Browns, Ruth sent a pitch from Bill Bayne deep into the right-field stands to eclipse his mark.

Newspapermen were frustrated. There was only one place readers could gather insights about Ruth. It was from the Babe's own column, syndicated by Christy Walsh. After his milestone, Ruth chalked up the record to "a matter of confidence and experience."[18] Of the pitchers he homered off of, Ruth said, "I have no 'easy marks' or particular favorites."[19] Once Ruth had achieved the record, the expectation grew for even more. The *New York Tribune* asked, "Can Babe Make It 60?"[20] A homer the next afternoon, then two against Cleveland, took his 1921 total to fifty-eight with five games to play. It was on the final day of the season that Ruth hit one last home run to establish a new single-season home-run record of fifty-nine.

The record-breaking season propelled the Yankees into the World Series. Walsh offered his clients World Series coverage and made another $2,000 from it. It offered a valuable lesson. For 1922, Walsh offered his clients a package of two articles a week for twenty-six weeks plus coverage of the World Series. It helped to increase subscribers and income. So, too, did the addition of more sports stars. For newspapers in National League cities, he signed up St. Louis Cardinals standout Rogers Hornsby. John McGraw, manager of the New York Giants, became a popular subject. To satisfy sports fans in the fall and winter, Walsh lined up Knute Rockne, the Notre Dame coach, to offer football insights. He diversified beyond sports and hired experts such as renowned Cornell University lecturer, Dr. Hendrik van Loon, and automobile expert Ray McNamara to write about non-sports subjects.

Walsh gained the trust and confidence of Ruth and his wife. When, in the summer of 1921, the couple adopted an infant daughter, Helen Ruth asked Walsh to act as a buffer between the family and the press, who were pressing to learn if Babe was the child's biological father. In June of 1922, when Ruth drew a suspension for arguing with an umpire, Walsh acted as his spokesperson. After the season, one in which Ruth was suspended four times and incurred the wrath of the press, Walsh organized a dinner for Ruth with New York City sportswriters to patch wounds and resolve differences.

In the fall of 1924, Walsh added promoter to his role with Ruth. He organized a breakneck tour, nearly two months in length, that took Ruth to fifteen cities in six states. The tour combined barnstorming with business. Walsh treated newspapers that subscribed to the Christy Walsh syndication service to a visit in their newsroom by the Yankees' great. He arranged for Ruth to play in fifteen exhibition baseball games with local players. With an eye on publicity for those games, he had Ruth make speeches to breakfast gatherings, luncheons, and dinner events—twenty-three in all. On the tour, Ruth headed four parades and paid visits to eighteen hospitals. A columnist for a newspaper in Stockton, California, called Walsh a "demon promoter."[21]

By the time Christy Walsh arrived at his in-laws for Christmas in 1926, he was Babe Ruth's full-fledged manager. Anyone who wanted anything from Ruth had to go through Walsh. Companies that wanted Ruth to promote their products had to negotiate with Walsh. He took charge of Ruth's fall barnstorming schedule, chased off fly-by-night promoters, arranged for local chapters of the Knights of Columbus to sponsor the games, raised Ruth's rate to $1,500 per game, and harkened his advertising savvy to publicize the games.

In August of 1926, Walsh negotiated his biggest deal yet for Ruth. He floated a proposal for a vaudeville tour. Ruth would give out autographed baseballs, crack a few jokes, tell some baseball stories, and even sing a couple of songs. Many in the entertainment industry believed such a show would be a big success. Keen to make the tour exclusive only to his chain of theaters, vaudeville impresario Alexander Pantages paid $100,000 to have Ruth conduct a twelve-week tour. For his work, Walsh received 15 percent of the sum.

The vaudeville deal was fodder for conversation at luncheons and other gatherings as Walsh renewed acquaintance with old friends and spent time with family in Los Angeles. Even though the holidays had him more than two thousand miles from his New York office, business was never far from his mind. As Christmas neared, Christy Walsh pondered an even bigger deal for Ruth. Calls were made. Meetings were set. Before boarding a train bound for New York in early January, Christy Walsh would lay the groundwork for his most significant deal for Babe Ruth yet. It had the potential to bring Ruth more money than any other deal previously struck. If it were possible, it might even bring greater notoriety. It was a deal that would make the baseball sensation the star of a motion picture.

3

Tarnished Stars

The merriment of Christmas wafted about Chicago's Michigan Avenue. Large, green wreaths of fragrant evergreen adorned lampposts. Snow fell, adding to the festiveness that blanketed hundreds of shoppers, some who walked ten abreast on the packed sidewalks. In the People's Gas Building on Michigan near Monroe, the frivolity of the fast-approaching, joyous day had yet to brighten the mood of one of the office occupants. Judge Kenesaw Mountain Landis was staring at not only what he said was "the hardest job I ever faced," he was about to engage in a power struggle.[1] His foe would be the man who, for the previous twenty-five years, was considered to be the most powerful man in the game.

Byron Bancroft "Ban" Johnson was not just the president of the American League; he created it. Urged in 1894 to leave his job as a sportswriter in Cincinnati to run a year-old minor league—the Western League—Ban Johnson, with his ideas and leadership, helped the eight-team, Midwest-based circuit grow far beyond anyone's wildest expectations. In 1901 Johnson withdrew the Western League from the minor league agreement with the National League. He renamed his league the American League and declared it a new major league. Johnson urged his teams to offer higher salaries and lure players from National League clubs. American League clubs drew larger crowds than those of the older league. Finally, in 1903, a peace deal was struck between the two leagues, one that included a championship series.

Johnson ruled with an iron fist. So strong was his grip on the game, he was called the "Czar of Baseball."[2] He operated on a lifetime contract. Johnson would allow clubs to be sold only to men he approved. Managers felt his wrath. He publicly second-guessed their tactics and moves. In some cases, he went so far as to have managers removed. Umpires weren't off-limits from

Johnson's ire, either. So strong was the unwavering support for Johnson from the owners of the eight American League teams, they were called Ban's "Yes-men."

It was in the fall of 1919 when Johnson's power base began to erode. Suspicion swirled about the World Series that year. It was suspected the outcome of games was not on the up-and-up. The American League champions, the Chicago White Sox, entered the Series a seven-to-five favorite. However, the day before the game, significant bets—$1,000, $5,000, and $7,000—were placed on the National League champs, the Cincinnati Reds. When the White Sox lost the first game, 9–1, suspicion was raised in some corners.

With each loss by the White Sox in the Series, whispers of fixed games grew louder. As Cincinnati celebrated winning the World Series, Dan Daniel wrote in the *New York Sun*: "It was said here that Eddie Cicotte had been bribed to throw his games. It was also said that five members of the Chicago club had been given $100,000 by a gang of gamblers to throw the series. These stories hurt baseball."[3] The integrity of the country's greatest sporting event was in question, its reputation sullied.

Neither law enforcement nor prosecutors in Chicago had any interest to investigate suspicions about the games. In a glaring example of the type of wrangling Ban Johnson was so adept at, he waited until the state's attorney was away in New York to approach his ambitious second-in-command. The man leaped at the opportunity and, much to his boss's ire, put the matter before a grand jury.

Almost eleven months after the nefarious World Series, a newly impaneled grand jury in Chicago took up the game-fixing probe. On the eve of his testimony, the White Sox star pitcher, Eddie Cicotte, entered the office of Charles Comiskey. "I don't know what you'll think of me," he said, "but I got to tell you how I double crossed you Mr. Comiskey. I did double cross you. I'm a crook. I got $10,000 for being a crook," Cicotte said. "Don't tell it to me," Comiskey replied. "Tell it to the grand jury."[4] Cicotte did, sobbing in the witness box, "I was a fool."[5] Once testimony concluded, eight White Sox players were indicted. All eight—Eddie Cicotte, "Lefty" Williams, "Shoeless" Joe Jackson, "Swede" Risberg, "Chick" Gandil, Fred McMullen, "Happy" Felsch, and "Buck" Weaver—were promptly fired by Comiskey.

Baseball's credibility was sorely damaged. A columnist for a Chicago publication, *Collyer's Eye*, called the game, "morally disorganized and out of repute."[6] In the smoldering aftermath, John Heydler, president of the National League, proposed radical change to the governance of the game. Since 1903, baseball had been governed by a three-person commission made up of the presidents of the National and American Leagues and the president of the Cincinnati Reds, Garry Herrmann. In 1920 it was Herrmann who served as the group's chairman. Heydler felt a national commission "was all right in fair weather, too frail to weather a storm." He proposed a new form of governance—one in which one man, a commissioner, would be given full authority to reign over the game. Heydler suggested they find a leader "so strong and of such unimpeachable reputation that its authority will be welcomed by every promoter, player, and lover of clean, honest sport."[7]

The reaction to Heydler's idea saw Ban Johnson's previously steadfast support begin to crumble. Three American League owners—Comiskey, Colonel Jacob Ruppert of the Yankees, and Harry Frazee of the Red Sox—broke ranks and voted with the eight National League club owners in favor of Heydler's plan. Johnson was incensed. He called Comiskey, Ruppert, and Frazee the "insurrectos." Less than sixty days after the grand jury indictments were handed down, Judge Kenesaw Mountain Landis was hired as the first commissioner of baseball.

Landis walked away from a lifetime position as federal judge of the United States District Court for the Northern District of Illinois to take charge of baseball. As a jurist, he was autocratic and stern, at times theatrical, and often abrupt. He took big and controversial cases with unflinching tenacity. Perhaps the most highly publicized of his rulings was the $29,000,000 fine he slapped on John D. Rockefeller's Standard Oil Company in 1907. It was later overturned on appeal. Beneath his gruff exterior was an unabashed baseball fan. During summer months it was not uncommon for Landis to conclude proceedings in his Chicago courtroom early in order to take in a few innings of a Cubs or White Sox game. Once fall arrived, everyone involved in court scheduling knew Landis would take time off to attend the World Series.

Landis never tired of explaining the origins of his unique name. His mother, he said, objected when her husband wanted their youngest to carry his first name, Abraham. Mary Landis suggested he be named for the Civil War battle in which Abraham Landis was wounded while in the Union army: the Battle of Kennesaw Mountain in Georgia. At the time of the boy's birth, two spellings of the site were used. Mary Landis chose the one with the single letter *n*, Kenesaw. Through the years, friends would simply call Mary Landis's son Kenny.

While, publicly, Ban Johnson praised the hiring of Landis for which he boasted of being primarily responsible, privately, he became a bur in the new commissioner's saddle. To his loyalists Johnson mocked Landis for what he considered a lack of aggressiveness in tackling the White Sox scandal. He pressed Landis to investigate allegations of National League crimes—in particular, claims that a New York Giants player or players had conspired to throw the 1917 World Series. Unbeknownst to Johnson, the new commissioner was pressing the newly elected state's attorney to set a trial date for the indicted White Sox players as quickly as possible. He had also dispatched members of his investigative team to delve into the 1917 World Series rumors.

Nine months into Landis's role, he faced the defining moment of his professional life. Jurors had acquitted the indicted Chicago White Sox players. Hours after the verdict was announced, Landis took prompt action. He imposed the harshest discipline ever handed down to any ballplayer in the game's history. The accused players—Eddie Cicotte, "Lefty" Williams, "Shoeless" Joe Jackson, "Swede" Risberg, "Chick" Gandil, Fred McMullen, "Happy" Felsch, and "Buck" Weaver—were banned from organized baseball for life. "No player who throws a ball game or sits in a conference with a bunch of crooked players and gamblers will ever play professional baseball," Landis said.[8]

The commissioner's forceful action was praised by the *New York Tribune*: "It is comforting, however, to realize the fate of the game rests with a man of such keen judgement and rigorous fearlessness as Judge Kenesaw Mountain Landis, the commissioner. Judge Landis has asserted himself on the case in unmistakable terms."[9]

The *Detroit Free Press* stated:

> The game demands something more than law honesty. It demands men whose pride in clean sport is such that they can not be approached by bribers and men who put money above the game. It is through such men that the game can live and continue to pay high salaries to ball players while it affords sport to millions.[10]

Babe Ruth devoted one of his ghostwritten columns to Landis's action. "Any baseball player who would actually or technically sell out millions of loyal fans who have made possible his success, is deserving of nothing less than exile."[11]

Now, five years later, Landis was faced with yet another baseball scandal. It was one that had the potential to be far worse for the game. "The baseball public can stand only so much," wrote *Honolulu Advertiser* columnist William Peet.[12] Where the White Sox scandal damaged the credibility of the World Series, the newest controversy involved two of the greatest—if not the most popular—players in the game: Ty Cobb and Tris Speaker.

It was during the summer of 1926 that the owner of the Detroit Tigers, Frank Navin, notified Ban Johnson of the letters possessed by Dutch Leonard. Navin was at first reluctant to believe his former pitcher. After mulling over the claims, he forwarded Leonard's letters to the American League president. In Johnson's mind the matter involved American League players and thus was strictly an American League issue. He dispatched his own team of detectives to investigate. But Johnson did not do as he was required under the game's new structure. He failed to bring the matter to the attention of the game's authority, the commissioner.

Following the 1926 season, Johnson ordered Cobb and Speaker to delay a planned hunting trip to Wyoming. He summoned the men instead to meet with him in Chicago. Ban Johnson laid out the information his investigators had assembled. Cobb admitted writing the letter but had no explanation for it. Asked about "Smokey" Joe Wood's letter, Speaker denied knowledge of it. While Cobb acknowledged meeting Leonard, Wood, and Speaker beneath the stands after the September 24, 1919, game, Speaker, on the other hand, claimed it never happened.

Johnson told the two that as player-managers, Cobb with Detroit, Speaker with Cleveland, they "were given positions of trust." Johnson added, the two men "had failed to keep that trust."[13] He banned the two stars from ever playing or managing in the American League again. Out of respect for their careers, Johnson vowed to keep the matter quiet. He told Cobb and Speaker they could resign or retire, but they were out of the game.

A secret meeting of the American League board of directors was assembled. Ban Johnson laid out the charges against Cobb and Speaker. He informed the men what action he had taken. About Cobb, Johnson explained it was "because he had written a peculiar letter about a betting deal that he couldn't explain and because I felt he had violated a position of trust."[14] Of Speaker, Johnson said the letter's contents did not surprise him. He revealed his investigators had been watching Speaker and his ball club for two years. Gambling, they reported, was rampant on the team. During games, chatter in the dugout had more to do with results at nearby racetracks than the ball game itself. "I'd call Tris cute," Johnson said. "He knows why he was forced out. If he wants me to tell him, I'll meet him in a court of law and tell the facts under oath."[15] Ernest Barnard, president of the Cleveland ball club, suggested Landis be notified. Once Johnson agreed, the board took a vote and gave unanimous approval to the actions taken.

Apprised of the claims made by Dutch Leonard, Kenesaw Mountain Landis sprang into action. He had at his disposal a small army of investigators, one so big the commissioner told team owners he kept every ballplayer in the big leagues under surveillance. Now Landis turned them loose to probe Leonard's accusations. Unable to convince Leonard to come to Chicago, the commissioner traveled west and to Central California for a face-to-face talk with the former pitcher. Then on November 27, Cobb, Speaker, and two other men connected to the scandal faced the baseball commissioner in his office in Chicago.

Three stenographers took turns taking down testimony during four hours of questioning. Damning information spilled forth. Falsehoods and half-truths were exposed. Investigators for Landis identified Fred West, a ballpark employee, as the man who carried envelopes with money that was allegedly bet on the game in question. When seated before Landis, West refused to take an oath. West was pressed about the money he had carried. "The money that figures in the case was not bet on a ball game, but on a horse," West said.[16] To support his contention, West showed the reporter a bookmaker's receipt for a wager on the first race at Aqueduct Racetrack on September 25, 1919. The bet was placed on Panaman, which went off at twelve-to-five and won. But when closely scrutinized by the commissioner's detectives, the bookmaker's receipt was found to be a forgery.

A man who operated the scoreboard in the ballpark in Detroit confirmed the game with Cleveland was fixed. He said a Tigers player gave him sixty dollars to bet on Detroit and to place a bet himself "because Cleveland is going to throw the game."[17] The man, George Barris, said two other Tigers players bet on the game and told him to keep quiet about what he knew.

Ty Cobb had announced his resignation as player-manager of the Detroit Tigers three weeks before the meeting with Landis. Now, forty-eight hours after a face-to-face talk with the commissioner, Tris Speaker handed in his resignation as well.

On the evening of December 20, 1926, Don Maxwell of the *Chicago Tribune* turned up at the front door of Landis's home in the Chicago Beach Hotel. Maxwell raised knowledge of the investigation. He sought confirmation. Landis became agitated. "This is against my whole nature," he said. "You know I've always acted frankly. You know I'm not afraid to tell the truth no matter whom it hurts. But I can't talk—NOW!"[18] Before Maxwell turned to leave, he warned Landis that enough was said to confirm allegations the reporter was privy to and that a story would be forthcoming.

The following day, Landis's worst fear was realized. Large bold type screamed from the front page of the *Chicago Tribune*: "LANDIS SILENT ON NEW BALL SCANDAL."[19] The commissioner knew the other seven daily newspapers in Chicago and, perhaps, those in other cities would soon be all over the story. Within his office, he ordered furious production of a report. He set a deadline that afternoon—December 21, at four o'clock—to share the report with the press. Twenty-four hours later, the newspaper headlines in Chicago and around the country would be far worse.

Release of Landis's report set off a frenzy. Large bold sensational headlines roared from atop newspaper pages in every corner of the country. "COBB AND SPEAKER IN BALL SCANDAL," headlined the *Los Angeles Daily News*.[20] "COBB, SPEAKER, LEONARD, AND WOOD UNDER INVESTIGATION," read the *Bos-*

ton Daily Globe.[21] "LANDIS LINKS TY COBB AND TRIS SPEAKER IN SCANDAL," touted the *St. Louis Post Dispatch.*[22] "TY AND TRIS SCANDAL ROCKS SPORTS WORLD TO ITS FOUNDATIONS," topped the *Oakland Tribune*'s story.[23]

Baseball was once again thrust into the throes of an ugly scandal. As to its magnitude, sportswriters around the country were in agreement that it was on par with or potentially worse than the 1919 World Series scandal. "A staggering shock," wrote *New York Daily News* columnist Marshall Hunt.[24] "Once again the hero-worshipping public learns its idols have feet of clay," stated Regis M. Welsh in *The Pittsburgh Post.*[25] Joe Vila, sports editor of the *New York Sun*, declared, "The fabric of the game is rotten. And that to maintain faith in it is to play the fool."[26] The most celebrated sportswriter of the day, Grantland Rice, wrote, "No further testimony is needed to show the unbelievable rottenness connected with so many features of the professional field."[27] *The Pittsburgh Press* sportswriter Ralph Davis suggested, "The whole fabric of baseball seems to be endangered."[28] To skeptics, Paul Gallico wrote in the *New York Daily News*, "Landis would not have blackened the lives of two men unless he had positive proof."[29] It was an opinion seconded by the renowned sportswriter Damon Runyon, who in his syndicated column suggested of Cobb and Speaker, "A man with a clear conscious does not commonly accept charges reflecting on his honor."[30]

Reporters flocked to Dutch Leonard's California farm for comment. They were greeted by a collie almost hoarse from barking at the many cars that drove onto the former pitcher's property. "I don't want to see any newspaper men and it will do them no good if they do see me," Leonard said before he turned away a reporter from the *Fresno Bee.*[31]

Nothing exposed the state in which the scandal placed baseball more strongly than the reaction of Colonel Jacob Ruppert, owner of the New York Yankees. Ruppert said, "If I felt that baseball couldn't be kept clean, I'd sell my club."[32] The revelation was only twenty-four hours old, and the storm that enveloped the game was about to get worse.

4

The Very Important Hero

An eagerness mixed with heightened anticipation flowed among young people in San Francisco. It was brought on by the date on the calendar—December 24—and the expected visitor this day was to bring. Among those youngest of the young, thoughts were of the impending arrival of a jolly, rotund man clad in a red suit and toting a large bag of gifts. Dozens at an older stage of their youth were anxious for an entirely different visitor due to arrive in the city that day—a figure they had only heard and read about but one as immortal to them as the anticipated Saint Nick. Babe Ruth was coming to San Francisco.

When the expected arrival time of train fifty-three drew near, it was hard to fathom how many young people had flocked to Third and Townsend in the city's east side. The platform at the San Francisco train station was teeming with children and teenagers. Ears strained for the first sounds of an approaching train. Eyes pierced the sky for the sight of billowing smoke that would signify their hero was near. The appearance of politicians and business leaders gave rise to an impending arrival. Once the large, black locomotive came into view, chatter along with anxiousness grew.

Squealing brakes with the hissing of steam filled the air as the large 220-ton locomotive slowed to a stop alongside the platform. Eyes darted in a quest for the first glimpse of this almost mythical figure. When a surge of youths swept across the platform, it told one and all that Babe Ruth had at last stepped from the train. The youths' exuberance paused while "Sunny Jim" Rolph, the mayor of San Francisco, presented Ruth with a key to the city. Introductions were made and hands shaken with business leaders. Then, once concluded, the kids were unleashed. They swarmed the large man, whose frame was covered by a double-breasted overcoat and atop his head, a flat cap

28

worn backwards. Scraps and sheets of paper, pencils, and pens were thrust at the Yankees' slugger, who chuckled, joked with the children, and obliged each and every request. Along with the young were adults, among whom were reporters. Each was keen for something entirely different from the baseball icon—his opinion of the accusations that produced headlines only forty-eight hours earlier. About the accusations of game-fixing and gambling against Ty Cobb and Tris Speaker, Ruth said, "I just can't believe it. I can't believe that it is true."[1]

It was vaudeville that brought Babe Ruth to San Francisco, the homestretch of his long tour. He was tired and suffering from a slight cold. "If there's a Santa Claus, he'll give me some rest and a lot of golf. These press agents are driving me nuts," he told the newspapermen.[2] Christy Walsh had Ruth on a breakneck schedule. For almost ten weeks, he had performed three shows a night. Days were filled with appearances at civic breakfasts and luncheons, talks to fraternal organizations, visits to hospitals and orphanages, and interviews at radio studios and in newspaper newsrooms. He presented championship cups to high school football teams and signed baseballs as rewards to essay winners. Then there were the photo ops. They ranged from ordinary poses to the utterly wacky, like the one in Spokane, Washington. There Ruth spent two hours taking batting practice. What made it unusual was that he swung the bat while outfitted in football garb, cleats, a leather helmet, and all. His swings were not at pitched baseballs, but rather tossed footballs. It wasn't until the second hour that he finally got hold of one and sent it sailing out of the stadium.

Ruth's most recent tour stop before San Francisco offered brief respite. Christy Walsh had friends in the Northern California town of Dunsmuir, a small town in the picturesque Trinity Mountains. Walsh knew he could count on his friends to take good care of Ruth, so he arranged a twenty-four-hour stay. Early in the morning, Walsh's friends collected Ruth and set out for a day of trout fishing on the Klamath River. When the group returned, Ruth beamed as he showed off his catch, a pair of healthy-sized steelhead.

San Francisco, however, would mark a return to the same hectic schedule Ruth had lived with since leaving New York in late October. His week would include a visit to KGO radio for an interview with Al Santoro, photos at the civic center with a San Francisco Boy's Club Little League team, and a banquet thrown in his honor by the Knights of Columbus. On New Year's Day, Ruth would suit up in football gear and perform a ceremonial kickoff to the annual East-West Shrine All-Star game at Kezar Stadium. It was all intertwined with the three shows a day he would perform at the Pantages Theatre on Market and Hyde Streets.

Ruth's show was well received. It was not his first foray into vaudeville—the live-performance genre that involved song, comedy, and other unique acts. Following the 1921 season, a man whom Ruth employed as his business manager, Harry Webber, proposed the idea of a stage show. Ruth would be joined by two veterans of vaudeville. Their act would involve joke telling, a bit of singing, and a mind-reading skit. Ruth's part in the show lasted twenty minutes. Webber organized a four-month tour and promised Ruth $3,000 a week. The plan came to an inglorious halt when Ruth lost his voice after the first four weeks.

By the winter of 1926–1927, Christy Walsh was no longer just a ghost-writer. He was Babe Ruth's full-blown manager. Since joining the Yankees, Ruth had become a magnet for every fast-talker, con man, or entrepreneur with a scheme, scam, or brainstorm. Most that he made deals with failed to deliver on their promises. Twice before Walsh entered the picture, Ruth had accepted offers of help. While with the Boston Red Sox, he entrusted John Igoe to handle his affairs. Once in New York, he placed matters in the hands of Harry Webber. Neither man did for Babe Ruth the things Christy Walsh did.

Walsh delivered for his client in a big way. In addition to his $52,000-a-year salary from the Yankees, the home-run slugger had money coming in from Walsh's newspaper syndication service. A number of products bore Ruth's name—sweaters, baseball equipment, even a Babe Ruth Home Run candy bar. The 1926 vaudeville tour was the biggest money-spinner yet, one which proposed to deposit $100,000 into the star's bank account.

In assembling the 1926 tour, Walsh arranged to bring Ruth to communities that did not have a big-league team—Minneapolis, Des Moines, Vancouver, Spokane, Portland, San Francisco, Los Angeles, and San Diego. To the locals, Babe Ruth was an almost mythical figure, someone they read about in the newspaper, heard about on the radio, or saw on the newsreels that played in their local cinema. His arrival in a town sparked excitement. Associated publicity schemes stoked the flames. It worked to pack Alexander Pantages's theaters.

Ruth's show was written by the New York columnist and humorist "Bugs" Baer. It began with a short movie showing highlights of Ruth's play in the just-completed World Series, followed by clips of his everyday life. The Yankees' slugger then appeared onstage, ushered by a song produced just for the show: "For He's King of the Swat, the Yankees' Best Shot." Ruth then told a few stories, demonstrated his batting technique, and offered a half-dozen autographed baseballs to any boy willing to come up onstage with him.

The show opened to skepticism, but the dubious theater manager in Minneapolis was won over when Ruth, demonstrating his famous home-run swing, comically stumbled and fell onto the stage lights to raucous laughter. What the critics liked about the show was Ruth's personable nature. He eschewed singing for conversation. "The Bambino soon steals his way into the affection of his audience," wrote the *Minneapolis Daily Star*.[3] After one of his shows in Spokane, Washington, a writer with *The Spokesman-Review* noted, "The baseball star proved a genial person."[4]

During the shows, the more youthful among the audience leaned forward in their seats with rapt attention as Ruth showed off his batting stance, how he gripped a bat, and finally, his ferocious swing. The ticket buyers reveled in the insights about the recently completed World Series. They were especially enthralled at Ruth's tales about Game Four, when he had perhaps the greatest-single-game performance in World Series history—three home runs, four runs scored, four runs batted in, and reached base five times in the afternoon.

The 1926 World Series had been a historic one for Babe Ruth. The very first time he came to bat, Ruth set a record for the most World Series appeared in: seven. With Boston, he pitched in three—1915, 1916, and 1918. On joining the Yankees, he led the team to its first-ever World Series appearance in 1921. He helped the Yankees return in 1922 and again in 1923.

Ruth already occupied a place in the World Series record book for his pitching exploits. He held the mark for consecutive scoreless innings pitched, twenty-nine and two-thirds, which spanned the 1916 and 1918 World Series. Now, Ruth entered the record books for hitting feats. Not only were the three home runs Ruth belted in Game Four a World Series record, but so, too, were his twelve total bases. In addition to his new record for the most home runs in a single game, the home run he hit in Game Seven helped Ruth to eclipse the record for most home runs in a World Series: four. During the 1926 Series, St. Louis Cardinals pitchers were reluctant to throw balls over the plate to Ruth. As a result, he walked eleven times in the seven games, which was also a new record, as was his mark for reaching first base nineteen times. In all, Ruth set ten records in the Series.

Though the Yankees lost the World Series to the St. Louis Cardinals and dropped the deciding seventh game when Ruth inexplicably tried to steal second base and was thrown out with two outs in the bottom of the ninth inning with the Yankees trailing, 3–2, his feats grew his legend. As astounding as was the tale of his three home runs in Game Four, especially the one that cleared the roof above the right-field stands in the St. Louis ballpark and shattered a window of a business across the street, it was a gesture Ruth made that garnered most of his World Series headlines.

Following the third game in the Series, the Yankees and Cardinals received urgent telegrams from a New York City banker. Horace Sylvester was in a state of despair. Doctors said his eleven-year-old son was dying. Weeks earlier, the boy had been thrown from a horse, then kicked in the head by the animal. He developed a bad infection that left him weakened and, by early October, near death. Johnny Sylvester whispered to his father his wish for baseballs autographed by the Yankees and Cardinals. The senior Sylvester, an avid baseball fan, sought to fulfill his ailing son's request. Two signed baseballs soon arrived by airmail from St. Louis, where the teams were playing. On one, Babe Ruth offered a special inscription, "I'll knock a homer for Wednesday's game."[5] Upon delivery of the gifts, the young Sylvester smiled and then, clutching the balls in his hands, fell asleep. When he awoke, his father held open a newspaper. Its headline told all. Babe Ruth had hit not one home run but three.

The boy's doctor offered encouraging news. Since receipt of the gift, Johnny Sylvester had improved. The morning after the World Series ended, the boy would receive an even more powerful elixir. Ruth was scheduled to play in a barnstorming game against an all-Black team in Bradley Beach, New Jersey. However, rather than take the scheduled train, Ruth hopped in his new roadster and, exceeding speed limits, made an unplanned stop, thirty miles away at the Sylvester home in Essex Fells, New Jersey. When Babe Ruth appeared at their door, the family was speechless, most of all Johnny. "Did your brother give you that black eye?" Ruth teased.[6] So mesmerized was the youth, propped up on pillows, that he could barely speak. All he managed was to whisper, "Thank you for knocking those homers for me."[7]

News of Ruth's home-run promise and subsequent visit to the ailing boy made its way into newspapers around the country. Heightened wonderment for Ruth generated by his World Series home-run-hitting prowess was soon accompanied by increased regard engendered by the compassion shown Johnny Sylvester. It was heart tugging. Fawning on sports pages gave way to laurels on editorial pages. The *Washington Evening Star* suggested the compassion shown by Ruth "has made this swatsmith more popular than any home run or cluster of home runs he has banged out in his successful career."[8] *The Pittsburgh Post* prodded more sports heroes to show similar kindness. "It is too bad that the inspiration of this vital personality can not be introduced into thousands of boyish sick rooms all over the country to the permanent banishment of ill health from many of them."[9]

To the editor of the editorial page of the *Daily Item* in Port Chester, New York, Ruth's empathy toward Johnny Sylvester had made the slugger a hero to many who may not have been fans before.

"Babe" Ruth's remarkable achievement of scoring three home runs in a single World Series game made him a hero with baseball enthusiasts everywhere. But even that feat did not gain for him the warmth of approbation and affection he has won from all Americans with his simple big-hearted kindness to little Johnny Sylvester who is said literally to have been called back from the grave by a cheery message from his boyhood idol, "The Babe."

He (Ruth) was touched, deeply, by the happiness he had restored to this tiny chap. Similarly touched have been hundreds of thousands of others as they have read of the scene. Thus has George Herman Ruth found his way into the hearts of untold numbers who might never have a second thought to him as an athlete.[10]

Evidence of Ruth's popularity was on display in abundance throughout his winter vaudeville tour. Large crowds, replete with high school marching bands and mayors with proclamations, greeted his arrival in towns and cities. Long lines snaked outside theaters for tickets to his performances. It was not uncommon for Ruth to find dozens of children pining for autographs outside the stage door after shows. When news spread through one small Montana town that Ruth's train would pass by, people gathered in hopes they might simply catch a glimpse of the Yankees' slugger, even though it was the middle of the night.

As Babe Ruth arrived in San Francisco, baseball was a game with problems. Just two months after the sport had reached a zenith of approval, public opinion was then spiraling from the accusations toward Ty Cobb and Tris Speaker. While public trust had been violated and integrity impugned, many fans could take comfort that, as Abe Kemp suggested in the *San Francisco Examiner*, "Ruth today stands as the only unblemished idol of baseball."[11] Paul Gallico, the *New York Daily News* columnist, wrote what many in baseball were no doubt thinking—that in light of the accusations against Cobb and Speaker, Babe Ruth was now "a very important hero, a most important one."[12] Baseball would soon need all the untarnished heroes it could find.

5

Ty Swings Away

Ty Cobb was an angry man. He was incensed by what he felt was betrayal on the part of Judge Kenesaw Mountain Landis. Cobb considered his position buoyed by the reaction of Detroit Tigers fans, baseball fans around the country, and loyal supporters and friends in his hometown of Augusta, Georgia.

It was the day after Christmas when reporters who had come to Augusta began their search for Cobb. None could find him. Inquiries at Cobb's home were rebuffed by the family maids. Cobb's wife could not be found, either. Similarly, in Cleveland reporters who sought out Tris Speaker were unsuccessful too. Unbeknownst to all, Ty Cobb had quietly slipped out of Augusta at two o'clock that afternoon. It was soon learned that not only Cobb but Speaker, too, were bound for Washington, DC, in what would be their first step in an effort to try and restore their reputations.

Tyrus Raymond Cobb was a consummate self-promoter. His skills at such dated back to his teenage years. A six-foot-one-inch dynamo of desire and talent, the then-seventeen-year-old Cobb hit on an idea that bordered on genius in his quest to earn a contract with a big-league ball club. Cobb penned dozens of notes under a pseudonym and sent them to *Atlanta Journal* sports editor Grantland Rice. In each, he assumed the role of a fan to rave about the exploits of a young ballplayer by the name of Ty Cobb, playing for the Anniston Steelers in the Tennessee-Alabama League. After receiving several of the notes, Rice finally bit and mentioned Cobb's success in a column. One year later, Ty Cobb was a member of the Detroit Tigers and beginning what would become an iconic big-league career.

On December 27, Cobb and Speaker spent the day walking the halls of the Congress. Cobb's father had been a state politician in Georgia. The younger

Cobb had many friends in politics—particularly, the senator from Georgia, William Harris. When Cobb and Speaker dropped by Harris's office, they received a pledge to investigate the matter. When later asked about it by reporters, Harris conceded he didn't know that there was anything Congress could do. Arthur Capper, the senator from Kansas, was perhaps the biggest baseball fan in Washington. After meeting with Cobb and Speaker, Capper said he would introduce a resolution asking for an investigation. "All the evidence so far has shown Cobb and Speaker were given a bad deal," Capper told reporters.[1] Despite his pontification, the senator later conceded he had no idea how he would go about such a probe.

Cobb and Speaker announced they were going to enlist the help of the Department of Justice. Claiming Dutch Leonard had used the mail to send the defaming letters, the besmirched ballplayers said they would ask the US Postal Department and the Interstate Commerce Commission to take on the baseball commissioner. Their pronouncements brought bemusement. George McGint, secretary of the Interstate Commerce Commission, told reporters he had no idea why Cobb would seek his help. His department, he explained, had no jurisdiction over baseball. Rush Simmons, chief inspector of the Postal Department, was equally nonplussed. When the two ballplayers left town, their one-day visit was successful in grabbing newspaper headlines but, in the end, proved more theater than any kind of effective tool for absolution.

In the days that followed the revelation of the accusations, Ty Cobb chose to defend himself much the way he played the game of baseball. He attacked. Cobb spewed threats and accusations with the ferocity that he sprayed line drives around American League ballparks. First, Cobb provoked threats of a congressional investigation of baseball. Next, after a meeting in Cleveland with Tris Speaker's attorney, W. H. Boyd, Cobb made loud threats of million-dollar defamation-of-character lawsuits against Dutch Leonard and Commissioner Landis.

Only a month earlier, Cobb had clearly accepted the banishment imposed by Ban Johnson. At a banquet in Asheville, North Carolina, Cobb told the crowd, "I said when I left Detroit, I had swung my last bat in a competitive game and meant just that."[2] He was even planning to take his family on a summer tour of Europe, something he had previously been unable to do because of baseball. Rumors sprang that Cobb, who had parlayed stock tips from admirers into millionaire status, might buy the Boston Red Sox or a minor-league ball club, the Atlanta Crackers. Through it all he was insistent, "I am absolutely through with baseball."[3]

That all changed on December 21, when Landis distributed his one-hundred-page report on the game-fixing and gambling charges to reporters. Ironically, only the day before, Cobb and Speaker met with Landis in

Chicago to answer questions and give their side of the story. While Cobb admitted to writing the letters, he and Speaker insisted they did not fix a ball game. Both men were blindsided by Landis's release of the information. Speaker was on the train bound for his home in Cleveland. Cobb, however, was still in his suite at the luxurious Congress Plaza Hotel. When he learned what Landis had done, he immediately went on the offensive.

Cobb summoned newspaper reporters to his room. For two hours they witnessed a man filled with anger and rage. Cobb's emotions ran the gamut as he professed his innocence. One minute, he paced about the room. The next, he barked at the men. Cobb derided his accuser as a blackmailer. Then, overcome by emotion, Ty Cobb slumped into a chair and sobbed. As tears rolled down his cheeks, Cobb spoke softly. Reporters strained to hear him. "It's the damndest thing ever pulled off," the thirty-nine-year-old said in his unmistakable southern drawl. "There are two fellows going out of the game absolutely clean. I know I am, and I think Speaker is."[4]

Only hours earlier, Landis had told reporters he would take no action. Cobb, Speaker, Dutch Leonard, and "Smokey" Joe Wood, he explained, were out of baseball. If any of them sought to return and play again, the commissioner noted, that would change things. He would likely hold a hearing to get to the bottom of the accusations and determine their eligibility to play once again. Little did Landis know that battle was going to take shape. As Cobb prepared to spend Christmas with his family in Augusta, Georgia, he told newspapermen, "I'll be back in the game next season."[5] Then exposing the core of his ire, he added, "I am not done with Dutch Leonard."[6]

It was Christmas Eve when Ty Cobb returned to his home in Augusta, Georgia. There he found a mountain of telegrams and letters—more than a thousand—piled high on the table in his home. At three o'clock, he was whisked to a testimonial that had been hastily assembled by the town's mayor. At the base of the seventy-six-foot-tall marble Confederate memorial on Broad Street in the city's downtown, Cobb was serenaded by a brass band, presented a basket of chrysanthemums, and cheered by hundreds, some of whom shouted for him to run for mayor. A large banner which read "Ty is still our idol and the idol of America" faced Cobb, who stood with his wife, Charlotte, son, Ty Junior, and daughter, Shirley. The mayor and two judges spoke first. Each extolled the respect and confidence all of Augusta had in Cobb. Then, standing not far from the inscription memorializing Confederate Civil War soldiers that read "None fell so pure of crime," Ty Cobb professed his innocence. "My conscious is clean and clear," he said.[7]

In the forty-eight hours Cobb was home, his emotions often erupted into fury. The object of his ire was not Judge Landis but Dutch Leonard. He excoriated his former teammate with words such as "rotten," "crooked," and "vengeful." He painted the former pitcher as a man with a thirst for revenge. Cobb claimed Leonard's decision to give Landis his letters was the "vengeful nature of a man I fired from the team."[8]

Cobb's claims soon coursed through every newspaper newsroom in the country. Headlines, articles, and columns in dozens, if not hundreds, of newspapers painted Leonard as a man after revenge. Such was the volume and intensity of Cobb's accusations that questions of the ballplayer's guilt or innocence became a vilification of Dutch Leonard.

Men in baseball stepped up to contradict Cobb's charges. Frank Navin, the Tigers' owner, pointed out that Leonard was let go because of a sore arm. John McGraw, manager of the New York Giants, told sportswriters that Leonard was pressured to turn over the letters by Harry Heilmann. None of it could stem the runaway fury of Ty Cobb's criticism.

It was then the scandal took a sensational twist. Cobb dictated a statement to the sports editor of the *Detroit News*. In it he made wild claims. Cobb insisted it was he who had uncovered Leonard's blackmail scheme as far back as June. "I was the first to apprise commissioner Landis," he said.[9] Cobb claimed he met with Landis in Washington, DC, during the 1926 season to inform the commissioner that Leonard was traveling in the East, offering to sell the letters. Cobb claimed he heard Leonard sought $30,000. The salacious charge heightened both support for Cobb and outrage toward Leonard. "He is the scum," wrote one sportswriter. "He sells because of personal enmity. He takes his gold but what is gold to an exile? He is a Judas. His life should be the life of a leper."[10] It was at this point that Dutch Leonard broke his silence.

On December 27, Muriel Leonard handed reporters a three-page, typed statement from her husband. In it Leonard sought to "emphatically set right the minds of the public."[11] He explained that the two matters, handing over the letters and receiving money, involved completely separate issues. The letters, he wrote, were handed over at the insistence of Judge Landis. What money Leonard received—$20,000—was from a contract settlement with the Detroit Tigers and was not connected to the letters in any way.

> When I presented a claim against the Detroit Baseball Club in Chicago in June 1926 to the proper authorities for damage sustained through loss of salary, those authorities, after a full jury, determined my claim was just and valid and settled the full amount of the claim. I received money from the baseball club for this claim only. I never received any money directly or indirectly for any letters or any information in my possession.[12]

Leonard then chided Cobb for accusing him of blackmail. "This term," he wrote, "is only used when one has no facts to sustain one's position."[13] While Leonard defended himself, Cobb expanded his attack. He called team owners untrustworthy and said they falsified turnstile counts and skimmed ticket moneys. The claim drew the ire of many, including Charles Comiskey, who shot back, "Cobb and Speaker did not protest when they were asked [by Ban Johnson] to resign. They did as they were asked, and if Speaker, a man who was managing a winning club, would resign without protest, it looks mighty peculiar to me."[14] The volley of accusations and retorts led a Nashville columnist to write, "Somebody is lying."[15]

Cobb enlisted the help of an attorney—an influential one: James O. Murfin. A former circuit court judge and member of the University of Michigan Board of Regents, Murfin was an unabashed admirer of Cobb. "Cobb's name will be cleared to the satisfaction of everyone," he declared upon his hiring.[16] The lawyer's first bit of action was to tell his client to be quiet. Cobb would not. One week of continued headlines became two. The outpouring of support for Cobb and Speaker was unrelenting. Soon it was not just sportswriters and columnists but entire organizations that chimed in with statements or actions to back the players. The Philadelphia Sportswriters Association sent telegrams to Cobb and Speaker to express "utmost confidence in [their] honesty and integrity."[17] The Chamber of Commerce in Jacksonville, Florida, invited Cobb and Speaker to their Orange Blossom Festival and the Geneva-Oglethorpe football game on New Year's Day. It was an invitation meant to "take this opportunity to assure you that all Jacksonville fans are back of you."[18] Even the Kiwanis Club of Texarkana, Arkansas, lent its voice to the fray when it passed a resolution condemning the charges against Cobb and Speaker.

Much to the chagrin of baseball, the scandal was seized upon as an opportunity to make money. Joseph Benjamin, whose Benjamin Candy Company made the Ty Cobb candy bar, took out ads in newspapers offering $500 to anyone able to provide proof that Cobb had been involved in a conspiracy to throw a game. Newspapers asked readers to weigh in on the guilt or innocence of Cobb and Speaker. The *Richmond Times-Dispatch* urged readers to reply with letters. The *Dayton News* printed ballots and invited readers to fill them out and mail them in. *Collyer's Eye* offered $50 in gold for the best essay about Judge Landis.

Players, both current and former, were sought out by reporters for their thoughts on the growing scandal. Many didn't just rally to Cobb's and Speaker's defense, they harshly disparaged Leonard. Some painted him as selfish, unwilling to pitch when the opponent used their best pitcher, and quick to beg off of pitching if he didn't feel his best. Dickie Kerr, the White Sox pitcher, told of running into Leonard in 1925 in San Francisco, where Leonard, he said, vowed he would one day get even with Cobb. "Pep" Young, who played second base in the game in question, said there was nothing out of the ordinary that afternoon, adding, "Dutch Leonard is an example of sour grapes."[19]

So sensational were the game-fixing charges that reporters even sought out celebrities for their opinions. "Why that rat," said Charles Lane about Leonard when a reporter caught the actor after a performance in Pittsburgh.[20] Frank Rippingille, the fourteen-year-old celebrated as America's youngest aviator, wrote in a special story for *United Press*: "I believe every boy in the United States who likes fair play will not believe this story about Ty Cobb."[21] Particularly persuasive were words from the popular evangelist Billy Sunday, who, at one time, played outfield for the Philadelphia Phillies and Pittsburgh Pirates before joining the ministry. Of Cobb and Speaker, Sunday said, "They are both my friends. It is impossible to imagine that two great stars would risk their fame and fortune for a few hundred dollars."[22]

Opportunists joined the fracas, none more opportunistic than William Randolph Hearst. Owner of the largest chain of newspapers in America and always on the lookout for the sensational, Hearst proposed to conduct a trial into the matter, judged by twelve New York baseball fans. Hearst offered Cobb, Speaker, and Leonard the best legal representation money could buy and to cover all costs. As an aside, Hearst said the commissioner could attend should he wish.

As voluminous as the negative ink was, equally damning was the volume of chatter throughout the Hot Stove League. So called by its origins, men warming from winter's chill around a store's potbellied stove while talking baseball, the Hot Stove League encompassed both the formal and the casual. Testimonial dinners in big cities honored star players. In small towns men gathered in a store, bar, or hall to hear yarns spun by the local baseball star, home for the winter. In any normal off-season, the hot topic of conversation would be the local ball club. Chatter or gossip would encompass what the Chickasha Chicks in Oklahoma should do to improve the team, whether the Topeka Senators needed a better shortstop, and all the way up to what trade the Cincinnati Reds ought to make to become a pennant contender. That was during a normal off-season. This had become no normal off-season.

As December 1926 turned to January 1927, team owners and league executives no doubt wished Burris Jenkins Jr., a columnist with the *Lincoln State Journal* in Nebraska, had been right when he predicted back in September that winter would be "one of the coldest seasons conversationally that fans had known in years."[23] Each day brought new developments. Headlines, columns, and articles further stoked the flames of the Hot Stove circuit, much to the ire of men in baseball, as noted by the *Lincoln State Journal*. "If the wishes of the commissioner and the league magnates are respected however, the scandal will die a natural death and the hot stove league will have to depend on the spring training camps for fuel during the next few months."[24]

Ty Cobb, however, would not comply. For six weeks Cobb not only kept the Hot Stove fires burning but made the flames white hot with incessant accusations. Cobb's incendiary attacks were a baseball version of General William Tecumseh Sherman's scorched-earth March to the Sea campaign during the Civil War. Rather than destroy cotton plantations and infrastructure, Ty Cobb verbally eviscerated Dutch Leonard. He challenged Kenesaw Mountain Landis. Cobb also drew the quiet ire of Ban Johnson. It was all done with claims and charges that were not only incendiary but—in many cases—inaccurate, unfounded, and damaging to the game.

Newspapers gave Cobb a largely unfettered pipeline to baseball fans and the public at large. Day after day Cobb criticized the target of his ire, Dutch Leonard. By choosing to remain quiet, the former pitcher was vilified in newspapers all across the country. In the *Muncie Evening Press*, the sports columnist suggested, "Dutch Squawk Leonard has our permission to be the first man to try to go over Niagara Falls in a paper drinking cup."[25] The *Arizona Republic* carried the headline, "Dutch Leonard Poorest Sportsman in Baseball," and it called the former pitcher the "Judas of baseball."[26] Billy Evans, the American League umpire who wrote columns for several newspapers, branded Leonard a "squealer."[27]

Each day reporters arrived at Leonard's farm, hopeful the former pitcher would comment. The men noticed Muriel Leonard peek through the curtains. If anything was spoken to them, it was by the pitcher's wife to inform them her husband had nothing to say. Leonard's silence enabled Cobb to shape public opinion. It led to incidents such as one at the Pacific Coast League owners' meeting, where two teams—the San Francisco Seals and Mission Bells—urged that Leonard be banned, not just from playing in the league but from ever again entering one of its ballparks. Concerned he might be on the receiving end of a similar reception in his hometown, Leonard withdrew from the championship golf tournament at his country club. It was a tournament title he was expected to contend for.

Finally, a day came when Leonard gave in. He agreed to speak with one reporter: Austin O'Malley of *United Press*. O'Malley found Leonard seated in front of a fire and willing to answer his questions. During their conversation, Leonard expressed anger that Landis had gone public with the contents of the letters. The pitcher said he did not talk about the letters for seven years, because "I feared by doing so I might be injuring the standing of baseball."[28] It was only after he was contacted by Landis that Leonard agreed to share their contents. "He impressed me with the fact that under baseball law, he was empowered to demand those things. So, I answered all his questions to the best of my ability."[29] As the conversation continued, it became apparent to the reporter Leonard harbored a great deal of animosity toward his former manager. Leonard confirmed such and explained that it stemmed from an arduous, ten-day stretch during the middle of the 1925 season and actions that destroyed both a friendship and mutual respect.

During the 1925 season, a number of rainouts packed the Tigers' schedule with makeup games in late June and early July, four doubleheaders in ten days. It taxed the pitching staff, and according to Leonard, "Cobb was desperate"[30]—so desperate that Leonard claimed his manager reneged on a commitment.

During the spring of 1922, Dutch Leonard considered his career in the major leagues closed. Farming consumed his time. It was then that letters began to arrive from Ty Cobb. Each one urged Leonard to return to the Detroit Tigers. Leonard declined. Finally, in 1924, with Detroit surging in the standings, Cobb wrote with a promise. "He wrote me that I would have four days rest between games," Leonard told the reporter.[31] It was under that promise that the pitcher agreed to return.

Now, according to Leonard, in the grueling stretch of 1925 games, Cobb grew desperate and ignored his promise. Leonard said he was asked to pitch two days after he had thrown all nine innings in a 7–4 win over Cleveland. The pitcher told the manager his arm was sore. By Leonard's account, Cobb became angry and accused him of "dogging it." Leonard acquiesced and pitched Detroit to wins over St. Louis and Boston, both with complete games.

On July 14, Leonard was on the trainer's table getting a massage. George Dauss was scheduled to pitch. Cobb entered the clubhouse and told Leonard he would pitch instead. When the left-hander explained that his arm was sore, Cobb berated him in front of his teammates. "Who do you think you are, manager of the team? Get out there on the field. Don't you dare turn Bolshevik on me."[32] That afternoon, Dutch Leonard endured the worst beating of his baseball career. Philadelphia battered him for twenty hits. They scored in six of the first seven innings and by the end of the seventh, they'd put twelve runs on the scoreboard. Ty Cobb never moved a muscle to replace Leonard. From the opposing dugout, Philadelphia's manager, Connie Mack, hollered to Cobb, "You are killing that boy," to which Cobb laughed.[33]

Leonard turned to the reporter and wondered aloud, "Why Cobb turned on me the way he did." Leonard suggested, "Money is his sole thought. Cobb may have figured he was too big to be touched. Well, he knows now that he is not."[34] The pitcher told the visiting reporter of yet another letter, one he had not shown Landis. It was prepared and sent by Cobb when the hitting great learned Landis was traveling to Dutch Leonard's farm. In it, Cobb wrote, "Dutch, I am in your power. Please take care of me and protect me." As Leonard ushered the reporter to the door, he told the man he expected criticism for talking. But, said Leonard, he wanted people to see Cobb and Speaker "for what they are."[35]

A research firm, NEA Service, was commissioned to gauge the fan reaction to the scandal. It found strong support for Cobb and Speaker. It was about that time when Cobb switched tactics. He jumped from accusing to demanding. At first, he insisted on a hearing, one where he could face his accuser. When his attorney pushed for a forum, the ballplayer changed his stance. No, he didn't want a hearing. "Let us have a verdict now," Cobb demanded.[36] Unbeknownst to Cobb, his visceral whirlwind wrought unintended consequences. Not only had investigators dispatched by Landis dug up more claims, but current and former players prompted by Cobb's accusations came forth with new information. Evidence was serious. The dark clouds shrouding baseball were about to get darker.

6

Baseball at the Abyss

In the minutes that led up to ten o'clock on the morning on January 5, the corridor outside the thirteenth floor, Michigan Avenue office of the commissioner of baseball was a compressed mass of sweaty anxiety. When the commissioner's secretary unlocked and then opened the doors, more than one hundred newspaper writers and photographers stampeded—jostling and sparring one another for one of the few seats. It was nothing short of a frenzy. It was driven by a series of sensational newspaper headlines:

"BASEBALL SCANDAL GROWS."[1]
"MORE BASEBALL 'CROOKEDNESS' UNCOVERED."[2]
"THREE BALL CLUBS ARE CHARGED IN TWO 'DEALS.'"[3]

For Ty Cobb, rather than help with his goal of vindication, the press coverage spurred by the former Tigers' endless interviews and accusations made things worse. Current and former players came forward with new claims. The most provocative happened purely by chance. A newspaper reporter traveling to a new job happened to stop over in Rochester, Minnesota. He found himself in a pool hall with "Swede" Risberg, the disgraced former shortstop of the Chicago White Sox.[4] Risberg, the admitted ringleader of the 1919 World Series game-fixing scheme, was on the outside of baseball looking in, banished for life by Commissioner Landis. He was running a small dairy farm just outside of Rochester. While the men shot pool, the reporter asked what Risberg thought about the allegations made against Cobb and Speaker. The response was stunning. "I can implicate 20 big leaguers in a baseball scandal, but Judge Landis will never ask me what I know," Risberg said.[5]

Risberg's claim made it into the local newspaper. A reporter for the *Chicago Tribune* who was in Rochester for medical treatment at the Mayo Clinic saw the story. He alerted his paper to it. Soon an offer of $500 was made to Risberg to tell what he knew. Risberg pointed a finger at Cobb's Detroit Tigers and said the team had thrown an entire series in 1917 to help the White Sox in their pennant fight with the Boston Red Sox.

Almost immediately, Landis sent Risberg a cable with an offer to pay for his travel and time if he would come to Chicago. Forty-eight hours later, on January 1, the former shortstop spent two hours in the commissioner's office, laying out his story. He answered every question put to him by Landis. Risberg offered specific details such as times and places. He fingered current and former players, managers, and even an umpire.

Reactions ran the gamut. Once their names appeared in print, the accused sent telegrams with terse denials to newspaper reporters. To others in the game, the accuser more than the accusations was what drew ire. "I would not believe anything that Swede Risberg might say at any time about anything," said Pittsburgh Pirates president Barney Dreyfuss.[6] Babe Ruth went one step further. "That bird ought to be hung by his toes until he is half conscious then be immersed in a vat of boiling oil. He was never a representative of good sportsmanship from the day he broke into big league baseball."[7]

Still, Risberg received support. Former White Sox teammates "Happy" Felsch and Buck Weaver confirmed what Risberg told Landis. Another former teammate, Chick Gandil, warned, "Risberg did not tell the half of it."[8] The flames of controversy grew higher. A Detroit newspaper carried a story in which its sports editor claimed Ty Cobb told him the St. Louis Browns had thrown an entire three-game series to the Tigers in 1923. Several Browns players, according to the account, wanted to spite the Cleveland ball club and help the Tigers finish ahead of them in the standings. On the heels of the accusation, the *Chicago Tribune* carried a story in which an anonymous source claimed the New York Giants had conspired with gamblers to throw the 1917 World Series. It was a charge made so often by Ban Johnson that Landis was certain the American League president was the newspaper's anonymous source.

For weeks Landis and his secretary, Leslie O'Connor, spent long hours poring over information gathered by investigators. On New Year's Eve, while Chicagoans were celebrating in restaurants and clubs on Michigan Avenue below, Landis was oblivious, working in his office. On New Year's Day, when Risberg concluded his session with Landis, the commissioner and his secretary hastily assembled addresses, then dispatched summonses—thirty-eight in all. Each recipient was offered travel expenses and compensation. All were given a date to appear, either January 5 or January 7.

Landis's plan for hearings ran into snags. A small number of players balked. One said he could not leave his lumber camp in Mississippi; another claimed illness. A third explained in a telegram that he was on a construction job in Mexico. The rejection that irked Landis most came from Dutch Leonard. The commissioner cajoled, urged, and even ordered to no avail. Ever since Landis had gone public with the news of Leonard's letters, the former pitcher had been barraged with abuse and threats. Some were from people like a former teammate of Cobb's, Charley "Boss" Schmidt, who lived ninety-five miles north of Leonard's farm in the town of Modesto. Amid the firestorm, Schmidt received a letter from Cobb, who wrote that Dutch Leonard "will never live a happy life." The former catcher wrote back, "If you want me to, I'll go down to Fresno and square things up with that Dutchman."[9] An exasperated Landis asked Leonard why he would not come to Chicago for the hearing. "They bump people off once in a while around there," the former pitcher replied.[10]

Through it all, the specter of Ban Johnson loomed. Stories that painted Landis in a negative light continued to find their way into print. The commissioner was accused of stonewalling requests to look into whether the 1923 World Series was fixed. Still more columnists predicted Landis would whitewash the current accusations to save baseball further embarrassment. The commissioner felt certain of the origin of the claims and was incensed by them.

On January 5, Landis opened the first of two one-day hearings. Outside of the People's Gas Building, where the commissioner's office was housed, it was cold, in the low thirties. A large crowd of fans, gawkers, newspapermen, and photographers massed on Michigan Avenue. Ty Cobb was swarmed when he arrived. Inside, tensions were high and temperaments were hot. Players waited in the corridor to be called. Some paced, others chatted. Cobb was particularly jovial, backslapping and shaking hands. He had been vindicated in the court of public opinion, and the greeting he received on the street below confirmed he was still the ever-popular "Georgia Peach."

The commissioner's office was packed. Reporters and photographers, forty in all, sat around a long table. Smoke from cigarettes and cigars choked the air.[11] Landis sat behind his office desk, smallish in a high-back chair that reached several inches above his tousled white hair. To his left was a witness chair. A second chair was positioned to place the accused less than a foot to the left of the man being questioned. Swede Risberg was the first called. "Will you repeat to me now the statements you made to me in my office on January 1 regarding the games between Chicago and Detroit in 1917?"[12] Landis asked as the hearing began.

Risberg leaned forward and then, in a strong, loud voice, spent more than an hour retelling his story. The games in question were part of a Labor Day series between the Chicago White Sox and Detroit—specifically, back-to-back doubleheaders on September 2 and 3, 1917. The White Sox, in a fight with Boston for the American League pennant, had entered September with a three-and-a-half-game lead. The pennant race was far from settled. At the behest of the White Sox first baseman, Chick Gandil, every player agreed to contribute forty-five dollars to a fund that would reward Detroit Tigers pitchers for laying down so the White Sox could win all four games. Risberg said it was the White Sox manager, Clarence Rowland, who told him everything was set, that the Tigers had agreed to the plan. Chicago won all four games and exited the series with a seven-game lead over Boston en route to winning the pennant and the World Series. Two weeks later, when the White Sox were in New York, Risberg recounted, it was then that Gandil approached each player for his contribution. Gandil and Risberg then took the money to Philadelphia, where the Tigers were playing the Athletics. At the Aldin Hotel,

Figure 6.1. The commissioner of baseball, Kenesaw Mountain Landis, here at a dedication ceremony in Los Angeles, called the Cobb-Speaker scandal the hardest job he ever had to do. *Courtesy: Security Pacific National Bank collection/Los Angeles Public Library photo collection.*

Risberg said he and Gandil gave what had been collected—$1,100—to Bill James, the Detroit Tigers' pitcher who coordinated his team's side of the deal.

Once Risberg completed his recitation, Landis peppered him with questions. The commissioner paced behind his desk. He sought specific details. Some felt Landis was trying to shake Risberg. Others thought the commissioner was trying to confuse the former shortstop. Risberg handled most of the questions deftly, but to some, he was vague, and to a handful more, he could not recall specifics. It was then that Landis summoned the men accused.

For the next four hours, Risberg sat silently as a parade—twenty-six men in all—followed one another to the second chair. Risberg puffed cigarettes and grinned as each was asked to respond to the accusations made. Clarence Rowland was first. "A damned lie!" he barked.[13] It was a line echoed by almost everyone who followed. Along with the denials were a few who were vague— "This happened a long time ago"—and a couple who proved evasive, saying, "It's hard to remember."[14] In between there were angry outbursts, profanities shouted, and menacing glares from accused toward accuser. Donie Bush shook a fist and challenged Risberg to fight. When Bernie Boland sat down in the second chair, the former Tigers' pitcher pivoted, faced Risberg, and barked, "I see you're still a pig."[15] There were dramatic moments as well. Ty Cobb took the stand and angrily denied to Landis that he confided to a Detroit sportswriter that a series with the St. Louis Browns in 1923 was thrown. About Risberg's charges, Cobb answered, "If there had been any dirty work, I'd have known it and recalled it."[16]

The most revealing testimony came when Eddie Collins was called. He walked toward the commissioner and slapped a checkbook on Landis's desk. Collins, the star of the 1917 White Sox, pointed to the entry for October 16, 1917. It was for a forty-five dollar check made out to Chick Gandil. Collins noted the date was after the World Series and proved, he said, the payment was for a gift and not a bribe. He went on to explain the money was not payment for games on September 2 and 3, but rather a thank-you to Detroit's pitchers for beating Boston on September 21, the day the Red Sox loss allowed the White Sox to clinch the American League pennant.

The day ended with Risberg's credibility in tatters. Even one of his former teammates, a man whom Risberg felt certain would corroborate his story, Buck Weaver said he knew nothing of the claims. Weaver used the audience with Landis to stress his innocence in the fixing of the 1919 World Series and plead for reinstatement to baseball.

As the commissioner's office emptied following the hearing, Kenesaw Mountain Landis began to prepare for the second day of testimony. He was keen to get Chick Gandil and Bill James on the stand. Much of Risberg's testimony involved the role of Gandil, the onetime first baseman of the White

Sox. Risberg had also accused James of being the point man for the Tigers. Gandil was already in Chicago, having received a summons from Landis. But before Landis could put him on the witness stand, the *Chicago Tribune* got ahold of him. On the morning of the second day of testimony, the paper ran a sensational banner headline: "SOX GAMES FRAMED—GANDIL."[17] In an article that filled an entire half page, the paper ran a signed, sworn affidavit in which Gandil confirmed everything Risberg had claimed.

It was three minutes past four o'clock on Friday, January 7, when Arnold "Chick" Gandil entered the commissioner's office. Wearing a tan, three-piece suit capped by a bow tie, Gandil removed his checked flat cap as he walked into the room. With him were two men he introduced as his lawyers. Landis motioned for Gandil to take the witness chair. The tension about the room was palpable. Rather than recite a story as Risberg had, Gandil responded to questions from Landis. He told of arriving at Comiskey Park before the September 2 doubleheader, when he passed Bill James beneath the stands. The two engaged in conversation. When they spoke of the pennant race, Gandil said the Tigers' pitcher told him, "You fellows get out there and hustle. The boys won't bear down on you."[18] When asked by Landis how he responded, Gandil answered, "I told him I would see that he got fixed up."[19] Gandil said some Chicago players thought a suit of clothes for each Detroit player would make an appropriate gift, but Gandil instructed cash was the best way to go.

Gandil explained the White Sox had a day off after a late-September series in New York against the Yankees. He went to his manager, Rowland, and suggested a team meeting to collect money they planned to give the Tigers. Gandil said Rowland gave permission to travel to Philadelphia to pay James. He recalled interrupting a poker game among several Tigers players when he handed James the envelope with their money.

Landis then shifted focus. He sought specifics about the allegedly fixed games. Holding up a newspaper, the commissioner said box scores of the four games did not show anything out of the ordinary. Gandil explained that the tipoff to the fixed games was in the numbers of walks and stolen bases. In this instance, both were much greater than normal. Detroit pitchers walked seventeen batters in three of the four games. Stolen bases were even more telling—three in game one, six in the second game, eight the next afternoon, and five in the series finale. Gandil explained that Detroit pitchers intentionally failed to hold the Chicago base runners. He made special note of the third game of the series, when there were eight stolen bases, including Fred McMullen's theft of home while Happy Felsch and Neimo Leibold each swiped third base.

When Landis returned to the matter of payoffs, he referred to Eddie Collins's testimony. Gandil remained insistent that Collins had paid him within an hour of being asked for the money. As for players who testified the money was a gift and not an inducement, Gandil laughed, then blurted, "That's a joke."[20] Where Swede Risberg had been, at times, evasive and vague under questioning by Landis, Gandil was calm, succinct, and thorough.

Bill James then took the stand. Now retired from baseball and living in Los Angeles, James proceeded to deny almost every claim Gandil had made. He said he never spoke with Gandil beneath the stands at Comiskey Park, only briefly on the field during the third game of the series. He claimed Gandil offered to reward any Detroit pitcher able to beat the Boston Red Sox in a three-game series on September 19 and 20. James did acknowledge receipt of an envelope with money from Gandil but insisted it contained far less than what was allegedly inside. As for Gandil's claim that the proof of the fix was in the poor performance of the Detroit pitchers, James answered, "We played rotten ball during that series which was customary for our ball club at that time. We were in and outers."[21]

After three hours of questions and answers in a stifling, packed room, the hearing was brought to a close. Thirty-seven men had been queried. Landis declared the need for a few days to review the voluminous testimony. He promised a decision at 10:00 a.m. the following Wednesday.

As reporters and ballplayers filed out of the commissioner's office, many were perplexed. Over two long days of testimony, not one question was asked pertaining to what brought about the hearing in the first place—Dutch Leonard's letters. That puzzlement appeared in print the following day. "What's the status of Ty Cobb and Tris Speaker?" asked Bob Shand in the *Oakland Tribune*.[22] Paul Gallico, sports editor of the *New York Daily News*, wondered, "Now, what about Cobb and Speaker? Are they in or out?"[23] The opinion editor in the *Detroit Free Press* wrote that Cobb and Speaker were "still shivering out in the cold, their cases unjudged and unsettled."[24]

In the aftermath of the hearings was an overwhelming belief that neither Risberg nor Gandil had offered the kind of evidence to substantiate their claims. In betting dens around Chicago, bookmakers were quick to lay odds at ten–to–one that Landis would exonerate the accused. Having heard everyone to take the stand call them liars, Swede Risberg and Chick Gandil left Chicago knowing full well where their credibility lay. "Some day the truth is going to come out and everybody will know that Gandil and I gave the facts. Those four games were fixed, and Detroit players got paid for it," Risberg said to reporters.[25]

None of it—not the odds, not the hearing, nor anything he heard—could shake Ban Johnson's position. The American League president had remained silent throughout the proceedings, but afterward, he told a friendly reporter his position regarding Cobb and Speaker would not change. His conviction remained the same. Cobb and Speaker, he said, were offered a hearing. Both declined. They accepted his decision and agreed to exit baseball. As far as Johnson was concerned, the former stars would remain banished from the American League, and no matter what Landis said or did, both had played their last game.

As Kenesaw Mountain Landis prepared to go into seclusion and study the testimony, he faced a challenge of daunting proportions. It involved the public perception of baseball's integrity. Wrote one newspaper columnist of the fans, "He must have his confidence restored."[26] Amid the myriad newspaper headlines in the aftermath of the hearings came one from a Tucson, Arizona, paper that succinctly captured the momentous challenge the commissioner held: "Landis Faced with Biggest Job of Regime."[27]

Decision Day

The weather was bitterly cold. Were a gauge visible, it would have registered just seventeen degrees. Bundled in heavy overcoats, a gaggle of newspapermen paced and chatted in hushed tones in the dark on Chicago's East Hyde Park Boulevard. Some among the group had waited longer than others, much longer, but for all of them, the wait had been nothing short of a marathon. Despite the chill and the hour, there was not a trace of surrender in any of those who toiled. Their place of encampment was the sidewalk outside the Chicago Beach Hotel, where Judge Kenesaw Mountain Landis lived. Their quest was a scoop—specifically, any indication be it a hint, inuendo, or even a suggestion of what the baseball commissioner would announce in seven hours' time.

It was three o'clock in the morning when the recognizable white-haired man appeared. His hands were stuffed in the pockets of his black overcoat. A floppy fedora topped his head. As the commissioner ambled toward the building, those gathered moved to intercept him. On sight of the reporters, Landis became agitated. Questions were barked. Landis responded but didn't; his words terse and unrevealing. With a wave of his left arm, the commissioner dismissed the throng. Then without hesitation or pause, he disappeared into the building.

While unsuccessful in their goal, the newspapermen had been more successful than Ty Cobb's attorney. Almost since the commissioner's hearing concluded five days earlier, James O. Murfin had sought answers about the status of his client and also Tris Speaker. The Detroit judge and attorney for Cobb spent thirty-six hours searching Chicago for Landis. By midday Sunday, an unsuccessful Murfin boarded a train and returned home.

Murfin was far from alone in his inability to find Landis. Following the conclusion of the hearings on Friday, January 7, the commissioner went into seclusion. Away from lawyers and newspapermen, Landis spent hours poring over the stenographers' transcripts of the testimony. He had spared no expense to get to the bottom of the accusations. By the time an accounting was made, Landis would show baseball's executive committee that close to $30,000 was spent to get to the truth—$20,000 on a team of detectives and another $10,000 to bring thirty-four witnesses to Chicago from as far away as Connecticut in the East and California out West to offer testimony.

While Landis worked in isolation, newspapers across the country fanned the flames of scandal. A Chicago sportswriter lent support to Risberg's and Gandil's testimony. Hugh Fullerton wrote of being around the White Sox at the time of their alleged deal with Detroit Tigers players. Fullerton recalled several of the White Sox expressing anger toward Eddie Collins for not contributing to the pot of money. Fullerton also told of overhearing Buck Weaver tell teammates he bought a purse for the wife of George Dauss to make up for his failure to contribute.

In the days after the hearings, accusations rose about more allegedly fixed games. A New York newspaper accused Ty Cobb of involvement in a 1923 game between his Detroit Tigers and the St. Louis Browns, which was also said to have been thrown. Cobb denied the accusation. Letters arrived at the commissioner's office with tips about even more games that were potentially crooked, specifically, during the 1921 and 1922 seasons. Once again, accusations about the New York Giants and a fixed 1923 World Series were also raised.

Columnists and sportswriters speculated on the potential ruling from Landis. Acquittals seemed the common expectation. Reporters went to Swede Risberg for his opinion. "The whole affair might be whitewashed," he said.[1] Men who worked with Landis in the legal profession reminded, however, of his unpredictability while on the bench.

On Wednesday, January 12, Landis entered his office at around 9:30 a.m. Several members of the media, nearly fifty in all, were waiting. The reporters were brought by the promise of a 10:00 a.m. announcement. Landis was still perturbed by his encounter with reporters hours earlier.

At five minutes of ten, Landis rose from his desk, checked his watch, and then began to hand out the report with his ruling. "By George that was the hardest job I ever faced," he said.[2] In the three thousand-word report, Landis cleared the twenty-one players who stood accused. The evidence, he concluded, was flimsy. Given their past, Landis felt he could not give credibility to Risberg or Gandil. Eddie Collins's checkbook records offered tangible evidence that the money collected for the Detroit Tigers' players was a gift and not a bribe. "An act of impropriety—reprehensible and censurable but not corrupt."[3] Swede Risberg was not surprised by the verdict. "There were too many witnesses against us," he said. "Those boys were there to testify as they did to save their job."[4]

In the report, Landis proposed changes to the game. He recommended several steps to combat gambling and game-fixing:

1. A statute of limitations with respect to alleged baseball offenses.
2. Ineligibility for one year for offering or giving any gift or reward by the players or management of one club to the players or management of another club for services rendered or supposed to be or have been rendered in defeating a competing club.
3. Ineligibility for one year for betting any sum whatsoever on any ballgames in connection with which the bettor has no duty to perform.
4. Permanent ineligibility for betting any sum whatsoever upon any ballgame in connection with which the bettor has any duty to perform.[5]

If the baseball commissioner felt his ruling would quell the game's winter of scandal, he was mistaken. Almost immediately, Landis found himself under assault from several flanks. Reporters were quick to notice no ruling was made on the matter that launched the controversy in the first place— the scandal involving Ty Cobb and Tris Speaker. "It's all in there," Landis snapped. "Read their testimony and judge for yourself whether they are inno-cent or guilty."[6] He reiterated what Ban Johnson had declared weeks before, that Cobb and Speaker were out of baseball and thus there was nothing to rule on. The only way that would change was if one or both were to petition for reinstatement.

A day later, Landis found himself under further attack in print. Newspapers across the country took up the case of Cobb and Speaker. The *New York Daily News* asked, "Now, what about Cobb and Speaker? Are they in or are they out? Is the word of Dutch Leonard any better than that of Gandil or Risberg? Or has Landis something that implicates them beyond any question?"[7]

On its editorial page, the *Detroit Free Press* fanned the flames by telling readers that Cobb and Speaker were "still shivering out in the cold, their cases unjudged and unsettled, though the accusation made against them was relatively trivial, and never has been in the least substantiated."[8]

In his syndicated column, Grantland Rice wrote:

So the wrath of the fans against Judge Landis, Leonard, Navin and Johnson can be understood. They figure that Cobb and Speaker gave them more entertain-ment and a greater number of thrills through twenty years than all the magnates combined. There is also the feeling that even if Cobb and Speaker were guilty on the Leonard counts it was only one slip and they are at least rigged out with average human honesty.[9]

An even bigger assault came from the commissioner's nemesis, Ban Johnson. The American League president chided Landis's ruling. "This is the
same case that was tried by the commissioner six years ago," Johnson said.[10]
He further said that Landis bore all blame for the Cobb-Speaker scandal, adding, "I don't believe Cobb ever played a dishonest game in his life."[11] The
growing intensity of the feud between Landis and Johnson raised a troubling
theory among some in the press. "There has been a persistent rumor that
the whole scandal outbreak was fomented by baseball interests opposed to
Landis's regime as baseball czar. It was argued that these interests were so
violently opposed to the commissioner that they were willing to risk shatter-
ing public confidence in the game if they could embarrass him or possibly
force him out of office and get the control of baseball into their own hands,"
wrote Will Murphy in the *New York Daily News.*[12] Dick Hawkins of the *Atlanta Constitution* theorized as much in his column. "Could it be possible that
Ban Johnson engineered the entire affair to force Landis to a resignation?"[13]

It was then that Ban Johnson overplayed his hand. A day after Landis's
ruling, an article appeared in the *Chicago Tribune.* In it a source identified
only as "one of organized baseball's leaders" stated categorically that no
matter what Landis were to rule regarding Cobb and Speaker, neither player
would ever again play or manage in the American League. "They have been
offered public hearings. Each of them declined."[14] The source went on to
claim that Cobb had been under investigation for two years and that the
letters belonging to Dutch Leonard were only a small part of the evidence
against Cobb and Speaker.

Upon reading the article, Landis became furious. He suspected Ban
Johnson to be the unnamed source. Similarly, Cobb's attorney (J. O.
Murfin, a Detroit judge) was not happy either. Murfin requested a meeting
with Landis and was granted one in two days' time. It was Saturday when the
two men met. Murfin pressed the commissioner on whether there was any
truth to what appeared in the article. Was there more evidence than just the
Leonard letters? Landis conceded that much of the information in the article
was news to him. He explained that four months earlier, in September, the
American League ordered all evidence forwarded to the commissioner. If
what the unnamed source claimed in the article was true, then Landis had
only a fraction of the information about Cobb and Speaker. Murfin said both
Cobb and Speaker wanted their baseball status clarified. Both men sought
to return to the game. Before the men parted, the commissioner promised
Murfin he would get to the bottom of the matter.

Before the day was done, Landis called a mandatory meeting of owners of
the eight American League ball clubs in Chicago in ten days' time. He told
the men he wanted every piece of evidence they had to bring resolution to the

Cobb-Speaker matter once and for all. Unspoken was an even more significant item on Landis's agenda. The commissioner wanted Ban Johnson dealt
with once and for all as well.

In the days that led up to the meeting, sides were drawn. Men once loyal
to Johnson jumped ship. Charles Comiskey, owner of the White Sox, declared himself on the side of Landis.[15] Similarly, Clark Griffith, who owned
the Washington Senators, said, "Johnson should have resigned two years
ago."[16] Colonel Jacob Ruppert, owner of the New York Yankees, bristled at
Johnson's persistent claim that the 1923 World Series—one in which his
Yankees beat the New York Giants—was not on the up-and-up. In spite of
the storm swirling around him, Ban Johnson dug in his heels. "It looks like
a merry session Monday. I stand by every charge I have made, and I am prepared to prove everything I say."[17]

On the eve of Landis's meeting, the American League's board of directors
gathered privately to discuss Ban Johnson's actions. The men were surprised
when Johnson entered the room. They were not surprised that he appeared but
found his appearance to be disturbing. Ban Johnson was clearly ill. The once
fiery leader struggled just to walk. Johnson's physician told the board that
his patient needed to take an immediate leave of his duties. The board, made
up of the owners of the Boston, Cleveland, New York, Philadelphia, and
Washington ball clubs, quickly agreed to the request. Johnson then rose from
his chair to leave. He momentarily wobbled, reached for the wall to steady
himself, and stumbled as he exited the room.[18] One director later remarked
that Johnson's doctor said that even after a six-week break, the American
League president was not likely to have the stamina to continue on the job
and would probably resign.[19]

Before their meeting concluded, Johnson provided the board with a
formal written statement that all information pertaining to Cobb and Speaker
had been turned over to the commissioner. When Landis was notified of the
development, he asked to meet with all eight American League club owners
that evening at the Blackstone Hotel. At five o'clock the commissioner stood
before the men. He opened with an expression of sorrow at Johnson's deterio-
rating health. Landis then said, in light of Johnson's statement regarding the
evidence in the Cobb-Speaker matter, there was no need for the meeting that
was planned for the next day. The club owners issued a statement to reporters, one that distanced them from Johnson's recent actions and threw their
complete support behind Landis.

The news of Ban Johnson's departure came as a bombshell. Even in their
questions about the stunning development, many reporters still pressed
Landis about the Cobb-Speaker matter. The commissioner promised he
would have a decision by the end of the coming week.

It was Thursday, January 27, and in Augusta, Georgia, Ty Cobb had just completed a round of golf when a telegram arrived. It was from Frank Navin, owner of the Detroit Tigers, and read, "This is to inform you that you are at liberty to do business with any club in the American League you can get the most advantageous agreement with."[20] Cobb had been exonerated and restored to good standing by Kenesaw Mountain Landis. So too was Tris Speaker. Just as Navin did not want Cobb back with the Tigers, the president of the Cleveland ball club let Speaker know he was not welcomed to return, either. "This would be a mistake," said E. S. Barnard, "both from the standpoint of the club and the standpoint of what would be best for Tris."[21]

Navin sent telegrams to the seven other American League clubs and all eight in the National League. He declared to each that he did not want Cobb back. Any team was free to negotiate with Cobb and no compensation for his services would be sought by the Tigers. Only moments after Tris Speaker received notice of his exoneration, a telephone message came from Clark Griffith, president of the Washington Senators. It extended the offer of a contract to join the team. Speaker accepted on the spot.[22] Within twenty-four hours, Cobb would hear from the St. Louis Browns and Philadelphia Athletics, both of whom were keen to sign the twelve-time batting champion.

In Chicago Kenesaw Mountain Landis was nowhere to be found when the decision was handed out. Once the pronouncement was typed up, Landis grabbed his hat and coat and made for home to pack for a trip to Florida and spring training camps. In the statement distributed by his assistant, Leslie O'Connor, Landis stated, "These players have not been found guilty of fixing a ball game. By no decent system of justice could such a finding be made. Therefore, they were not placed on the ineligible list."[23]

Particularly frustrating to Landis was his inability to get Dutch Leonard to face Cobb and Speaker in a hearing. The attorneys for the two players were insistent on it. From his visit to Leonard's farm in October 1926, to the day he issued his final ruling three months later, Landis had been unrelenting in his quest to bring Leonard to Chicago. The former pitcher was equally unflinching in his outright refusal to do so. Without Leonard's presence to either corroborate claims or be impeached, Landis lacked conclusive evidence to determine whether Cobb and Speaker had been part of a plot to fix a game or games.

Reporters traveled to Leonard's farm for comment. They were met by the former pitcher's wife, who said her husband was ill and "would have no statement to make anyway."[24] A reporter found Ban Johnson in Excelsior Springs, Missouri, convalescing at the home of a friend. "My health is poor and has been poor for some time and I don't feel like making a statement of any kind at this time," he said.[25]

Speculation about a landing spot for Cobb ran rampant. "Right now, I don't know where I will play but I'll be back in the big show," he said.[26] The front-runner quickly became the woeful St. Louis Browns. While the idea of a player of Cobb's stature joining a last-place ball club seemed perplexing to many, insiders felt it was not far-fetched. "Cobb and Dan Howley have been friends for years. That makes the idea look sound," said Ed Barrow, business manager of the New York Yankees.[27] Within two days of Landis's announcement, Howley, the new Browns' manager, stepped off a train in Augusta, Georgia, anxious to meet with his friend. "I don't know if Cobb is going to play baseball but if he is I want him," Howley said to reporters.[28]

Howley wasn't Cobb's only suitor. Connie Mack, rebuffed in his efforts to land Tris Speaker, also sought an audience with the hit king. "I hope we have better luck in getting Ty Cobb than we had with Tris Speaker," Mack said.[29] Rumors flew that the Boston Red Sox and New York Yankees also had an interest in signing Cobb. Both, however, proved to be unfounded.

While Cobb and Speaker emerged from the stain of scandal, the same could not be said for professional baseball. Four months of scandal had painted the game with tarnish. "In my eyes baseball has a blacker stain on it now than any scandal put on it," wrote *New York Daily News* sports editor Paul Gallico.[30] For weeks, the winter hot stove season (normally a vehicle for building anticipation for a new season) was instead dominated by the negativity of controversy—so much so that Ralph McGill opined in the *Nashville Banner*, "Old John Q Public is weary of the charges."[31] Now, reputations were damaged. The integrity of wins and losses was left to question. It was all enough to push the preeminent baseball publication in America, *The Sporting News*, to declare: "Enough filth for one winter."[32]

8

The Red-Faced Cardinal

The greeting was warm and genial. Smiles, strong handshakes, and a slap to the shoulder peppered this reunion. To passersby in the opulent Union Station in St. Louis, there could be no denying that the man just off the train from Louisville, Kentucky, and the local who met him were friends. Their meeting was noticed. It was attention getting because of who the greeter was: Rogers Hornsby, one of the greatest players in baseball. His guest hadn't come to St. Louis entirely on a social matter. This was business. The Kentuckian was invited to Hornsby's home. He instead suggested they meet at the visitor's hotel later in the evening. Hornsby told him to phone his home in forty-five minutes. When the man did, he was given the brush off, told to speak instead with Hornsby's lawyer. Within twenty-four hours, that brushoff would precipitate yet another baseball scandal.

During the month of January 1927, Rogers Hornsby would not be a stranger to Kenesaw Mountain Landis. He first came to the baseball commissioner's attention in an innocuous sort of way. It was during the week that led up to Christmas in 1926. Landis was about to go public with information about Dutch Leonard's letters when the St. Louis Cardinals stunned baseball fans by trading Rogers Hornsby. The five-time National League batting champ and player-manager of the Cardinals was sent to the Giants for New York's star shortstop, Frankie Frisch, and a pitcher, Jimmy Ring. The trade sparked outrage in St. Louis. Hornsby held hero status, and why not? He was undeniably the best hitter in the National League. In 1926, his second season as a player-manager, Hornsby guided the Cardinals to their first World Series. When they beat the mighty New York Yankees to earn the championship, euphoria erupted in St. Louis.

Thirty thousand people jammed the ballpark, Sportsman's Park, to welcome the team home. Celebrating wasn't limited to the city of St. Louis. Jubilation blanketed the entire region. In Poplar Bluff, 150 miles to the south, residents celebrated with an auto parade—cars festooned with banners and noisily dragged tin cans. Town leaders speculated that very few of the ten thousand citizens of Du Quoin, Illinois, were not celebrating in the street once the final out of the World Series was recorded. Merchants in St. Louis showered Cardinals players with gifts. The biggest was for Hornsby: a brand-new automobile bought with $5,000 collected from grateful fans.

And now, sixty days later, Hornsby was traded. Fans were furious. Letters that expressed rage poured into the Cardinals' office. Threats were made to hang the Cardinals' president, Sam Breadon. Three angry fans leaped onto the running board of the Breadon family car and screamed nasty epithets at Mrs. Breadon before a police officer noticed and chased the men away. Such was the depth of outrage at the trade that the St. Louis Chamber of Commerce appealed to Landis to void the deal. In a telegram to the commissioner, Victor Miller, the mayor of St. Louis wrote, "We appeal to you as arbiter of the baseball world to refuse to sanction the trade."[1] The commissioner replied back that he could not.

Soon after, another matter involving Hornsby came to the attention of the baseball commissioner. Rogers Hornsby hadn't been just player-manager of the Cardinals, he owned a piece of the ball club—1,167 shares of stock, which accounted for a 10 percent ownership stake. Hornsby was the second-largest shareholder in the team. This presented a problem. No one who owned part of one club could play for another. "He can't play any championship games for New York as long as he holds stock in the St. Louis club," said John Heydler, president of the National League.[2] Hornsby was ordered to divest his interest in the Cardinals. It was a matter that would soon become thorny.

Upon news of the trade, the entertainer Al Jolson contacted Hornsby with an offer to buy the shares. Jolson was already a part owner of the ball club. Once Jolson entered into negotiations with Hornsby's attorney, the depth of the problem was bared. When Rogers Hornsby received his shares, they were valued at $43 apiece. On the heels of a World Series championship and a profitable year at the box office, Hornsby presumed the value of the shares to be between $300 and $600. It was a price far too high for even Al Jolson to afford.

The league took on the problem. Heydler informed the Giants that while Hornsby could participate in spring training and exhibition games with his new ball club, he would not be permitted to play in any regular-season game until his Cardinals shares were sold. Sam Breadon, principal owner of the

Cardinals, agreed to bring in accountants, conduct an audit, and let them determine the value of the team and its shares of stock.

By late January 1927, the commissioner of baseball had finally cleared his desk of the Swede Risberg and Cobb-Speaker matters. If Kenesaw Mountain Landis thought, however, that he had put to rest the last of baseball's scandals, he was sorely mistaken. Another one, both ugly and damaging to the game, was about to erupt. It involved Rogers Hornsby.

The man Hornsby met at Union Station wasn't just a friend visiting town from Louisville, Kentucky. Frank L. Moore was a bookie—Rogers Hornsby's bookie. Moore had traveled to St. Louis out of exasperation. Ever since the end of the World Series, he had tried to collect moneys he claimed Hornsby owed. When on arriving in St. Louis he was rebuffed, Moore resorted to his next tactic, one that would prove both damaging and embarrassing to Hornsby and to baseball. Frank L. Moore went public.

On January 11, Moore summoned reporters to the hotel where he was staying. There he revealed stunning news: that Rogers Hornsby was refusing to pay money that he owed—$92,800 in gambling debts. "I can prove," he said, "with little effort that I paid the amount in question, $92,000 or a bit more on Hornsby's wagers."[3] Moore showed canceled checks. He displayed telegraphic receipts of money transfers. He explained how Hornsby began betting small amounts on horse races, but as he won, the size of his wagers grew from tens to hundreds. The bookie added that during the 1926 season, Hornsby gambled away his entire season's salary—$30,000—in just one month, making wagers every day of the month. Moore told the newspapermen that he advanced Hornsby money, paid some of his debts, and placed bets at the ballplayer's request. "It has cost me dearly to be a hero worshiper," he said.[4]

Though it was suspected, few in the team's inner circle actually knew that Hornsby's friendship with Frank L. Moore was a big reason Sam Breadon ordered his trade to the Giants. The bookie and the ballplayer were first introduced between innings of a game in Cincinnati during the 1925 season. "Got any tips?" Hornsby bluntly asked.[5] The bookie offered a few from which Hornsby won. A friendship was quickly forged. Stories abounded that when Hornsby won $5,000 on a race at a track near St. Louis, Fairmount Park, he was hooked.

As the friendship grew, so too did the amount of time Moore spent around the ball club. He was Hornsby's guest at spring training in San Antonio, Texas. During the season, every weekend that the Cardinals were home, Moore was not only at the games but before each game was also in the team's dugout. When the Cardinals reached the World Series, Moore was Hornsby's guest at every game. Breadon voiced his disapproval. "Drop this man," he urged Hornsby.[6] The manager refused. Breadon felt Hornsby's gambling was a big reason his batting average dropped eighty-eight points from the 1925 season. A rift developed. It became so bad that over the final two months of the season, the manager and team president did not speak to each another.

As the World Series jubilation subsided, it became clear that Hornsby and Breadon could not coexist. Though the player-manager had a year to go on a contract that paid $30,000, Hornsby used the World Series success to seek a pay raise. He demanded a three-year contract with a salary of $50,000 per year. Breadon said he would not go longer than a one-year deal. He also wanted Hornsby to agree to stop betting on horse racing. It was then that things reached a stalemate. In mid-December at the league meetings in Chicago, Breadon let the owner of the New York Giants, Charles Stoneham, know that Hornsby could be available in a trade. Stoneham made his manager, John McGraw, aware of the opportunity, and within an hour the swap was done. "Hornsby had a wonderful opportunity here, but he kicked it all away," said Breadon.[7]

Earlier in the off-season, McGraw made an attempt to sign Ty Cobb. It came not long after Cobb resigned from the Detroit Tigers. When Kenesaw Mountain Landis found out, he put a stop to it. The commissioner was still in the midst of his investigation and not prepared to rule on Cobb's standing in the game. Landing Rogers Hornsby more than made up for losing out on Ty Cobb.

Rogers Hornsby was a collection of tenacity and talent. He was a hardscrabble Texan, as quiet verbally as his bat was productive, prickly in nature (which bred loathing), and yet one whose play commanded the ultimate in regard. For eleven years Hornsby had been undeniably the greatest player in the National League. From 1920 to 1925, he won a record six consecutive batting titles. Three times during that span he hit over .400. Hornsby was a rare combination of hitter, able to both hit for a high average and for home runs. Twice, in 1922 and 1925, he won the triple crown, leading the league in the three golden statistical categories: home runs, runs batted in, and batting average. The New York Giants were a team in need, desperate need. For nine seasons, from 1917 to 1925, they had been the preeminent team in the National League. During that span, they went to the World Series five times and won it twice. The other four seasons, they finished second. But in 1925 the Giants tumbled in the standings to fifth place.

In truth, what the Giants really needed was a star, "a rival attraction to Babe Ruth," wrote *The Sporting News*.[8] Throughout the second half of their dominant run, winning failed to prevent their attendance from slipping. From a high of 973,477 paid customers during the 1921 season, the Giants' attendance plummeted to 700,362 in 1926. A big reason for the huge drop was Babe Ruth.

In 1919, the season before the New York Yankees acquired Ruth, they drew a paid attendance of 619,164. In 1920 Ruth's home-run-hitting exploits saw the Yankees' attendance double to 1,289,422, making them the first team to ever draw more than one million fans over a season. In 1923 the Yankees rubbed salt in the wound, building a palatial new ballpark on the opposite side of the Harlem River from the Polo Grounds, where the Giants played. They continued to lead baseball in attendance and revenues, something the Giants hoped to counter with a star player like Hornsby.

The Giants and their just-acquired second baseman quickly agreed to a new contract, one that would give Hornsby a raise to $40,000 per season and cover two years. It was when he returned home to St. Louis after signing his Giants contract that Hornsby stepped into controversy—via the revelation by Frank L. Moore.

Around St. Louis and to many in the National League, Rogers Hornsby's gambling was hardly a secret. Those who knew him described a man who gambled with the same degree of tenacity he displayed on the diamond. Hornsby had two additional phones installed in his home with which to place bets. On one, he would phone Moore to place his bets, while his wife used the other to learn prevailing odds from St. Louis-area bookies. There was talk that Hornsby won $100,000 on horse racing and baseball bets the month of September in 1926 alone. Others, however, said his losses grew so deep that St. Louis-area bookies would no longer take his wagers unless Hornsby paid in cash. After the season it was said Hornsby gave the car he had been gifted by grateful Cardinals fans to a bookie, Mark Gumbert, to pay off his gambling debt. He admitted to Moore that things looked "pretty bad."[9]

While Rogers Hornsby was known to be a prolific bettor on horse racing (particularly in Kentucky) talk grew late in the 1926 season that he had expanded his wagering. Hornsby was also betting on baseball. Tom Kearney, one of the biggest bookies in St. Louis, said the Cardinals' player-manager and some of his players "feel me out on prices in the National League race."[10] Kearney told confidants the manager and some of his players bet one-to-two on their team's chances to win the National League pennant. Suspicions were raised about Cardinals games in an early September series against Cincinnati and more games two weeks later against Philadelphia. Observers expressed the opinion that both Cardinals opponents played well below their capabilities. Word of Hornsby's activities got around. John McGraw, the Giants' manager and well-known for being a wintertime bettor on horse races in Cuba, said, "He must realize he is bringing disgrace upon the great national game. Reports that he has been betting on ball games do not help him."[11]

When in mid-January Frank L. Moore made his accusations, surprise was not a reaction for many within professional baseball. What reporters were keen to pin down was whether Hornsby did, in fact, bet on baseball. Moore replied, "I frequently make bets on baseball. I bet on the Cardinals every time I had a chance," he said.[12] As for Hornsby, Moore was adamant that he had never known his friend to bet on baseball, only the horses.

Moore's accusations generated headlines. "ANOTHER BASEBALL SCANDAL!" screamed the Chicago sports paper *Collyer's Eye*.[13] Stories of Hornsby's gambling appeared in newspapers throughout the country. Hornsby fired back. He painted Moore a liar. Hornsby insisted he never placed bets through Moore. He said the money he owed was for a loan to buy an apartment building in St. Louis. Hornsby added that he had missed two payments but had just put a check in the mail to Moore.

Moore was not deterred. The Kentucky bookmaker arranged to meet with Sam Breadon. He sought to attach the Cardinals stock shares Hornsby owned and thus get his money back. Breadon said he considered Moore's beef with Hornsby to be a private matter, one that neither he nor the Cardinals would get involved with. Angered by the response, Moore then threatened to take the matter higher. He told Breadon he would travel to Chicago and share Hornsby's dereliction with the commissioner of baseball, Kenesaw Mountain Landis. It was then that Frank L. Moore got a response.

Rogers Hornsby's attorney agreed to sit down with Moore. He told Moore that if he could provide an itemized list and purpose behind the money Hornsby owed, he would discuss payment with his client. If Hornsby and his attorney thought this would make Moore go away, it didn't. It merely put the assault on pause, and just for a few days at that. Moore was a man who kept meticulous notes. When he turned over the requested information, it involved eleven separate items: ninety-day notes, an accommodation note, checks and loans paid to Hornsby's wife at the ballplayer's request, a $7,500 loan to buy an apartment house that Moore claimed was still unpaid, and even an investment in a greyhound-racing organization. Everything, Moore said, he had paid at the request of Rogers Hornsby with the promise of repayment.

Hornsby held his ground. He remained steadfast in his contention that he owed Moore nothing. That's when Frank L. Moore went to his last resort. He sued Rogers Hornsby. Moore placed everything in the public record: the specifics about the expenditures and details about the debts. It was then that Rogers Hornsby came clean. He admitted to prolific gambling.

Moore wasn't alone in trying to collect debts from Hornsby. In short order several more lawsuits were filed against the ballplayer. Sonnenfeld Millinery went to court to try to recover $505 owed by Hornsby's wife, Jeanette, for dresses she had bought. The Hornsby's family physician sued, claiming the couple hadn't paid the $387 owed for treating Mrs. Hornsby. Rogers Hornsby argued the doctor's fee was exorbitant. A former attorney of Hornsby's not only sued the ballplayer for unpaid bills amounting to $5,250 but, in filing suit, attached Hornsby's stock, bank account, and real estate equities.

None of the controversy would mute the loud ovation Hornsby received when he was introduced at the annual Baseball Writers Association Dinner in New York City on February 7. The event was a pinnacle event of each off-season, a highlight to the Hot Stove campaign. But rather than favorable news, the headlines in the New York papers on the days surrounding the event focused on the controversy over Hornsby's ownership of stock in the St. Louis Cardinals.

Hornsby had no shortage of offers to buy his shares. A former Cardinals manager offered $66 a share, which was rejected. So too was Sam Breadon's offer of $80 a share. Breadon conducted an audit. Based on the findings, Hornsby said he would agree to a price of $105 per share. He found no takers.

Rumors flew that the trade would be rescinded and Hornsby sent back to the Cardinals. It was quickly shot down. "You can't undo baseball trades any more than you can unscramble eggs," said Charles Stoneham.[14] The day after the Baseball Writers Dinner, the National League held a league meeting in New York. Stoneham and Sam Breadon conferred on the Hornsby stock matter. The Giants' president had been in the brokerage business and offered to use his contacts to try to sell Hornsby's shares.

The problem became a nagging nuisance for baseball. It was frustrating for the Giants, who wanted Hornsby to be a ticket seller but instead saw article after article mention his gambling and stock problem. It was problematic for baseball because it allowed controversy to fester. Arbitration was offered to try to resolve the stock matter. Hornsby accepted. Breadon said he would not. No resolution could be reached until the eve of Opening Day. Under threat that Hornsby would not be permitted to play for the Giants, the player and his former team reached an agreement on a sale. The stock was purchased by the Cardinals and retired. Hornsby received $116,700. Any hope Frank L. Moore held that part of that money would be used to pay his claim against Hornsby was quickly dashed. Hornsby's attorney took a strong stance to defend his client. In a legal filing, William Fahey pointed out that gambling was illegal. Thus, he wrote, Hornsby could not be compelled to pay Frank L. Moore. Moore sought a speedy court resolution. Fahey and Hornsby wanted just the opposite. They wanted any hearing into the matter postponed until after the season. A judge granted their request, and the matter was delayed until January 1928.

Without resolution, another batch of bad press raged. "When they tumble, they carry an unmeasured wreckage with them," wrote Washington columnist Robert T. Small of the game's fallen heroes.[15] To many, it placed emphasis, if not pressure, on Babe Ruth. In the aftermath of the Cobb-Speaker scandal, one newspaper headline read: "Ruth, Landis Saved Baseball Once; Can They Do It Again?"[16] *United Press* sportswriter Henry Farrell was among those to suggest Ruth as a solution. "Professional baseball still has Babe Ruth and Commissioner Landis, but they are not novelties now and what the club owners will do to get the minds of the paying public off a scandal involving two of the greatest players of all time is a question they will have to solve."[17] It was true Ruth's power-hitting exploits shifted the public's attention from the scandal and the banishments of September 1921. Five years had passed, however. Ruth was among the older, everyday regulars in the game now. He had shown himself in 1925 to be mortal. Was his bounce-back season in 1926 proof that he was still the game's premier star or a last flash from a dying comet? Few questions held more importance as the 1927 baseball season loomed.

9

Stealing the Show

All about the diamond, men moved large equipment into position. Wrigley Field, a two-year-old, double-decked jewel of minor-league baseball and home to the Los Angeles Angels of the Pacific Coast League, was being transformed into a movie set. Two large cameras on tall tripods, lights on even larger tripods, and screens to block unwanted sunlight were positioned about.[1] Near the dugout one of the stars sat on a canvas-backed chair stitched with his name, Babe Ruth. To any of the baseball fans among the cast and crew, this Ruth sported a look they had never seen before.

Announcement of the lucrative deal Christy Walsh secured for Ruth couldn't have come at a better time for baseball. Sports pages were consumed by the Ty Cobb–Tris Speaker game-fixing scandal. News of the deal distracted, at least in small part, from the controversy that had torn at baseball's integrity for three months. Attention-grabbing were the headlines that touted a six-figure movie payday for Ruth. In reality, the Yankee star's motion picture compensation merely had the potential to reach such an eye-catching figure. The sum guaranteed Ruth was actually much less: $25,000. The rest would come from a percentage of the profits should the picture gross more than $40,000. In all, there was the potential for Ruth to net $75,000 for his one month of acting work.

This was not Ruth's first foray into motion pictures. In 1920 Adam Kessel and Charlie Bauman, owners of a small production outfit, convinced Ruth to star in a movie they conceived. The men saw Ruth as a ticket to success, a celebrity of such magnitude that fans would line up at the box office, anxious to see him on the big screen. Once the picture *Headin' Home* was released in September 1920, the pair cut Ruth a check for $10,000. He was giddy at the windfall—so giddy, in fact, that for weeks he took delight in showing off the check to many of his friends. It was several weeks before Ruth finally went to his bank to deposit the check. When he did, it bounced. The film, so it turned out, had been a flop at the box office, and the ballplayer never got his pay.

This project, however, promised to be far different. Now Ruth had representation in Walsh, who had proven successful in sifting the serious from the suspicious. Unlike Ruth's earlier motion picture foray, this deal was with a legitimate company, one making a splash in the motion picture industry. Along with Paramount and MGM, First National was one of the biggest motion picture companies in the industry. Its founders, Tom Talley and J. D. Williams, were shelling out big bucks to buy film rights to books and to sign big-name actors. The men gave Charlie Chaplin the industry's first one-million-dollar contract. Their fledgling compound of four large sound stages, a half-dozen office buildings, dressing rooms, and storage warehouses was teeming with activity.

Among the many books and plays First National purchased for adaptation was a magazine story, "Said With Soap." It had been written by a sportswriter, Gerald Beaumont. First National's production manager John McCormick pondered a potential male lead for the project. The more he and others at the studio discussed possibilities, the more Babe Ruth's name came up. All agreed that while the story was not written with Ruth in mind, he was perfect for the part. Discussions with Christy Walsh and then Ruth himself produced agreement. "For what we may safely say is the first time in the history of the motion picture business, a celebrity from the sporting world has been cast because of his fitness to play a certain screen story role," said Wid Gunning, the person assigned to produce the film. "Ordinarily the celebrity is signed for the sake of his fame and a story is built around him."[2]

When the deal to star in the film was struck, Ruth was in the latter stages of his vaudeville tour. Christy Walsh arranged with Alexander Pantages to conclude the tour in Salt Lake City on February 1. The heralded baseball slugger arrived in Los Angeles amid fanfare two days later. The WAMPAS Baby Stars, a half-dozen attractive female actresses who made appearances on behalf of the Western Association of Motion Picture Advertisers, greeted Ruth as he stepped from the train at Le Grande Station just before 10:00 a.m. The ladies presented Ruth with an oversized baseball bat made of redwood. Two kissed the baseball star on the cheek.

The enthusiastic greeting Ruth received was in sharp contrast to the feelings of the woman who would costar in the picture. Anna Q. Nilsson, cast to play the female lead, was an unmitigated star in the profession. Described in *Filmplay* magazine as "a talented actress with beauty, charm, distinction, and a conscience—she is real people," Nilsson regularly appeared opposite the leading actors in the business.[3] In *The Lotus Eater*, she starred alongside

Figure 9.1. On his arrival in Los Angeles, Babe Ruth was welcomed by the WAMPAS Baby Stars. *Courtesy: Security Pacific National Bank collection/Los Angeles Public Library photo collection.*

the industry's top romantic actor, John Barrymore. She was paired with Walter Pidgeon in *Miss Nobody* and George M. Cohen in *Seven Keys to Baldpate*.

Studio heads considered Nilsson influential to box-office success. This translated to considerable work. From her first year in the business in 1912 (when she appeared in twenty-one films), Nilsson had performed in at least four or more per year. Most recently, Nilsson starred in ten motion pictures in 1924, six in 1925, and five in 1926. Telegrams and phone calls to her manager's office portended a busy 1927 as well.

Nilsson's own personal story generated almost as much publicity as did her roles or her long, wavy, "polar bear blond" hair, as one writer liked to call it.[4] She emigrated to the United States from Sweden in 1907 at the age of seventeen, having picked beets to earn money for the trip. Once in New York, Nilsson sought work as a nursemaid. While on her way to a job interview, she became lost on Fifty-Seventh Street. As she searched for the address, Nilsson was stopped by an elderly man who asked if he could paint her. The man was Carroll Beckwith, a portrait painter of renown whose subjects included Mark Twain and Theodore Roosevelt. His painting of Nilsson drew the attention of the celebrated artist Penrhyn Stanlaws, who asked Nilsson to model for him. Stanlaws's work frequently appeared on the cover of popular magazines, and it was in this way that she became noticed by Kalem Company, a New York motion picture company. Sidney Olcott, the head of the studio, signed Nilsson to a four-year contract. During that span, she became one of the studio's most popular performers.

Nilsson had an impetuous streak about her and carried a penchant for dancing in clubs and playing baccarat in speakeasies. Once she became involved in the production of a motion picture, however, the wild side was pushed aside, and the actress became totally consumed with work—so much so that when she felt the wardrobe department could not find an adequate dress for a scene, Nilsson made one herself.

At the time Nilsson agreed to the role in *Babe Comes Home*, the male lead had yet to be cast. When it was, Nilsson's enthusiasm for the role changed. She became angry, unhappy at the idea of playing opposite an acting novice. Nilsson griped that she had worked with most, if not all, of the leading men in the industry. She worried that a first-time actor would portend a flop, something that, at this stage of her career, she worried might curtail future film offers. Both her friends and studio executives explained Ruth's popularity and coaxed Nilsson to a state of enthusiasm for the project.

Hiring a sports star to headline a motion picture involved risk. First was the question of acting ability; next was the history of such films. The track record of films that featured sports stars was not good. Though football star "Red" Grange displayed personality on the big screen, his film *One Minute to Play*, grossed barely more than a quarter of a million dollars at the box office. Universal Pictures signed the hugely popular boxer Jack Dempsey to make a series of eleven fight films. They did not renew his contract once the deal expired. Bill Tilden, the Wimbledon and United States Open champion, appeared onstage in tennis-instruction films and was recruited to perform in motion pictures.

Studio executives could not be faulted for thinking Ruth might generate a different result. After all, his popularity was quantified by turnstile counts in every city in the American League. It was well-known that rival teams saw attendance spike whenever Ruth and the New York Yankees came to town. Yet the baseball phenomenon came with a far different dynamic than what movie houses might experience. It wasn't just Ruth the man who pulled the curious and the trend chasers into ballparks. Most in the throngs came to see Ruth do what he did greater than anyone ever had in baseball before: hit home runs. Still, what helped to reinforce the studio's decision to use Ruth was the breadth of his popularity. Those who flocked to see Ruth play ball weren't limited to those in American League cities. Masses traveled from neighboring communities, even outside the state. There were many instances of both businessmen and entire families who planned a summer vacation just to see Ruth play. At the extreme was the personal physician to the king and queen of England, who traveled to America to see Ruth play. While he did take in a Yankees game, the man returned home disappointed, unable to tell friends he had witnessed Ruth hitting a home run. The numbers who traveled to witness Babe Ruth firsthand were not lost on business. Many seized on opportunity. One example was the Louisville and Nashville Railroad, which offered four-dollar Babe Ruth specials, a round-trip ticket to see Ruth and the Yankees play the Browns in St. Louis.

Those unable to attend wrote, and their letters arrived in droves. Ruth received more than twenty thousand pieces of fan mail each season.[5] They came from all over the world—from India, Cuba, Germany, and Japan.[6] Ruth sought help with the barrage. Teammates were recruited, asked to screen letters. Those from children or invalids were set aside for a swift reply.[7] Most wrote for autographs. What they received didn't always come from Ruth, though. Doc Woods, the team trainer, became adept at forging Ruth's signature. In many instances his was the signature that arrived in reply.

The popularity of Babe Ruth transcended sports. In speeches during his campaign for the presidency of the United States, Warren G. Harding invoked Ruth's name. In one, he urged four thousand tradesmen and labor union members in Ohio to strive for the sort of excellence Ruth displayed on the ball field. "What is the big inspiration in life? The natural desire to excel. Why do we all applaud Babe Ruth?" Harding asked before explaining that "the workman who performs his tasks better than another has satisfaction in his soul."[8]

Labeling someone with the name "Babe Ruth" became a means to measure exceptionality. Boxing champion Jack Dempsey was called the Babe Ruth of the heavyweights. The seemingly invincible racehorse Man 'o War was hailed the Babe Ruth of the equine world. The skill of English golf sensation Abe Mitchell was explained not by heralding his three United States Open titles but by referring to him as the Babe Ruth of golf. Similarly, Scottish soccer sensation Andy Wilson was lauded not as a prolific goal scorer but as the Babe Ruth of soccer. Sportswriters called Belgian tennis standout Jean Washer the Babe Ruth of tennis.

Yet for all of Ruth's renown, there were actually those unaware of the baseball star. When the fourteenth edition of *Who's Who in America* was released sans the name Babe Ruth, the editors were soundly criticized. While on concert tour, the famous tenor Enrico Caruso was asked his thoughts about Babe Ruth. "I will have to admit," he said, "I don't think I have ever heard her sing."[9]

First National Pictures invested heavily in Ruth's motion picture project, both financially and with resources. Ruth would be surrounded by an experienced cast and crew. Ted Wilde was hired to direct the picture. Normally the handpicked director to comedic actor Harold Lloyd, Wilde was loaned to the studio for the project by Lloyd himself, an avowed baseball fan. Wid Gunning was made producer of the film. He was almost immediately given his first challenge—what to call the film? "Lilly of the Laundry" was kicked around. So too was "Babe in the Laundry." Ultimately, *Babe Comes Home* was the title agreed on and registered for the film.

Just as acting represented a challenge for Ruth, *Babe Comes Home* offered one as well for Nilsson. The woman knew little of anything at all about baseball. Louis Stevens was engaged to adapt the magazine article into a movie script. In the story, Nilsson plays the part of a laundry woman, Vernie. Ruth is a ballplayer, Babe Dugan. Vernie grows frustrated trying to get the tobacco juice stains from Babe's jersey and decides she is going to reform him. Vernie and Babe become romantically involved. Once Babe gives in to Vernie's pleadings and stops chewing tobacco, he goes into a batting slump. Babe's hitting grows so cold that he gets relegated to the bench. During a critical game, Vernie appears at the railing. She surprises Babe with some chewing tobacco. With a cheek bulging from a plug of tobacco, Babe steps to the plate and hits a home run that wins the big game.

When the deal to make the picture was initially struck, nobody knew what to expect from Babe Ruth—not the producers, not the director and, least of all, not those who wrote the script and concocted the gags. "We first began work on this comedy by protecting ourselves. Nobody knew how Ruth would screen, or how he would respond to instructions given him," said Wid Gunning, the film's producer. "We had the scenario written so Babe could just 'walk' through the film."[10] The reason for their concern was manifest during the first three days of filming. Ruth was nervous, made so by the other actors watching him execute his scenes. There were flubs, missed marks, and mistakes. During a scene in which Ruth was to show anger, the director suggested he slam a door shut behind him when he exited a room. Ruth complied but slammed the door so hard he tore it from the hinges.[11]

By the end of the first week of filming, the baseball star caught on to the ins and outs of acting. Ruth became much more comfortable. His confidence grew. It grew so much that Ruth felt comfortable making suggestions, recommending changes to comedy gags—a half dozen of which the director, writer, and producer liked and agreed to insert into the script.[12]

Ruth's costar came around too. As the Babe's skills improved, Anna Q. Nilsson's anger at being made to share the screen alongside the acting neophyte abated. "Babe is marvelous to work with," Nilsson told a reporter.

"Every girl I have heard talk about him thinks the same as I do, that he is a prize, just a jewel."[13]

Studio heads were pleased by what they saw from the end-of-day dailies. They agreed with the director's assertion that there were scenes that could be improved by new comedic skits. Reshoots were agreed to, and the studio pledged to increase its financial investment in the project. More comedic actors such as Arthur Stone and Louise Fazenda were added to the cast to enhance the many new gags being added.[14]

The first several days of production took place in Wrigley Field. For Ruth, his scenes involved very little acting. In fact, during the first few days, all he was required to do was bat. To the handful of children who managed to sneak into the park and hang over the railing from front-row seats, Ruth looked different.[15] His face was caked with thick makeup. Rather than the familiar Yankees pinstripes, Ruth wore the uniform of the local club, the Los Angeles Angels: white baseball flannels with an overlayed LA on the left breast and a ball cap adorned with the letter *A*.

Ruth was asked, at first, to simply do what he did best—hit home runs. Mixed in was a scene in which the director instructed Ruth to guide a foul ball into the upper deck. Through shots from another scene and creative editing, it would be made to strike Vernie in the eye, precipitating the initial meeting of Babe and the girl, when he brought her flowers as an apology. But what the director Ted Wilde wanted most from Ruth during the first week of filming was home runs, lots of them. To the cheers of several hundred extras, each paid five dollars a day, Ruth drove a succession of pitches from former New York Giants standout "Doc" Crandall over the right-field wall.[16] He estimated to friends that on one day, he hit somewhere in the neighborhood of two hundred balls into the parking lot beyond Wrigley Field's right-field wall. "Just to get one home run for the picture," he said. "Boy that was work."[17] In the syndicated *Ripley's—Believe It or Not*, Robert Ripley wrote that Ruth hit 125 home runs in one hour at Wrigley Field in Los Angeles.[18]

From hitting home runs, the shoots moved to specific baseball tasks. The baseball action was hardly the flowing kind of a real game. Instead, much of it involved the director, Ted Wilde, instructing Ruth to perform a certain baseball task, then another. To Wilde's cry of "Ready!" Ruth would position himself to dash from the batter's box or, for another scene, prepare to run from a spot halfway down the third-base line. On cue, operators would crank a handle to bring the manually powered cameras up to speed, at which time Wilde would bark, "Camera!" and Ruth would perform his task.[19] A sprint to first base with Ruth made to round the bag as if he were heading for second, or a dash down the third base line followed by a hook slide across home plate as an umpire thrust his arms out in the safe signal,

Figure 9.2.   Babe Ruth bats during filming of *Babe Comes Home*. Ruth estimated in one day, he hit two hundred baseballs out of Wrigley Field in Los Angeles. *Courtesy: Security Pacific National Bank collection/Los Angeles Public Library photo collection.*

brought Wilde three-to-five-second insert shots. Once the scene concluded, Wilde would shout, "Cut!" and Ruth was given pause but only momentarily, however, for each such scene was performed over and over, shot and reshot as many as four, five, and a half-dozen times.[20]

Provisions were made for reporters to watch the filming. During the breaks they would descend upon Ruth with a plethora of questions. "I like the work," Ruth said of acting. "It gets rather tiresome at times," he said of the tedium common on a motion picture set.[21] For Ruth, acting brought insulation from the baseball controversy that raged two thousand miles away in Chicago. It was only when a reporter from the *United Press* news service brought up the subject of the claims made against Ty Cobb and Tris Speaker that Ruth's friendly demeanor changed. "The baseball scandal? It's over. Those men have been vindicated. Let's forget about it if we love the great American game."[22]

By the second week of filming, Ruth's confidence grew. He offered suggestions to improve the script and became quick to criticize baseball scenes. The slugger frequently huddled with Wilde after takes from which the director emerged nodding. But a day came when Ruth's objective critiques spilled into frustration-grounded criticism. It involved the performances by extras who were cast as ballplayers. To observers it appeared many had been hired for comedic purposes and not because they could play the part of a baseball player with any amount of credibility. Ruth, it turned out, was a stickler for accuracy. During a particular scene, he reached a boiling point with the ballplayers. He snatched a megaphone the director used to communicate with staff and performers. "You, you, leftfielder and you center fielding guy," Ruth hollered. "What league do you think you're in?"[23] He moved the outfielders into a defensive position used with a left-handed batter at the plate. Wilde stood alongside and nodded his agreement to the changes Ruth ordered.

As Wilde worked to complete filming of the scenes in Wrigley Field, a distraction occurred that left the director exasperated. The Los Angeles Angels were scheduled to begin spring-training workouts. As several of their players appeared in the team's dugout, two got Babe Ruth's attention. "Truck" Hannah and Johnny Mitchell had been teammates years earlier with the New York Yankees. Ruth soon drifted away from the film crew. When the Angels began to take batting practice, Ruth was coaxed to the plate to hit. A teenager had been recruited to pitch batting practice, but on seeing the greatest player in the game step to the plate, the young man became nervous. Offerings sailed wide of the strike zone and got progressively wilder. Teasing intensified. Ruth burst into laughter, a laugh that grew so hard he could not swing the bat. Finally, Ruth regained his composure, and when the young pitcher sent a ball into the strike zone, the slugger belted it high over the right-field wall.[24]

Hijinks between Ruth and his former teammates continued for close to an hour before a noticeably perturbed Wilde convinced his star to return to his work in front of the cameras. He moved Ruth's scenes to a place in the outfield away from where the Angels were training. Even that failed to stop the shenanigans, for as Ruth resumed the particular scene, members of the Angels intentionally whacked baseballs in his direction in an attempt to make the star flinch, duck, or completely botch whatever he was tasked to perform.[25]

The final day of shooting in Wrigley Field called for capturing what would be the pinnacle scene of the movie, the game-winning home run. Several thousand extras were recruited to fill the stands. On cue some were to adversely gesture and boo the Babe, while others followed directions to cheer wildly. As Ruth stepped into the batter's box, he carried with him a favored bat. It was one he had used for several seasons. Such was his attachment to the bat that he would not allow any other player to use it. With the camera operators turning the crank to roll the film, the simulation of the championship game got underway. On the director's command, the pitcher went into his delivery. Ruth swung hard. Heads turned to follow the flight of the ball over the right-field wall. Ruth, however, reacted to something entirely different: a sound and a feeling. He knew in an instant what both meant. When he made a more thorough check, it only confirmed what he feared. His cherished bat, the one he had swung with such devastating effect in the recent World Series, had split from end to end.

While the crew gathered up equipment and prepared to vacate Wrigley Field, Babe Ruth made a forlorn figure. He slumped into his canvas-backed chair. The look on his face told one and all how upset he was about the loss of his prized bat. To some it may have seemed trivial, but not for Ruth, who sat downcast with emotions the same as the condition of his once-cherished home-run maker.

10

Reinvigorating Babe Ruth

A simple buzz gained quick attention from the hotel switchboard operator. One lone call was not entirely uncommon for this early hour of the morning. When, suddenly, more buzzing sent multiple operators stuffing plugs into jacks amid the sound of a hornet's hive, it could only mean one thing—trouble. A large volume of calls at six o'clock in the morning was extremely unusual for the Alexandria Hotel. But so too was the sort of noise that awakened and sent a great many of the guests on two floors of the first five-star luxury hotel in the city of Los Angeles to their telephone in anger. The calls complained about loud noise, noise that interrupted sleep. A manager was dispatched to quell the trouble. When the man knocked at the door of the offender's room, the noise inside stopped. The door pulled open, and before him stood a large man drenched in sweat, hair disheveled, and dabbing moisture from his face. It was Babe Ruth. The cause of the disturbing early morning ruckus was his exercise routine.

To those in baseball who knew him, Babe Ruth and exercise seemed an implausible, if not entirely impossible, marriage. After all, the man's drinking and late-night carousing were as legendary as his home run. "The Playboy of Baseball," he was called.[1] Ruth's habits incurred such wrath from the Yankees' manager that the slugger was ordered home during a road trip and suspended. Doctors had been aghast at Ruth's eating habits, which they said bordered on gluttonous. He was, as Thomas S. Rice wrote in the *Brooklyn Daily Eagle*, "an irresponsible big boy and joy rider through life."[2] Why and how Ruth changed traced back to Asheville, North Carolina, in April 1925.

Since joining the New York Yankees, Babe Ruth had been an invincible giant. The 1924 season proved a watershed year for Ruth. He once again led the American League in home runs for the sixth time in seven seasons.

His forty-six was best in both leagues. However, this time, he accomplished more. Ruth had long been chided by his detractors as a feast-or-famine hitter. Statistics bore out their claim. While no player hit more home runs than Ruth each season, neither did anyone strike out more than the Yankees' slugger. But in 1924 he muted the home-run-or-strikeout criticisms by winning the batting title for the first time in his career. Ruth amassed a stellar .346 average to lead the American League. Six months later, however, Ruth was knocked from his pedestal and toppled back to mortal, or as *The Sporting News* suggested, he fell "from King to Jester."[3]

Each February, Ruth and a handful of teammates would travel to Hot Springs, Arkansas, where for up to three weeks they would take advantage of the spas, warm weather, and the local golf course to get in shape for spring training. When Ruth arrived on February 11 to ready himself for the 1925 season, people were aghast. The player who came into professional baseball as a 185-pounder tipped the scale at 246 pounds. News reached the ears of reporters. They wrote of Ruth being obese, called his gut a "bay window," his weight "tonnage," and raised alarm that being so overweight could lead to injury and hamper his home-run hitting.

Throughout spring training, the newspaper throng made the focus of their stories more about Ruth's struggle to lose weight than the Yankees' struggle to construct a pennant contender. Some days, as many as a dozen cameramen followed him around, jockeying for the perfect photo to illustrate Ruth's girth. Miller Huggins, the Yankees' manager, went out of his way to try to slim his star player down. Ruth was instructed to do extra running in the outfield. He was made the base runner in rundown drills. When Ruth questioned why, Huggins snapped, "You look like the side of an Iowa barn."[4]

At the end of March, the Yankees and Brooklyn Dodgers set out on tour, playing several exhibition games throughout the South. In Nashville fans heckled Ruth as a fat, old man—a jibe he answered with a single and a double. In Chattanooga Ruth silenced barbs with two home runs. He hit two more when the teams met in Atlanta. But it was the next day, as the Yankees pulled into Asheville, North Carolina, when catastrophe struck. Ruth collapsed as he stepped from the train. Six teammates carried him to a waiting taxi, which hurried the slugger to the Battery Park Hotel. A doctor was summoned. "Too much food in one stomach," Dr. Charles Jordan said, citing indigestion, a touch of flu, and Ruth overdoing it in his quest to lose weight.[5] The next day, the headline in the *New York Daily News* read, "BAMBINO DIGGING GRAVE WITH TEETH."[6]

Reporters scurried after details. One Yankee player told a writer he had witnessed Ruth down a half-dozen hot dogs, then wash them down with a pint of bicarbonate before running onto the field to begin a game. After a night of rest, the Yankees sent Ruth home to New York with Paul Kritchell, a Yankees scout, as his chaperone. Unbeknownst to Ruth, as his train passed through Georgia, a report emanated from media in Canada that he had died. Newspapers in England picked up the story, causing a full-blown stir. Telegraph operators were asked to get clarification from rail stations along the route. When the train arrived at Union Station in Washington, DC, employees boarded in a search for Ruth. To their relief, they found him alive and feeling much better than when he boarded.

As Ruth's train drew near Newark, New Jersey, the slugger moved through his Pullman car toward a small washroom. With their destination just fifteen miles away, Ruth wanted to freshen up. He asked Kritchell for a comb, and the scout retreated to retrieve one. Moments later, Kritchell reached the washroom and found Ruth on the floor, unconscious. A doctor traveling on the train responded to the summon for help. Upon arriving at Penn Station, angst broke out when there was no ambulance waiting on the platform. The vehicle had broken down en route, so another was hastily dispatched. Police held gawkers back. It was almost thirty minutes after arriving before Ruth was finally placed on a stretcher and, with the aid of five men, removed from the train through a window. Now conscious but delirious, the ailing Yankee fought to rise up from the stretcher and was forcefully held down. Police threatened to smash the cameras of any photographer who dared take a picture. Christy Walsh was notified and rushed Ruth's wife, Helen, to St. Vincent's Hospital, where the Babe was taken.

Dr. Edward King, the Yankees' team physician, met with reporters. He chalked the episode up—again—to a touch of flu and indigestion. As for being found unconscious, King explained that Ruth had passed out in the train's washroom, then hit his head on a pipe. He was checked but did not appear to have suffered a concussion. The hospital switchboard was inundated with calls inquiring about Ruth's condition. A police lieutenant in plain clothes was posted outside of room 19 with orders that no one was to be allowed inside.

Opening Day of the 1925 season was just three days away. Edward Barrow, the Yankees president, declared Ruth's condition was not serious. He was optimistic the Yankees would have their right fielder in the Opening-Day lineup against the Washington Senators. In his hospital room, Ruth was restless, keen to be discharged and insisting he be allowed to play. But then a complication threw a wrench in that plan. Ruth's temperature would not subside. It continued to hover above one hundred degrees. Five days after his admittance, it was determined Ruth did not have a touch of the flu, but rather an intestinal problem: abscesses. Surgery was needed. Ruth would miss one, maybe two, months of the season. "That news sure comes as a shock," said Miller Huggins.[7]

With concern there was gloating. Billy Evans, an umpire with a widely read newspaper column, wrote, "When Babe Ruth starts to slip physically, he will pass out of the picture quickly."[8] Ty Cobb added, "When he breaks, it's going to come quickly."[9] Ruth was made an example at a meeting of the Pennsylvania Dental Society, where Dr. Albert McCann said Ruth "could be batting out home runs today if he had used his teeth properly and selected right foods."[10]

For Babe Ruth, the 1925 season was an utter disaster. The twenty-minute procedure to repair Ruth's lower intestines kept him out of baseball for six weeks. Without the slugger, the Yankees plummeted toward the bottom of the standings. They finished the season in fifth place. Attendance fell by almost half. Ruth's batting average took an eighty-eight-point dive, and his home-run tally, twenty-five, was the lowest since he had begun to play in the field in 1918.

Ruth's problem was driven home by fan mail. Instead of requests for autographs, fan mail now contained weight-loss remedies. A woman from Cleveland urged Ruth to eat ten pineapples a day. Another, from Detroit, said drinking three glasses of vinegar a day was the answer to Ruth's weight problem. Of course, the sportswriters continued to prod. A California newspaper chronicling the biggest failings in sports in 1925 wrote, "Babe Ruth, of course, draws the title of the biggest bust," which it attributed to his appetite.[11] To the criticism Ruth said, "I have been the sappiest of saps, alright I admit it."[12]

In the aftermath, Christy Walsh went to work. In December he didn't just put Ruth together with Artie McGovern; Walsh demanded Ruth hire the personal trainer and follow his instructions. A former club fighter from Hell's Kitchen, Artie McGovern parlayed failure in the ring into a successful fitness business. He was so badly battered in his more than two hundred professional fights that plastic and dental surgeries were needed to repair his injuries. A badly broken hand had to be surgically rebuilt. During the hours spent with doctors, McGovern learned and developed a philosophy about health and fitness. He created a system of exercises and used them to help charity cases at a New York City clinic. In 1910 at the age of thirty-three, McGovern opened a small gym above a riding academy on Sixty-Sixth Avenue in the city's West Side Physicians sent patients. McGovern trained the wealthy in their homes. In December 1926 Babe Ruth turned up at his door.

When Ruth first came to McGovern's gym, the fitness guru was quick to realize the Yankee slugger was driven by a competitive nature. While he put Ruth through a few basic exercises, he felt competitive activities would better motivate Ruth. McGovern played handball with Ruth. He had Ruth box and also put him in the pool to swim. Ruth took to it. He spent three hours at McGovern's gym almost every day, and when he arrived in Tampa, Florida, for spring training he was "not as fat as he has been," in the words of Warren Brown of the *St. Petersburg Times.*[13] The Babe Ruth of 1926 was more akin to the pre-1925 Yankee star. Over the season he played much more like the Bambino whom fans had grown to love. Ruth blasted 47 home runs, drove in 153 runs, and posted a batting average of .372. Though Ruth's legs weakened late in the season, his play helped return the Yankees to the World Series.

When motion picture work brought Ruth to Los Angeles for three weeks in February 1927, Christy Walsh recognized opportunity and seized it. He ordered his client to pay Artie McGovern $1,000 to come to Los Angeles for the duration of filming and to follow his training regimen. In New York, McGovern could work with Ruth. In Los Angeles, 2,800 miles from friends, temptations, and bad influences, Artie McGovern could control the Bambino. Ruth's exercising, eating, and even sleep would be in accordance with what McGovern wanted. While it was not uncommon for ballplayers to do baseball activities or resort to manual labor to build strength during the off-season, never before had a ballplayer done indoor training with a fitness expert. The program Walsh orchestrated for Ruth was a first for any professional baseball player.

When news of McGovern's hiring was made public, Ruth was concluding his vaudeville tour in Salt Lake City, Utah. Otis Pusey, in the local *Deseret News*, called the arrangement between Ruth and McGovern "unequaled in baseball history. For the first time in baseball records a player has sent across the country for a trainer."[14]

Artie McGovern's program was both intense and extensive. He woke Ruth each morning at 6:00 a.m. It wasn't always voluntarily and, on occasion, took stern cajoling to get the Babe going. Once he had Ruth up, the men were out the door by 6:30 for a run, one that grew in time to cover more than five miles. The timing of the daily run became so consistent, people gathered on street corners to gawk and even applaud as Ruth jogged down Hollywood Boulevard. Christy Walsh negotiated use of a room at First National Pictures, which McGovern turned into a workout room. The trainer equipped it with dumbbells, a medicine ball, boxing gloves, and a rope. Between takes or at the end of the day after shooting, Ruth and McGovern would box, usually five rounds (but the men occasionally added a sixth), after which Ruth would skip rope for several minutes. Following the 1925 season, McGovern worked principally to improve Ruth's cardiovascular level and endurance and to strengthen the ballplayer's midsection. It had taken a good portion of the season for Ruth to heal from his surgery. The aggressive twist and powerful follow-through of the slugger's swing put tremendous stress on that section of his body. In Los Angeles McGovern added more strength-building exercises, games of catch

Figure 10.1. Babe Ruth's trainer, Artie McGovern, oversees a workout. McGovern placed particular emphasis on building Ruth's abdominal muscles. *Courtesy: Security Pacific National Bank collection/Los Angeles Public Library photo collection.*

with a heavy medicine ball, bicep curls, chest and shoulder presses with the dumbbells, and duels of tug-o-war, often with actors recruited to challenge the Yankees' star.

Being isolated in Los Angeles gave Artie McGovern the chance to have a far greater impact on Babe Ruth than he could in New York. There his work with Ruth was limited to the three or four hours the ballplayer spent in his gym. Here he had control of Ruth for almost the entirety of each day. That gave McGovern the chance to correct one of Babe Ruth's biggest problem areas, how he ate. Now every meal Ruth ate and all that he drank was prescribed by McGovern. For starters, the twelve cups of coffee Ruth drank each day were replaced with cups of hot water.

Breakfast changed dramatically. No more was Ruth given free rein to wander into the hotel dining area and order his customary waffles, pork sausage, coffee, and donuts. Under McGovern's watchful eye, Ruth's first meal of the day was fruit and a bowl of cereal—preferably, bran with skimmed milk. Lunch was soup, a broth with vegetables, and one slice of bread.

Figure 10.2. Between filming takes, Babe Ruth gets in a workout as extras watch. Boxing was a favored activity. *Courtesy: Security Pacific National Bank collection/Los Angeles Public Library photo collection.*

For several seasons the newspaper brigade had chided Ruth for his penchant to snack on hot dogs. A half dozen with several soft drinks were frequently downed to satisfy hunger pangs before games or during train travel. But Ruth's biggest appetite was reserved for steak, planked steak. He liked his steak rare, almost raw, and he seldom stopped at just one. People who dined with Ruth were aghast, seeing him eat sometimes four steaks in a sitting. A particular favorite of Ruth's was steak smothered in pork chops. But McGovern put a stop to it. "No red meat," he declared.[15] It would be only chicken or fish for Ruth during the duration of his stay in Los Angeles. In time, as a reward for his hard work, McGovern permitted Ruth a steak as a reward, but desserts were out—no sugar and no fried foods either.

McGovern did not just dictate, he taught. He explained calories and put them in the context of a car, its fuel, and what would be needed for a specific journey. Where one would expect grumbling and even resistance from someone used to having his way, McGovern received none from Ruth. "He is absolutely the most sincere worker I ever handled," he said.[16]

Christy Walsh arranged for Ruth to meet Bill Tilden and for the two to play a friendly game of tennis at the Los Angeles Tennis Club. Tilden, the six-time United States Open and two-time Wimbledon champion, was in town to appear in a movie, *The Music Master*. After their game, Tilden told the celebrated sportswriter Grantland Rice that Ruth "had about the worst tennis form I ever saw," but added, "it was remarkable what he could do. His reflexes were amazing. His judgement of distance was remarkable. So was his timing. He was quick with feet, hands, and eyes. He was a study in instinctive knack."[17]

Tilden's unscientific observation of Ruth jibed with that of professional scientists. In 1921 Christy Walsh, in a quest for publicity for Ruth, arranged for the Yankees' outfielder to be tested at the Psychology Research Laboratory at Columbia University. The session took place two hours after Ruth completed a game. At the direction of Columbia professors Albert Johnson and Joseph Holmes, Ruth underwent an array of tests. Over three long hours, the professors tested Ruth's eyes, ears, mental skills, concentration, breathing, and

Figure 10.3. After a friendly game between the two men, tennis great Bill Tilden (right) expressed amazement at the natural quickness, speed, and reaction times of Babe Ruth (left). *Courtesy: Security Pacific National Bank collection/Los Angeles Public Library photo collection.*

reaction time. The goal was to evaluate Ruth's nervous system and its reaction to outside stimuli. Ruth was made to tap steel plates, press keys to bursts of light while seated in a dark room, climb stairs, cross out letters on cards to time, and recite numbers that were flashed for a millisecond. The tip of his tongue sticking from a corner of Ruth's mouth said he was focused. That he took the tests seriously was confirmed by the results. Johnson and Holmes called Ruth's results extraordinary. The baseball sensation, they concluded, functioned at 90 percent efficiency, compared with the average human's 60 percent. Ruth's eyes reacted in 160 one-thousandths of a second, 12 percent faster than the average human. He responded to sound in 140 one-thousandths of a second, a time 10 percent faster than normal. Ruth's intelligence, attention, quickness of perception, and accuracy of understanding was well above normal.

Ruth was taken to a room and handed a replica of the bat he used in games, only this one was connected by wires to a machine. Ruth was instructed to react to a flash of light and swing the bat as he would at a pitch during a game. A strap was wrapped around the slugger's chest to gauge his breathing during the swing. The speed, strength, and quickness of Ruth's swing was measured. Johnson and Holmes announced the speed of Ruth's swing as 110 feet per second. His most effective point of contact was a spot over home plate at a height less than an inch above his right knee. The researchers calculated that when Ruth made contact with a fastball at that point, he was likely to send a pitch, on average, between 450 and 500 feet. It could be farther, they noted, were Ruth to hold his breath for a fraction of a second less during the swing.

A stir accompanied publication of the professors' findings in the October 1921 issue of *Popular Science Monthly*. Copyeditors produced headlines that called Ruth everything from a freak to supernormal, even a superman. Sportswriters theorized that these findings accounted for Ruth's superiority on the baseball diamond. But that was then, and now was now. Ruth was twenty-six when the study was conducted. When he began training with McGovern in Los Angeles, he was days from celebrating his thirty-third birthday. Most considered an athlete of thirty to be "over the hill." That was perhaps confirmed by the players who donned uniforms during the prior season. Of the 265 American League players who saw the field during the 1926 season, only 10 everyday regulars who played in more than one hundred games were over the age of thirty.

Much of Artie McGovern's work was based on a premise that the human body does not use oxygen as effectively once past the age of thirty. It was the trainer's belief that this phenomenon caused a decrease in muscle strength and a gradual, irreversible decline in a ballplayer's skills. It was a big reason the fitness expert concentrated so much effort the previous winter on rebuilding Ruth's fitness, his cardiovascular level.

Three weeks into Ruth's Los Angeles regimen, the Yankees' trainer dropped in for a visit. Al "Doc" Woods was a chiropractor by training. Through the years his expertise had grown, as had a reputation that led the Yankees to employ him to treat their players. Woods observed Ruth's workouts with McGovern and was more than just a little impressed. He was perhaps most surprised to see the illustrious night owl in bed each night by ten o'clock. Once back in New York, Woods lavished praise. He told all that Ruth's waistline had shrunk eight and a half inches. "Ruth looks great right now," he said. The trainer predicted a big season for the slugger: "If condition will turn the trick, it will be done."[18] *Los Angeles Times* writer Bob Ray went even further. Ruth, predicted Ray, "figures to have his greatest season if spring condition counts for anything."[19]

11

Digesting a Cobb Salary

The pictures told the story. On one side was Ty Cobb, smiling, holding aloft a Philadelphia Athletics jersey. Opposite was Babe Ruth, seated in chair, donning the uniform of the minor-league Los Angeles Angels while a makeup artist dabbed pancake on his face in preparation for the shooting of another scene of *Babe Comes Home*. The telling sign was the look on Ruth's face—stern, perhaps even brooding. Were Ruth actually angry, he had good reason to be. A large headline in the *Los Angeles Times* was the reason: "COBB SIGNS WITH MACKS AT $60,000 SALARY."[1] Ty Cobb had eclipsed Babe Ruth. Ruth was no longer the highest-paid player in baseball.

Once Ty Cobb was cleared to resume his playing career, his services were hotly coveted. His good friend Dan Howley, recently made manager of the St. Louis Browns, desperately tried to convince Cobb to join the team. The Browns made a tempting contract offer, $50,000 per year. But Cobb wanted more than just money. He wanted to join a ball club that would compete for a pennant. The Browns had finished seventh in 1926. Cobb was not convinced the club had the talent to be competitive in 1927.

The Philadelphia Athletics were a different story. Like Howley, Connie Mack, traveled to Cobb's home in Augusta, Georgia. He laid out a tempting offer. The package totaled $60,000. He would receive a $25,000 sign-on bonus, a salary of $25,000 for the 1927 season, and a separate $10,000 bonus. The ultimate selling point, however, was the strength of Mack's ball club. The Athletics finished third in 1926 and second in 1925. Already Mack had signed Eddie Collins, a .344 hitter with the White Sox in 1926, and Zach Wheat, who had twice driven in more than one hundred runs in the last four seasons with the Brooklyn Dodgers. Mack convinced Cobb that his addition would make the Athletics a legitimate contender for the American League title. Cobb agreed and signed with Mack's team.

Tris Speaker returned to the game as well. His was not the bidding war waged for Cobb. Though both the Yankees and Athletics sought him, Speaker expressed gratitude for the chance and accepted the first offer he received. It was from the Washington Senators, who offered a $25,000 salary for the 1927 season, a sign-on bonus that was not disclosed, and two additional bonuses—one for reaching the World Series and another should the Senators win the World Series. It was rumored that the total sum of Speaker's pay was comparable to Cobb's.

Ruth's irritation at seeing Ty Cobb eclipse him as the highest-paid player in the game grew to fury twenty-four hours later. That's when his own contract for the 1927 season arrived. The New York Yankees' offer was the same $52,000 salary received the previous year. Ruth was furious. "I am worth $100,000 to the New York club and if they won't give me that much, I'll quit baseball," he declared.[2] McGovern seconded the assertion, saying Ruth is "far better than he was a year ago, and if a year ago he was worth $52,000 he should be worth $100,000 today."[3] When pressed by reporters about his plans should he quit baseball, Ruth said he would partner with McGovern to open a chain of gyms. Colonel Jacob Ruppert refused comment on Ruth's demand. He did concede that the contract was sent merely to comply with baseball rules, which said a player must receive his new contract by February 15 or become a free agent. Ruppert said the Yankees' offer was simply a feeler and that he and Ruth would confer once the player had completed his movie responsibilities.

Ruth's salary demand and his threat to quit buried the baseball scandal from newspapers throughout the country. Rather than the Cobb-Speaker or Hornsby issues, now large headlines filled newspapers from Connecticut to California blaring the declaration of the Yankee star. Accompanying articles were equally inflammatory. "Terrible! Astounding! Dismaying! There aren't enough words in the dictionary," wrote Thomas Holmes in the *Brooklyn Daily Eagle*.[4] Next came the rumors, suggestions that the Yankees might actually trade Ruth. One report in particular by sportswriter Davis J. Kelly claimed the Yankees were in discussions on a deal that would send Ruth to the Philadelphia Phillies. A day later, the reporter backtracked.

While Ruth continued work on his motion picture, his worth was debated around the country. Grantland Rice estimated Ruth had made the owners more money than legendary stars such as Rogers Hornsby, Christy Mathewson, Honus Wagner, Ty Cobb, Walter Johnson, or Tris Speaker combined. Westbrook Pleger stated in his syndicated column that if Kenesaw Mountain Landis was worth $50,000 a year as commissioner, Ruth would be cheap at even three times that salary. A Southern California columnist wrote that Ruth "can name his price and baseball, if it is wise, will pay that price."[5] Experts were sought to weigh in on whether the slugger was worthy of the game's first six-figure salary. In his syndicated column, the American League umpire Billy Evans wrote, "It is impossible to say just how much any star is worth. The form that he is showing and the success that his club may be enjoying are more or less the determining factors. I would say Babe Ruth is worth just as much as he can get."[6]

A *United Press* story suggested that just as pressure from fans and the media led to hearings that brought Ty Cobb and Tris Speaker back into baseball, there was likely to be a similar backlash if fans felt Ruth received a raw deal from the Yankees.

Ruth's demand for the game's first six-figure salary filled newspapers. In both large cities and small towns, it seemed everyone, whether columnists, editorial page writers, and even the average man and woman on the street, had an opinion about what Babe should be paid. Papers large and small posed the question of Ruth's worth to readers. The *Chicago Tribune's* Inquiring Reporter column asked people on Madison Street what salary Ruth deserved. One replied $75,000 per season. Another answered, "Babe is the best drawing card in baseball and should be remunerated accordingly."[7] A third respondent said Ruth should be paid $85,000. In the small California town of Monrovia, the newspaper asked townspeople if Ruth was worth such a big salary. "Absolutely not," answered the town's fire chief. The secretary of the Chamber of Commerce stated, "Babe Ruth or any other athlete is not worth $52,000 a year as a ball player, but as a drawing card for the New York team he is worth that much and more."[8]

Colonel Jacob Ruppert, owner of the Yankees, needed no schooling when it came to Ruth's value to his ball club. The New York Yankees that Ruppert and Tillinghast Huston, his partner at that time, purchased in 1915 were a miserable club. During the first four seasons of their ownership, the team never finished higher than fourth. The New York Yankees were tenants, existing under the thumb of the National League New York Giants, in whose ballpark (the Polo Grounds) they played. During the first four seasons of Rupert's ownership, the Yankees never reached a half million in attendance for a season. The Giants, on the other hand, eclipsed the figure three times.

Everything changed on January 5, 1920, the day Harry Frazee sold Babe Ruth to the Yankees for $125,000 and a $350,000 loan. The acquisition was fortuitous for Ruppert in many ways. Only twelve days after acquiring Ruth, Ruppert, who owned one of the largest breweries in New York, was hit with a devastating blow—Prohibition. The Eighteenth Amendment to the Constitution banned the manufacture, transport, and sale of alcoholic beverages.

Over the ensuing six months, however, Babe Ruth offered salve to Ruppert's financial wounds.

Ruth erupted from phenomenon to icon during that summer of 1920. He smashed a record fifty-four home runs and fans streamed into the Polo Grounds like never before. The Yankees became the first team to surpass one million in fan attendance. They drew 360,000 more than their landlords. The shift in dynamics so incensed the Giants' owner, Charles Stoneham, that he kicked his tenant out. His action painted Stoneham as jealous, but at the heart of the rub was scheduling—specifically, preferred game dates. Baseball was played solely in the afternoon. Saturdays and Sundays, when most fans were off work, were prime dates. The Giants took the majority of weekends, leaving the Yankees to stew. On Stoneham's pronouncement, the league presidents became involved. Negotiations allowed the Yankees to use the Polo Grounds for two more seasons while they went to work on a ballpark of their own. In 1923, when Ruppert threw open the gates to Yankee Stadium, he unveiled a grand palace. His was the game's first three-decked stadium and offered the largest seating capacity in baseball: 56,886. It would soon come to be known as "the house that Ruth built."

Ruth's slugging sent the New York Yankees on an unprecedented rampage. In 1921 they reached the World Series for the first time and re-turned to the championship series again in 1922 and 1923. They finished second in the American League in 1924 and played again in the World Series in 1926. Ruth led the American League in home runs in five of his first seven seasons with the Yankees. There were some statisticians who felt it was more impressive that Ruth led the league in runs scored in five of his first seven seasons with the ball club and also runs batted in during four of those seven years. Of greater importance to Ruppert were the attendance figures and the related income he deposited into his bank account. The Ruth-fueled Yankees led baseball in attendance in each of his seven seasons, never drawing less than one million fans. They consistently outdrew the Giants, often by more than 20 percent.

As the Hot Stove talk of Ruth's impending contract negotiations began to heat up, one figure quietly loomed large in the background. The influ-ence of Christy Walsh had swelled in the six years of his association with Ruth. From syndicating ghostwritten articles about Ruth, Walsh became the spokesperson for Ruth and his wife, Helen. When Ruth ran afoul of Commis-sioner Landis for violating baseball barnstorming rules in the fall of 1921, Walsh had interceded and took control of future barnstorming tours. He kept the commissioner abreast of Ruth's commercial endeavors through telegrams and packets of newspaper clippings he sent through the mail. In time Ruth en-trusted Walsh to handle the many pitches from entrepreneurs and businesses who sought to use Ruth's name in connection with their product. In short, Christy Walsh was Babe Ruth's manager, the first such for any ballplayer in the game. Now Christy Walsh would orchestrate Babe Ruth's salary negotiations but in a covert and not overt way.

During the 1926 World Series, it was well known among sportswriters that Ruth's three-year contract with the Yankees would expire at the conclusion of the season. In Game Seven, a rumor made its way through the press box at Yankee Stadium. Ruth, it said, would demand $150,000 per year, almost triple what he was paid in 1926.[9] The rumor quickly found its way into print. "He won't get it," snapped Rupert when the rumor reached the Yankees' owner's ears.[10] When Ruth arrived in Montreal on his postseason barnstorming tour, he denied having made such a demand and said he wouldn't turn his attention to contract talks for another six months. Puzzled sportswriters then realized the origin of the rumor: Christy Walsh.[11]

Reporting on Ruth's impending contract negotiations was pushed to a back burner of Hot Stove news by the outbreak of the Cobb-Speaker scandal. It was not until Cobb and Speaker were cleared and Ruth arrived in Los Angeles to perform in *Babe Comes Home* that the receipt of his contract from the Yankees made his salary negotiations leap to the forefront.

Throughout the month of February, questions and even controversy over Babe Ruth's 1927 contract dominated baseball coverage. Every few days another log was tossed on the fire, and the ensuing firestorm generated valuable publicity for baseball—"pro bono publicity," suggested one sportswriter.[12]

In the days that followed Ruth's receipt of his 1927 contract, his mere mention that acting paid more in a month than what he earned from baseball would set off an uproar that Ruth would quit baseball for acting. Reports, such as "the movies threaten to lure Babe Ruth from baseball," appeared in several newspapers.[13] The syndicated news service *Universal Service* wrote, "Reports from the coast have Ruth so adept in the movies that baseball will have to come high to keep its own brightest star from becoming one of those cinema celebrities."[14] Members of the film crew were asked about Ruth's acting skills. Their evaluation stoked the flames. Dave Thompson, production manager for First National Pictures, praised the ballplayer's comedic acting skills. "Ruth's sense of comedy is very keen," he said. Thompson compared Ruth to the comedic acting star "Fatty" Arbuckle and said, "Ruth can command a very big salary in pictures if he wants to stay in the business."[15]

Several writers, however, pointed out astutely that Ruth's popularity with the public was the result of his feats on the baseball diamond. Should he give up the game, his popularity would wane, and his income opportunities in motion pictures would wither as well. As for Ruth, his own ghostwritten columns steered clear of the matter. They instead focused on his exercise program and offered advice on fitness, weight loss, and proper nutrition. All of it led writers close to Ruth to call the controversy "ingeniously concocted threats."[16]

A week prior to Ruth's planned departure from Hollywood, he returned his unsigned contract along with a letter to the Yankees. Stories abounded that the letter contained an ultimatum. Ruth was noncommittal. During a pause in filming, Ruth was pressed by Bill Kelley of *Universal Service* and Marshall Hunt of the *New York Daily News* to reveal the contents of the letter. Ruth replied that the decision was entirely up to Colonel Ruppert. If the Yankees' owner agreed, Ruth said he had no problem sharing a copy of the letter. Hunt then phoned Ruppert, who initially gave his consent. But when Ed Barrow, the Yankees' business manager, found out, he insisted Ruppert reverse his decision. Hunt was thus surprised to receive a telegram from Barrow that conveyed a change in the Yankees' position.

> This is to notify you that neither Col. Ruppert nor myself have given permission to any newspaper or individual to make public any letter or telegram addressed to the Yankee baseball club by Babe Ruth.[17]

Perplexity was short-lived. Even before Ruppert received Ruth's letter, it was leaked to two news services, *Associated Press* and *United Press*. In twenty-four hours, the letter appeared in dozens of newspapers across the country. The Yankees' owner was angry, not at the contents so much as the violation.

> Dear Col. Ruppert:
>
> You will find enclosed contract for 1927, which I am returning unsigned because of the $52,000 salary figure. I am leaving Los Angeles Feb 26 to see you in New York and will be prepared to report at St. Petersburg, but only on the basis of $100,000 per year for two years plus refund of $7,700 held out from my salary in the past.
>
> I think you are entitled to know what terms I honestly expect and therefore the figure is not padded with intentions of accepting less. Nor is it based on the suggestions I have received from thousands of fans nor from newspaper articles that have appeared in many parts of the country, but on what I feel I am worth from past performance and prospects.[18]

In New York, a quest began to determine who leaked Ruth's letter. Colonel Ruppert had an idea who the culprit was. "It was a good letter," he said to a reporter. "Even if the Babe didn't write it."[19] While Ruppert was coy, the *Los Angeles Record* was not. Their sports columnist Harry Grayson declared in print just who the leaker was, Christy Walsh.[20] "O, Mr. Christy Walsh, how could you," chided the *New York Daily News*, which held release of the letter on instructions from Ruppert and Ruth.[21]

Ruppert suggested to reporters that just as screenwriters had furnished Ruth with his lines for *Babe Comes Home*, so too had Christy Walsh through the entire salary controversy. If Ruppert chaffed, it was because Walsh was successful in shaping public opinion. The weeks of headlines brought many fans to back Ruth's position.[22] Ruppert grew testy with newspaper columnists who sided with Ruth. "You, Farrell," he snapped at a writer for *United Press*. "You sent a story all over the country that if Babe didn't nick me for $100,000, he was a sucker. That's a lot of money."[23] Some writers who backed Ruth went so far as to suggest every club in the American League should contribute to his pay, given what the slugger meant to their ticket sales. Added pressure on Ruppert came from the club on the other side of the river, the Giants. Rogers Hornsby represented a box-office threat. And the press predicted the National League club would get off to a hot start behind their new sensation.

Ruth continued to stress that he would quit baseball if offered a penny less than $100,000 per year. Few, however, bought it. The New York press especially knew from being around him just how much the game meant to Ruth. How hard Ruth was training was not lost on the reporters in Los Angeles. Whenever they asked Ruth about the upcoming 1927 season, his answers reflected an eagerness, such as the afternoon when he said, "I would hate to leave baseball. I have my greatest season coming."[24] It was a statement that bared to all just where his heart lay.

12

That's a Wrap

The large figure dropped into one of the room's thickly upholstered chairs. Not long after, the lights were turned off, a projector whirred to life, and images filled a screen on the opposite wall.[1] Viewing the dailies, all that had been shot during the previous day's filming, was a staple of the end of a day in the motion picture industry. The review involved the director, producer, writers, and those tasked with supervising sound, cameras, and other key responsibilities. They hurried from the set to scrutinize their work in the comfort of a projection room on the studio's lot. On this day, the large figure in one of the chairs, Babe Ruth, was made part of the group of scrutineers.

When a comedic scene appeared on the screen, one that involved Ruth kicking a diminutive shortstop in the seat of his pants, the slugger's laughter bellowed about the room. Once the viewing concluded and the lights came back on, Ruth beamed, "Cripes, that's good! That's good comedy!"[2]

With the baseball scenes done, filming shifted to another off-site location, an amusement park. Cast, crew, and, most importantly, equipment moved twenty-five miles west to the beach community of Venice, which Ruth continued to erroneously call "Venison." There at Kinney Pier, known as the Coney Island of the Pacific, Ruth and Anna Q. Nilsson would film a date scene. The arrival of the Yankees' star set the park buzzing. It wasn't long before Ruth had a long train of children following his every move.

Once lighting was established and the cameras were cranked, Ruth and Nilsson were instructed through several scenes. The couple was filmed as they strolled the arcade. They cuddled on the Big Dipper roller coaster. It was during filming at a dunk tank that the inner child in Babe Ruth was set loose.

The scene called for Ruth to throw a ball and hit a target five inches in diameter from a distance of thirty feet. By striking the target, a man would be knocked from a perch and into a tank full of water. Ruth found this not only an easy task but a particularly funny one too.

Ruth howled the first time the man kicked up a loud splash. He quickly grabbed another ball. "Watch this!" he hollered to his costar. As Ruth raised his left arm to throw, Ted Wilde realized what was going on. "Babe! Babe! Wait!" cried the director. "The camera didn't get you and this is valuable stuff! We can't waste these shots." Ruth turned toward Wilde, a perturbed look on his face, and said, "Awe, I can hit that thing pretty near every time."[3]

Soon laughter filled the set. Ruth threw and threw again. With each successful toss, a prize was handed to Nilsson. Ruth's throws were made with such precision that it was not long before Nilsson struggled under the weight of the many stuffed dolls she tried to carry in her arms. While Nilsson squealed with giddiness, the man continually plunged into the water found little humor in Ruth's actions. In fact, after one too many falls into the water, the man barked to Wilde that he quit, and the scene was brought to a halt.

The frivolity of the evening at the amusement park belied issues enveloping Babe Ruth. While working on the motion picture, he was dealing with a legal matter in San Diego, 120 miles to the south.

Ruth's headache began when his vaudeville tour came to that city during the second week of January. As part of his act, Ruth often called up children, a half dozen or less, to receive an autographed baseball. After a show, the theater manager noticed a forlorn-looking boy leaving the building. The man found out the boy was from a neighboring community of Escondido and was disappointed because he didn't get a ball signed by Ruth. The theater manager told the boy to stay for the beginning of the next show. Early in the second show, Ruth called four boys and two girls to the stage. A seventh child sprang from his chair, strode up the center aisle, and sparked an exchange with Ruth.

"Wait a minute, Babe. I'm coming too!"

"Who are you?

"I'm Bill Brewer from Escondido."

"I didn't ask you where you were from."[4]

Ruth waved the boy up onstage, where he and the other six children received their coveted prize. It was often a part of Ruth's show that brought smiles and laughter from the audience. But in San Diego, either the Brewer incident itself or one similar raised the concern of one Stanley M. Gue, who charged Babe Ruth with violating child labor laws.

Stanley Gue was the deputy state labor commissioner. He was viewed as a political opportunist, a man with eyes on higher office. Gue charged Ruth with two counts of violating child labor laws. The first was for using children in his act without a permit. The second count was for making children work after ten o'clock at night. When his office notified Ruth's show of the charge, a spirited telephone exchange ensued. Ruth offered to eliminate children from his show, but the theater manager refused. Both Ruth and the theater manager were perplexed by the charges. Gue's staff said children were made to do a skit in order to receive a baseball. It was a claim that was vehemently denied. Theater management pointed out the children simply came onstage, offered their name, received a baseball, then exited without doing anything more.[5]

Ruth's vaudeville tour next took the show north to the coastal town of Long Beach. His show was in its final weekend in that city before it was to move east to Salt Lake City, Utah. Early on a Saturday morning, January 22, Ruth and several friends traveled seventy-five miles east to the town of Redlands. By 9:30 a.m., they arrived at the Rainbow Angling Club in nearby Mill Creek for a morning of trout fishing. The fish were biting, so much so that Ruth lost track of time. It was 11:45 a.m. when one of the men hollered to Ruth that his show would begin back in Long Beach in an hour and a half.[6]

A frenzy broke out. A call was made to arrange for an airplane to fly Ruth from Redlands to Long Beach. The group hiked to their car, then hustled Ruth to the nearby airport.[7] When Ruth arrived for his show, he learned that Stanley M. Gue's assistant, Martha Moore, had obtained a warrant for his arrest. "Gue ordered me to so that Ruth might be represented before he left the state in connection with his vaudeville show," she said.[8]

Wearing the garb of his show—baseball pants, stirrups, white socks, and black shoes—Ruth walked into the Long Beach Police Department. A photographer snapped a picture as Ruth paid Sergeant Joe Hale and booking clerk Harry Knable the $500 for bail.

The following week, a Monday afternoon chaos erupted into Tuesday turmoil. Newspapers all across the country ran headlines similar to that of the *Los Angeles Daily News*, which read, "BABE RUTH SOUGHT ON BENCH WARRANT."[9] None of it was true.

When Ruth's case appeared on the court docket in San Diego the day before, neither Ruth nor an attorney had been present. Gue's office was quick to notify the press of the ballplayer's failure to appear and that a new bench warrant was being ordered. Later that afternoon, though, notice of Ruth's bail payment arrived at the court by mail from Long Beach. Following the last case of the day, the judge, Claude L. Chambers, was notified of the payment. The new warrant was invalidated.

Christy Walsh leaped to the forefront on Ruth's behalf. He arranged a lawyer for Ruth. Walsh notified the court that Ruth would be back in California for a movie role in two weeks. On that information, the judge set February 6 as Ruth's new court date. When Walsh informed Ruth, he got resistance. The date, Ruth later told the press, "is my thirty-third birthday. I didn't want to have to spend it in court."[10] Walsh's and Ruth's attorney persuaded the judge to reschedule the matter for February 25.

While Ruth was filming, Christy Walsh was never busier. He was busy doing the same thing over and over—saying no. No sooner had Ruth arrived in Los Angeles to film *Babe Comes Home*, than Walsh was inundated with requests from groups and events that wanted Ruth to appear. Ted Wilde's shooting schedule and Artie McGovern's workout plans left Walsh little opportunity to deliver his client. Ruth did attend the sixth annual WAMPAS Frolic and Ball, where he regaled the three thousand guests with bits from his vaudeville routine. Ruth gave a brief talk to seven thousand Boy Scouts at an annual rally. Before a packed house at the Hollywood American Legion Stadium, Ruth was introduced and said a few words in the ring prior to the "Kid" Brown–Dick Hoppe fight. On his last night in town, Ruth awarded the winner's cup at a college dance contest. Each generated column inches of publicity and, in some cases, accompanying photos.

When filming of *Babe Comes Home* entered its final week, intensity and activity were ratcheted up several notches. Cast and crew moved to the First National lot in Burbank. Several issues—the time involved to bring Ruth up to speed on performing and the myriad baseball scenes shot by a crew that did not understand the game—put the production well behind schedule. Ruth's schedule was inflexible. He had a hard-and-fast departure date to be in New York for his contract meeting with Colonel Jacob Ruppert and then to Florida for spring training with the Yankees.

Wilde was left with no choice but to insist upon ultra-long days. Shooting would sometimes encompass an exhausting fourteen hours. There were nights where it didn't conclude until the wee hours of morning. On one Herculean night of filming, the cast and crew performed twenty-six scenes. The schedule was particularly difficult for Wilde. One week into the project, his wife had given birth to a baby girl. As the director entered the final week of the project, his wife and young daughter came home from the hospital.

The scenes shot on the studio lot were the indoor scenes, scenes in the baseball team's clubhouse or Ruth's love scenes with Anna Q. Nilsson. Ruth took the shoot seriously. He practiced his love scenes in front of a mirror in his hotel room. Ruth playfully tried to persuade Artie McGovern to practice a heavy romance scene with him. No amount of coaxing could get the trainer to comply. Ruth instead rehearsed with his golf bag.

As Ruth wrapped up his work, word came from San Diego. Judge Chambers dismissed the charges against him. Stanley M. Gue would not be deterred. He vowed to refile.

On Ruth's final night of filming, Wilde kept the crew working until 3:00 a.m. It had been that way for six straight days. Ruth was exhausted. So was most of the crew. Yet throughout the breakneck shooting schedule, Ruth never squawked. "We've never had a person on any set who was more genuinely liked," said Wilde. "He is never late, works overtime without a murmur, and does anything asked of him."[11]

In the waning days of production, there were talks between the studio, Ruth, and Christy Walsh about more motion picture projects. "This acting business is getting just as easy as playing baseball," Ruth said.[12] By the time Ruth left town, he had a verbal agreement—nothing in writing or yet official—but the studio wanted him to return the following winter and make one and, perhaps, even two more films. Compensation discussed was more than generous.

When Ruth, Walsh, and McGovern arrived at the Burbank station, they were greeted by a royal sendoff. Banners were strung. Many of the biggest names in Hollywood were on the platform to shake Ruth's hand. Flashbulbs from newspaper photographers illuminated the crowd. Ruth was presented flowers, then his fellow cast members broke out harmonicas and played "Aloha" as he boarded the train bound for New York. Before disappearing into his Pullman, Ruth gave the gathered a farewell wave.

As Ruth's train pulled away from Burbank, acting faded into the background, much like the skyline behind. Each mile journeyed toward New York brought baseball more and more into focus. Awaiting him was a clash of the titans. Sensational media had a nation interested, anxious, and even nervous about the potential outcome of Ruth's impending sit-down with Colonel Ruppert. Each town Ruth's train passed through filled the windows of the Overland Limited with evidence of the Yankee star's popularity. In Riverside, a group of Boy Scouts waited patiently on the platform to wave as Ruth's train chugged past. When Ruth disembarked to stretch his legs on a vacant platform during a brief stop in Ogden, Utah, it made the local newspaper. His train's mere passing through Grand Island, Nebraska, drew a writeup in the town's paper. Whether in small towns, outposts, villages, or cities, the public thrilled to a smile or wave from Ruth as his train passed by.

Artie McGovern was not about to let travel get in the way of his work. He arranged for a portion of the baggage car to be made a gym. A door was rolled open, and as the train passed through burghs and towns, people captured a brief glimpse of Ruth, shirtless, boxing or skipping rope. In North Platte, Nebraska, Ruth disembarked to get in some running. He trotted back and forth on the station platform. As he did, Ruth was chased by adoring fans.

By the time Ruth's train reached Northwestern Terminal in Chicago, anticipation of his meeting with Ruppert was peaking. "One of the biggest financial transactions of the fiscal year will be the signing up of Babe Ruth," wrote W. O. McGeehan, sports editor of the *Oakland Tribune*.[13] It was Tuesday morning, March 1, when Ruth stepped from his train. A gaggle of reporters was waiting. "Do you really hope to get $200,000 for two years?" one asked. "I hope to tell you," a confident Ruth replied.[14] In New York, tension was high. Sportswriters from the city's many papers pestered Yankee president Ed Barrow about the impending contract talks. "We have nothing to say," Barrow said.[15]

In Chicago an hour passed. Whistles signaled the end of the layover. Ruth was on board the Pullman, ensconced in his compartment, left to ponder and to prepare. The final half of his journey would take place through the night. Newspapers in New York told when Ruth's train would arrive the following morning. It was information that would drive a horde of thousands to the station to cheer his return to New York City. While Ruth appreciated the crowds, only one man was on his mind. Ruth's anticipated salary showdown with Colonel Jacob Ruppert was now less than twenty-four hours away.

13

The Plan Goes Awry

The limousine pulled to a stop outside the large, fortress-like building at 1639 Third Avenue. There was a time when stepping from a car at this site would fill one's nostrils with the smell of hops, barley, and malt, scents which had wafted about the neighborhood. But that was before January 1920 and the implementation of the Eighteenth Amendment to the United States Constitution, more widely known as Prohibition. At that time Colonel Jacob Ruppert's brewery had employed more than one thousand workers and produced 1.25 million barrels of beer per year, including his brewery's signature beers, Ruppert Pale Ale and Knickerbocker Lager. Now the Yankees' owner was lucky to churn out 350,000 barrels annually, all of it so-called near beer—beer with a low 3 percent alcohol content to comply with government regulations.[1]

That Colonel Jacob Ruppert summoned Ruth to his office at the brewery and not Yankee Stadium gave some men cause for concern, chief among them Christy Walsh. Only Ruth exited the limousine for the meeting with Ruppert. While the Yankees' owner would include the team's business manager, Ed Barrow, and an executive of his brewery, the idea of a player employing a representative in contract talks was simply not something done in baseball. Walsh could only hope that a month of rehearsing for this very meeting would stick with Ruth and that his client would stay true to their plan.

It was 11:00 a.m. and had already been a busy morning for Walsh and Ruth. On arriving at Grand Central Station, the train from the West Coast was met by almost five hundred enthusiastic fans. Ruth was perturbed by the jostling and shouting from the throng. When he escaped the horde, he ordered his limousine driver to St. Vincent's Hospital, where Helen Ruth was convalescing from illness. The couple had been estranged now for almost two years. Still, Ruth brought her flowers and sat by her bedside, offering comfort. From St. Vincent's, Ruth went to Artie McGovern's gym to get in a workout. After a game of handball, he showered, changed, and made for the Ruppert Brewery to talk contract with his boss.

For Christy Walsh, the contract negotiations were a pinnacle moment in what had been a challenging three months. He knew that Babe Ruth's peak earning power in baseball was nearing its end. This was perhaps the most important contract his client would receive. Ruth, who was thirty-three, would be thirty-five when the proposed two-year deal expired. Just eighteen players of that age played in the American League in 1926, and of them only a small handful were still productive. To Walsh, it was extremely important that Ruth extract all he could from this negotiation.

Throughout the winter, Walsh had worked to prepare Ruth for life after baseball. It was not an easy task. As prolific as Babe Ruth was at losing baseballs during his seven seasons with the New York Yankees, he was equally, if not even more, prolific when it came to spending money.

By 1925, Babe Ruth was broke. His spending was out of control. He owned nine cars, each among the most expensive cars made in America. Extravagance seeped from his closets, filled to excess with suits, coats, shirts, and shoes. During a road trip to play the Browns in St. Louis, Ruth wore twenty-two silk shirts over three days. He cavalierly left each behind in hotel rooms. "Money is to the big likeable Babe like water that runs through the mill race. None of it sticks to his fingers," wrote L. H. Gregory in *The Morning Call*.[2]

Yankee players assigned to share a hotel room with Ruth didn't. "Why I room with the big monkey's luggage," said Ping Bodie.[3] Mike Gazella and Jimmie Reese made similar comments following seasons in which they were assigned to room with Ruth on the Yankees' road trips.[4] Ruth's late-night carousing brought trouble. He was the victim of blackmail attempts by a number of women, some of whom he had trysts with, but many he had not. In each case, Ruth spent thousands on detectives to prove the claims were false.

Before the 1922 World Series, an attorney threatened to go to the papers with a story that Ruth took his client across state lines in violation of the Mann Act, a federal law that prohibited interstate transport of women or girls for debauchery or any other immoral purpose. The attorney proposed he and his client would stay silent in exchange for a sizable sum of money. A year later, an attractive nineteen-year-old, Dolores Dixon, did make a claim public. The girl's guardian filed a lawsuit in which she claimed Ruth was the father of Dixon's unborn child. She sought $50,000. Ruth insisted he had never heard of the woman. He turned his investigators loose. In both cases, the men found the women were being used by blackmailers.

In 1921, Ruth and his wife, Helen, adopted an infant. The baby girl was actually the product of a fling Ruth had with a married model who did not want the child.[5] By 1925, infidelity cost Ruth his marriage. It proved expensive. Both Catholics, Babe and Helen Ruth agreed to separate but not divorce. In October 1925, Ruth signed a costly separation agreement. He would pay Helen $100,000 in four installments—$20,000 in October 1925; $30,000 in October 1926; $25,000 in October 1927; and $25,000 in October 1928. In addition, Helen Ruth was given ownership of the couple's 125-acre farm in Sudbury, Massachusetts.[6]

There were lawsuits, speeding tickets, and unpaid taxes. When the Yankees arrived in Boston for a game in 1921, Ruth was served a subpoena for unpaid vehicle taxes while he lay soaking in a bathtub. Two weeks later, Ruth was sued for money owed an automobile dealer.

Before Christy Walsh entered the picture, Ruth had lost thousands on business schemes. One left Ruth holding the bag for $37,500.[7] He was labeled a sucker in the press. Sportswriters accused him of "preferring to listen to pinhead advisors."[8]

For all of his selfish overindulgences, Babe Ruth was a generous man. He exuded kindness. Visits to orphanages and hospitals arranged by Christy Walsh on barnstorming and vaudeville tours tugged at Ruth's emotions. It was not uncommon for him to press as much as fifty dollars into the hand of a child with debilitating injuries or disabilities. In Detroit, when he noticed the clubhouse boy shaking from cold weather, Ruth pulled two twenty-dollar bills from his pocket and gave them to the youth with instructions to go buy a coat.

Among those closest to Ruth was a belief that his frivolous spending habits stemmed from the rejection he endured in childhood. Ruth was seven when, on June 13, 1902, his father turned the boy over to the brothers of St. Mary's Industrial School. Ruth was deemed incorrigible, an out-of-control truant. Influenced by workers at the Baltimore docks, the boy's cursing, smoking, tobacco chewing, and alcohol consumption pushed his parents to an extreme point of exasperation.

St. Mary's Industrial School was a combination boarding school, reform school, and orphanage. It was a Catholic institution, created in 1866 by the order of Xaverian Brothers. It housed eight hundred boys in a six-building academy, which was spread over several acres outside of downtown Baltimore.[9] Such was the local regard for the work of the school that the juvenile court sentenced many truants, runaways, and incorrigible youths to serve their sentence at St. Mary's. It was here George Herman Ruth would reside for twelve years.

The thirty brothers at the school were strict but caring. Counselors, mentors, teachers, and advisors—all imposed unyielding structure, the kind needed to break, reshape, and direct wayward boys. It was one of these men,

Brother Matthias, who changed the direction of George Herman Ruth's life. Martin Leo Boutilier was born in 1872 in Lingan, a hardscrabble, coal-mining town in the eastern Canadian province of Nova Scotia. It was after his family moved south to the United States that he joined the order and was christened Brother Matthias. At St. Mary's Industrial School, his titles were prefect of discipline and assistant athletic director.[10] At six feet six inches tall and 250 pounds, his was an imposing figure able to quickly quell the unruly.

Equally stern and compassionate, Brother Matthias helped Ruth navigate the homesickness of his early weeks at the school, then deal with the rejection that followed. Ruth frequently faced an empty chair on visiting day. Neither his parents nor his sister, Mary, came to visit. "I guess I'm too big and ugly for anyone to come and see me," he said.[11]

Other than for extreme offenses, corporal punishment was eschewed for a reward-denial philosophy. The school subscribed to the belief that "idleness breeds trouble" and kept the boys busy with myriad activities. In addition to academic work, religious training was a staple of each day's activities. Boys were taught a trade. Ruth took up shirt making. Participation in sports was mandatory.[12]

Bigger than most of the boys his age, Ruth was initially steered into sports, where it was felt his build might help him excel. He didn't like that the school's football field had sticks and broken glass scattered about. Basketball held little interest. Boxing was fun, but it was another sport, one Brother Matthias was involved with coaching, that sparked Ruth's enthusiasm: baseball.[13]

Matthias taught Ruth the basics, then invested hours to hone his skills. He pitched batting practice, oversaw bunting drills, then with a mitt on his left hand and a bat in his right, Matthias would hit groundballs to infielders, catch the throw, flip the ball from the mitt into the air, and whack a fly ball to an outfielder. He insisted every boy learn all nine positions. Ruth initially took to catching. When a pitcher lost his privileges, Ruth was tabbed to replace him. From Ruth's ensuing performance, it was felt pitching might just be his niche.

St. Mary's Industrial School had forty-four teams. They were broken into levels based upon ability. While many of the boys strived to move up to the next level of competition, those who were most competitive longed to reach the first team, a travel team that played wearing real flannel baseball uniforms. Ruth quickly moved up the ladder of teams, quicker than most. He was seventeen when Brother Matthias instructed him to report to the equipment room and receive a uniform. The teen was ecstatic.[14]

In February 1914, Baltimore was hit by a fierce snowstorm. A group of St. Mary's students were sliding on ice at a pond near the school when a younger boy appeared and told Ruth he was wanted immediately in Brother Matthias's office. Fearing he was to be punished, Ruth responded reluctantly.

When he stepped into the brothers' office, Ruth removed his cap and was surprised that nobody in the room had a stern look on their face. Brother Matthias introduced Ruth to a visitor. The man was "Jack" Dunn, owner and manager of the local ball club, the Baltimore Orioles. The Reverend Brother Gilbert, the school's athletic director, was a friend of Dunn's. He contacted the Orioles' owner and manager to tell him about Ruth. Based on the word of Brother Gilbert and without ever having seen Ruth pitch, Jack Dunn offered the nineteen-year-old a contract for $600 and a train ticket to join his ball club for spring training in Fayetteville, North Carolina. As Ruth left the office, he threw his cap in the air, let out a yell, and jumped into a handstand. Five months later on July 9, the Boston Red Sox paid Dunn $25,000 for three of his players. The most heralded was praised, "one of the most sensational moundsmen who ever toed the slab in the International League."[15] Babe Ruth had reached the major leagues.

In the years that followed, Babe Ruth's gratitude toward St. Mary's Academy and Brother Matthias in particular was unyielding. In 1919 fire sparked by a workman's torch destroyed much of the school.[16] Ruth worked tirelessly to raise funds and help the school rebuild. He brought the Yankees to Baltimore for a charity game, where he waved a personal check for $2,500 and issued a challenge to the six thousand fans to match it. He arranged for the school's fifty-member band to accompany the Yankees to Cleveland, Detroit, Chicago, and St. Louis. In each city they played at the games and performed fund-raising concerts at which Ruth appeared and signed autographs. In all, $100,000 was raised.

In 1926 Ruth invited Brother Matthias to New York. He took him to a car dealership and asked what he thought about one particularly expensive car. "If you think you can afford it, George," Matthias replied.[17] The very next day, the car was delivered with a note, "For you with many thanks for what you and St. Mary's have done for me."[18]

Ruth's generosity extended to his Yankees teammates. He loaned teammates money but refused to accept interest when they paid him back. Ruth frequently took teammates to dinner after games. When he did, the Babe always picked up the check. Yet he did so with a wary eye. If he ever noticed a teammate fail to reach for the check, that teammate was never invited back.[19]

But when it came to spending, there were few areas where Babe Ruth threw away more money than at the horse races. During spring training, he was a regular at Florida horse races and dog tracks. Fans were quick to give him tips on supposedly sure things. But none of them ever were. Ruth felt his best chance to win was if he bet at least $1,000. The most he dropped on a single race was $10,000. He was sued by bookies for moneys owed. Their claims were almost always met with protests from Ruth. Umpires told the story of Ruth being ejected from a 1921 game on purpose so he could get to a local racetrack in time to place wagers on hot tips he'd received for the sixth and seventh races. Ruth carried so much cash at times that he sought and was granted a permit to carry a handgun. But nothing in Ruth's history of reckless spending became more legendary than his gambling on a trip to Cuba following the 1920 season.

Ruth agreed to a proposal for a fifteen-game barnstorming tour of the Caribbean island. He would be paid $1,000 per game. When Ruth left New York, he took $5,000 in spending money. He knew full well the horses were running at Cuban racetracks. During his visit to the island, Ruth was either on a baseball diamond or at a racetrack. In almost no time, he lost the $5,000. Ruth also lost the $15,000 he received for playing in the exhibition games. He wired his bank for another $15,000 and lost that as well. "You tell 'em I'm off the ponies for life—maybe," he said.[20]

Ruth's exorbitant gambling was curtailed by a stunning discovery. He met a man, a bookie, who agreed to place bets for him at racetracks around New York. They became friends. Ruth, however, became suspicious when none of the man's tips paid off. He was shocked to learn the man was a private detective who was sending nightly reports on his gambling activity to Colonel Jacob Ruppert.[21]

When Ruth arrived in Los Angeles on his vaudeville tour in January 1927, a man at the train station hollered, "I'll see you in Tijuana." Knowing the man was referring to the racetrack in the Mexican border town, Ruth shouted back, "The hell you will!"[22] At a luncheon the next day, a reporter asked Ruth about his losses at the track. "If I had all the dough I lost I could own a ball club now, but I'm through."[23]

Convincing Babe Ruth to curtail his excessive spending was a futile exercise for Christy Walsh. He insisted, he pleaded, he cajoled. Walsh told Ruth stories of ballplayers who were broke soon after their playing days ended. He warned Ruth that he was on a similar path. Pleas to save money drew curt replies. After all, Ruth pointed out, he was "the home run king" and was simply "living up to the title."[24]

Shortly after the 1923 World Series, Walsh recruited help and concocted a plan. Harry Heilmann, the Detroit Tigers' right fielder, worked in the off-season for Equitable Life Insurance. Ruth liked Heilmann. Together Walsh and Heilmann met with Ruth to convince the slugger to invest in a deferred annuity. Walsh explained that it would give Ruth a guaranteed income once his baseball career ended. He would be financially independent. Ruth was initially reluctant. As tables were laid out showing investment and return probabilities, he came around. He agreed to invest his World Series share and other moneys made outside of baseball. His initial investment was $50,000.

Sold on the idea, Ruth invested again. This time, in February of 1927, Walsh proposed a plan designed to generate publicity. On Ruth's thirty-third birthday, he would invest $33,000. It was money owed Ruth from his syndicated newspaper column. The money was put into yet another annuity. There were plans to make more investments that would build the fund to $250,000.

While Babe Ruth was in New York City, negotiating with Colonel Ruppert wasn't his only appointment. There was another pressing matter that required his attention: his taxes. From his 1926 earnings, Ruth owed between $40,000 and $50,000. Rumors swirled about the city that Ruth was to be arrested. A large crowd gathered outside Custom House, home in New York to the Internal Revenue Department. Reporters clamored to know if an arrest was imminent. After his workout at Artie McGovern's and before traveling to Colonel Ruppert's office, Ruth, his attorney, and Walsh visited Custom House. Ruth was presented with his tax bill. Walsh arranged for it to be paid before Ruth left town for Florida and spring training. It was left to Frank K. Bowers, head of the regional Internal Revenue office, to calm the reporters and explain that Ruth was not and never was going to be arrested.

When Babe Ruth walked into Colonel Jacob Ruppert's office, it was over. Baseball would not have its first $100,000-a-year player. It was an outcome that was predetermined, based both on Jacob Ruppert's business acumen and his personality.

A third-generation brewer, Jacob Ruppert inherited his father's brewery in 1915. A year later, he partnered with a friend, T. L. Huston, to buy the New York Yankees for $450,000. Six years later, Ruppert bought Huston out for $1.25 million. In addition to baseball, Ruppert expanded his business ventures to include real estate, owning several office buildings in Manhattan and a resort in Florida. In time Ruppert grew the $6 million his father left to $40 million. A bachelor who worried that women only showed interest in him because of his money, Ruppert was short in stature, wore a signature clipped mustache, and spoke with a German accent. He carried the title of Colonel, earned from service in the National Guard. Called "Jake" by his friends, Ruppert could be curt while also persuasive. At the brewery employees considered his manner brusque. Rarely were others called by anything but their last name. Yet his relationship with his ballplayers was paternalistic, more father–son than employer–employee. And no ballplayer tried Ruppert more or held a closer relationship with the man than Babe Ruth.

In the seven seasons Ruth was a Yankee, the player took Jacob Ruppert on a roller coaster ride of unimaginable home-run hitting and World Series–winning highs to detestable depths of suspensions, tantrums, and perplexing contract negotiations. Ruppert handled his star player with a combination of sternness and compassion. He was strong in his support of the commissioner

when Judge Landis suspended Ruth for the first six weeks of the 1922 season for violating barnstorming rules. Ruppert took a different tact, stripping
Ruth of his captaincy when just five days after he had returned from that
suspension, the slugger threw dirt into the chest of an umpire, spewed vile
language, had to be restrained by opposing players from hitting the man, and
then leaped into the stands in pursuit of a heckling fan.

An outburst by Ruth in August 1925 finally taxed Ruppert's patience.
It happened in St. Louis when Ruth pushed the Yankees' manager, Miller
Huggins, to a breaking point. Angered by the late-night carousing, missed
curfews, and ignored bunt signs, Huggins suspended Ruth indefinitely and
fined him $5,000. Huggins told Ruth he was being sent back to New York
immediately. Enraged, Ruth traveled instead to Chicago, where he told
reporters he would never play for Huggins again. He sought a meeting with
Kenesaw Mountain Landis to ask the commissioner's help to lift his suspension. Ruppert ordered Ruth to drop his pursuit of the commissioner and return
to New York at once. There the men had a private sit-down. In a fatherly
tone, Ruppert told Ruth, "it was a pity he should shatter the ideal people
have of him."[25] He urged Ruth to change his ways, then laid down the law.
Ruth, he said, would not play again until he made things right with Huggins
and the teammates he let down. After allowing Ruth to stew for another four
days, Huggins invited him to face the team. Ten minutes before the Yankees'
September 6 game with Philadelphia, Huggins summoned his players off the
field and into the clubhouse. Reporters were allowed in the room as well. A
remorseful, humbled Babe Ruth stood before the room and issued an apology.
He promised to respect and follow the direction of Huggins in the future as
well. When Ruppert arrived in St. Petersburg the following February for the
start of spring training, he grinned broadly when he learned Ruth was fishing.
His fishing partner for the day was a local minister. It moved one reporter
to write that Ruppert "made Ruth jump through hoops like a talented ring
master."[26]

Ruth's past contract negotiations with Ruppert had been devoid of dispute.
When Ruth joined the Yankees, Ruppert and his co-owner, T. L. Huston,
promptly hiked his pay from $10,000 to $25,000. Just prior to the start of
spring training in 1922, Ruth and the Yankees were stalemated over a new
contract. Ruth sought $52,000 per season for five years. When neither side
would budge, Ruth proposed a coin flip to settle the matter. Ruppert agreed.
Ruth won and received what he wanted.

Now, with spring training getting underway in Florida, both Ruppert and
Ruth were keen to reach a deal. Inside the Ruppert Brewery, a malty aroma
filled the air. Ruth rode the elevator past a glass-enclosed room filled with
large copper vats. Arriving on the sixth floor, he walked down a marble

corridor until he reached the office of his boss. Inside the large room with its marble floor and mahogany walls, the men shook hands, then engaged in brief small talk.[27] Ruppert was quick to get straight to the point. Ruth had asked for $200,000—a salary of $100,000 a season for two years. "Well Babe, how will $210,000 for three years suit you?" Without hesitation Ruth blurted, "O.K.," and five minutes after the meeting began, the two men shook hands on a deal.[28]

The press was then invited in. Ruth took a fountain pen in his right hand and, as flashbulbs popped, acted as if he were signing a contract on the tabletop. Both men called the deal amicable. "I'm tickled to death with the Colonel's treatment of me," said Ruth. "Babe and I have always been good friends. He respects my judgement and I respect his desire to make all he can out of the game in his prime," Ruppert added.[29]

When Christy Walsh learned the news, he was crestfallen. For weeks he had schooled Ruth, preparing him for the meeting; to find out that in five minutes Ruth acquiesced and agreed to Ruppert's first offer—$70,000 a year ($30,000 less than what they wanted)—left him angry. He knew that his client was not a good negotiator. Walsh wished he could have been allowed to join the meeting, to kick Ruth under the table and force him to stick to their plan. Baseball, Walsh felt, owed Babe Ruth. It wasn't the other way around. Ruth's business manager had done calculations. He showed Ruth that the Yankees generated an extra $300,000 at the box office each season because of Ruth. On the road, Ruth meant anywhere from an extra $25,000 to $50,000 to each of the other seven American League teams. He told Ruth that if Ruppert argued that a $100,000 salary would leave the Yankees with no profit, he had to counter that exhibition games in spring training and on the off days during the season brought in plenty and that Ruth was the only Yankee required to play in every exhibition game.[30]

Such was the level of disgust he felt that Walsh would never speak a word of this salary negotiation to Ruth.[31] Jacob Ruppert, on the other hand, was giddy. While reporters chattered away with Ruth, the Yankees' owner exited his office. He approached Edward Barrow, the Yankees' business manager, and instructed the man to "wire manager Miller Huggins in St. Petersburg, Florida that all is well."[32]

14

A Different Babe

The small ballpark in Orlando was enveloped by a state of frenzy. It was the fourth year the Cincinnati Reds made the burgeoning central Florida town their spring-training home, and on this day, March 10, 1927, that relationship between team and town was about to reach a zenith.

Interest had been percolating since the day after Christmas 1926, when the Reds' president, August "Gerry" Herrmann, announced the schedule of games that would be played at Orlando's Tinker Field. The second of the four was the one that raised excitement. It would be a first. Never before had the New York Yankees played in Orlando. Herrmann went one step further. To maximize both potential ticket sales and game revenue, the Reds' owner declared the game "Babe Ruth Day." It was an announcement made with a purpose—to ensure the Yankees' sensation would play that afternoon.

Babe Ruth had only been with the Yankees seventy-two hours after the meeting with Ruppert in New York when he and his teammates boarded three buses for the 125-mile trek east from St. Petersburg to Orlando and their first exhibition game. The ink on his new contract was scarcely one week dry. After the signing, his tax meeting, and a visit with his wife, Ruth made the thirty-seven-hour trek by train from New York to Florida. On arriving in St. Petersburg, Ruth's first stop wasn't the Yankees' spring-training site. It was a golf course. Getting in eighteen holes with members of the press, Ruth astounded his playing partners with a 365-yard drive on the final hole.[1]

Two dozen Yankees greeted Ruth when he arrived at Crescent Lake Park, a fifty-six-acre public park with baseball diamonds the Yankees would call home for six weeks. Many of the players sported sunburns, a side effect from two weeks of workouts under the Florida sun. When Ruth stepped into the batter's box for the first time, his mighty swing promptly sent the ball out of the park. The baseball landed at the feet of a farmer working in a nearby field. "I see Babe Ruth is in town again," the man said when a batboy turned up to retrieve the baseball.[2]

A day later, Ruth was at it again. In the morning workouts, he fouled off the first pitch he saw, then knocked the next two well beyond the right-field fence and into Crescent Lake, an achievement he would replicate later in the afternoon. Onlookers said it was the best Ruth had ever looked early in spring training.[3] Miller Huggins was delighted, too, as he watched Ruth run the bases.

It was clearly a different Babe Ruth. What his strength on the golf course and in batting practice didn't reveal, his clothes confirmed. Huggins had left a sweatshirt in Ruth's locker to wear during training. It was the size he had worn the year before. Now, however, it was loose and baggy. Ruth laughed that none of his suits fit either.[4] Sportswriters could see the difference. The player who'd weighed 254 pounds during the 1926 season was now 218 and "positively slender and willowy," as one wrote.[5] "He is taking the task of getting in his best shape quite seriously," wrote another.[6] When asked if Ruth's form made winning the pennant a cinch, Huggins chuckled, "Let [Connie] Mack have his week."[7]

When the first two Yankees' buses pulled to a stop in front of the team's Orlando hotel, nearly everyone on board was taken aback at the reception they received. One thousand children cheered the Yankees and flocked after Ruth.[8] The game was an important one, not only to the Cincinnati Reds but also to the town of Orlando. The Chamber of Commerce made a $4,000 guarantee to convince the Reds to make their town its spring-training home. A baseball committee was established, headed by the mayor L. M. Autrey, with a goal to sell enough tickets to recoup the committed moneys. Plans were launched to sell season tickets. Box seats for the four Orlando exhibition games were priced at $11. Grandstand seats were sold for $5.50. The Lions Club, the Exchange Club, the Bank of Orlando, and the Chamber of Commerce itself committed to purchase $200 worth of tickets apiece. The local newspaper the *Orlando Sentinel* ran quarter-page advertisements to promote the effort.

The Chamber of Commerce was not the only one faced with a financial commitment. Herrmann, too, had obligations to meet. Three of the exhibition game opponents—the Washington Senators, St. Louis Browns, and Cleveland Indians—were promised $1,000 for traveling to Orlando. The New York Yankees demanded more and got it, a whopping $4,000. Essential to the goal of both parties was that one player in particular, Babe Ruth, had to play.[9]

Two days before the game, Herrmann announced that all children between the ages of six and sixteen would be admitted to the game free of charge. Tom Lantz, the superintendent of public recreation, issued a plea for vehicles—one thousand in all—that could transport children to Tinker Field. Lantz distributed stickers that drivers were to place on the windshields of their cars. They read, "Jump In Kid! See Babe Ruth! Free Baseball!"[10] He further instructed drivers to go to the nearest school and pick up youths who wanted to go to the game.

When the gates were opened at Tinker Field, workers were overwhelmed. A long line of fans paid their three dollars at the box office, and the 1,500-seat grandstands were quickly filled. Music from the Orlando Pythian Huzzar Band mixed with the buzz of the crowd. Ruth came onto the field to a loud ovation. He was affable, shook hands with children, posed for pictures, and doffed his cap as he bowed to the crowd. The local newspaper called it "the biggest day in the history of Orlando."[11]

Even though Ruth had trained with the Yankees for only two days, Miller Huggins put him in the starting lineup. He instructed Ruth to play center field and wrote his name in his customary spot in the batting order, third. At 3:30 p.m. the game began. Shortly after, Ruth came to bat for the first time. Tinker Field's grandstands were filled beyond capacity. Still more fans stood with their backs pressed against the outfield fence. They made noise, lots of it. Children and adults encouraged Ruth. Children pleaded to see a baseball deposited over the right-field fence. Instead, in Ruth's first turn at bat, they saw a pitch grounded softly to second base and their hero retired for an out.

It was in the fourth inning when Ruth came up again. By this time, Syd Dyer, a young prospect in an audition for the Reds, succeeded the starting pitcher Carl Mays. Whether from nerves, poor pitching mechanics, or just a lack of strike-throwing ability, the young Kansan had difficulty putting his pitches in the strike zone. Mark Koenig was already on first base via a walk when Ruth stepped into the batter's box. Groans filled the air when he walked, as did the next hitter, Lou Gehrig.

After two Yankees were retired, Mike Gazella lined a single to right field. Ruth broke from second base and was soon in an all-out sprint to try to score. As Ruth rounded third base, he stumbled. The spikes at the bottom of his left shoe caught on the third-base bag. He went down. In severe pain, Ruth hopped on his right foot the rest of the way to home plate. When the inning ended, Ruth limped from the Yankees' dugout, intent on returning to his position in center field. It was no use. By the time Ruth reached the first-base line, the pain was too great. He turned, hobbled back to the dugout, and said, "It's no use Hug." Miller Huggins arranged for Ruth to be driven to the team's hotel and receive attention from the team doctor.[12]

While box office staff at Tinker Field gleefully reported its highest-ever one-game take, $6,700, Ruth lay atop a bed in his hotel room, writhing in agony.[13] Dr. Albert Woods applied wraps and told Huggins that Ruth had suffered a tendon injury to his left calf. It was either torn or strained. The ire from it all was capsulized the following morning by Marshall Hunt in the *New York Daily News*. "There was exploitation this afternoon, but tonight Mr. Ruth is suffering the consequences."[14]

It was left to Miller Huggins to be the bearer of bad news to the Florida village of Auburndale. Ruth would not play in the much-anticipated game there against his former team, the minor-league Baltimore Orioles. In fact, Huggins said it would be at least a week before Ruth played again. It actually turned out to be nine days before Huggins could write Ruth's name on a lineup card again, save for a game against the Boston Braves five days after the injury in which a stir-crazy Ruth talked his way into pinch-hitting, then struck out.

Until his return to the Yankees' lineup, Ruth hobbled about with the aid of a cane, his left leg heavily wrapped from foot to thigh. During that time, he worked with Tony Lazzeri to level out his swing. He was almost giddy the next day when the young second baseman hammered out four hits and predicted Lazzeri "is going to be one of the greatest batters in the league this year."[15] Ruth commiserated with Walter Johnson after the Washington Senators' ace pitcher was struck by a line drive and suffered a broken left ankle one day after Ruth endured his injury. At a boxing match, the emcee introduced Ruth, then urged him to climb into the ring and wave to the crowd. Ruth instead tossed his cane into the ring to make the statement that he couldn't.

Eight days after his injury, Ruth fielded fly balls during outfield drills. He ran effortlessly, with only a slight limp. Huggins declared his slugger would return to the lineup the next afternoon against the Boston Braves. Promotion efforts to generate a big crowd went into overdrive. Large headlines promoting that Ruth would play appeared in local newspapers.

For St. Petersburg, Florida, the New York Yankees meant far more than the dollars taken in at the box office. True, the thirty-seven players pumped money into a local hotel and area restaurants during the team's six-week stay. The three weeks of exhibition games brought tourists to town. But civic leaders in St. Petersburg saw the Yankees and, in particular, their star player Babe Ruth as far more than March dollars. The team and Ruth were an essential catalyst in plans to grow the town. While the Boston Braves also trained in St. Petersburg, it was the Yankees, the American League champions, and Ruth who appeared in articles almost daily during spring training in newspapers all around the country. Every article had either St. Petersburg, Florida, as its byline or a mention of the town within the story. St. Petersburg rode the coattails of baseball's most popular team and its star player. While people living in snow-covered parts of the country read about the Yankees' frolics in sunny

St. Petersburg, they came away with an impression that "St. Petersburg is still progressing," said Byrd Latham, president of the Chamber of Commerce.[16]

During the nine days that Ruth was unable to play, local leaders bemoaned a decrease in attendance at Yankees games in Waterfront Park. All that changed once Miller Huggins announced Ruth's impending return. When Babe Ruth trotted to right field on Saturday afternoon, March 19, he was cheered by 3,500 fans, the largest crowd of the exhibition game season in St. Petersburg.[17] He was removed after five innings, during which he'd walked, grounded out to the first baseman, and struck out.

It was in Ruth's third game back that, despite still limping, his swing convinced all he was recovered. He received a loud ovation when he came to bat in the sixth inning. An inning earlier, he had doubled. Now, with two teammates on base and a one-ball, one-strike count, Ruth tagged a pitch and sent it over the right-field wall for his first home run of the spring. Two innings later, Ruth homered again, and the Yankees defeated Cincinnati, 16–7.

When March came to an end, the Yankees broke camp for an exhibition-game tour with their opponent in the 1926 World Series, the St. Louis Cardinals. It was a breakneck schedule of six games in seven days over four states. The teams would play in Jacksonville, Florida; Montgomery, Alabama; and Savannah and Atlanta, Georgia, before concluding with games in Knoxville and Nashville in Tennessee. No sooner would each game end than the players would be on a train headed for the next town. The games promised to bring in big money and were billed the "Little World Series."

At each game Ruth was the player in the spotlight. Demands were incessant. Local newspapermen sought interviews. How many home runs would he hit? "I hope to get 61."[18] Ruth said he liked the Yankees' pennant chances, then grew annoyed when questioned about his salary. It was when reporters strayed from baseball that his patience expired. "Sorry," Ruth said, "I can't talk longer but you know how it is."[19] One thing he never wavered from was signing autographs. At each ballpark, paper and baseballs were thrust toward him. Ruth obliged every request and even spent time between innings during the games signing balls in the dugout.

Each game brought fans from all over the state. An overflow crowd of ten thousand came to the ballpark in Jacksonville. The turnout in Montgomery was hailed the largest to witness a sporting event in Alabama. Organizers were elated with a crowd of five thousand on a Monday afternoon in Atlanta. So big were the games, society columns noted which of the town's leading citizens saw Babe Ruth play.

Ruth gave the fans memories. When the series began, his batting average for the spring exhibition games was below .300. By the time it ended, he was on a torrid tear. Ruth doubled and scored a run in Jacksonville. He doubled home the game winner in Savannah, doubled twice in the game in Montgomery, and then did it again the next afternoon in Atlanta.

By the time the tour reached Tennessee, things became frenzied. Eager promoters in Knoxville anticipated five thousand would show up. At least 10 percent were traveling from out of town. But the teams had opted to travel from Atlanta by morning rather than at night. The Yankees arrived late, barely two hours before game time. Compounding anxiousness, heavy rains fell during the morning. When Miller Huggins reached the local ballpark, he was adamant that the field was far too wet for a game. With no game to see, the throng flocked instead to the Farragut Hotel, intent on seeing Yankees players up close and getting autographs. The lobby was jammed when the ball club arrived.[20] "Gee what a crowd," a tanned Babe Ruth exclaimed when he entered the hotel.[21] Ruth shook hands and signed a few autographs before retreating to his room, where he locked the door and refused to answer phone calls from local reporters.

The "Little World Series" tour ended in Nashville. For weeks iron and concrete workers put in long hours to construct new stands and increase the seating capacity of Sulphur Dell, the local ballpark, from 2,500 to 7,000. Their efforts were rewarded when a full house cheered the Yankees and Cardinals. It wasn't long into the game when Babe Ruth gave the crowd something to remember. In the bottom of the first inning, Ruth lined a shot that sailed over the fence in center field for a home run. The Cardinals won the game, 10–8. "But," as Blinkey Horn wrote in the *Tennessean*, "you are not likely to hear a bunch of excited urchins on the street corner chattering about that. They will be buzzing about the four-bagger which Babe Ruth sent buzzing over the palisades."[22] Columnist Ralph McGill of the *Nashville Banner* concurred. "There was many a man who went home to his supper last night with an inch or so extra on his chest—he had seen the 'Big Bam' hit one."[23]

From Nashville the Yankees hurried for home. Two final exhibition games remained on the schedule before Opening Day of the 1927 season. On the 870-mile train trip, a sportswriter asked Ruth about his ailing left leg. "Can't tell it ever hurt," he answered.[24] The Yankees arrived home to a cold, wet New York City. In spite of bad weather, thirty-five thousand fans pressed through the Ebbet's Field turnstiles to witness the two games. A three-run home run by Ruth was the highlight of a 6–5 Yankees win in the first game. His three singles topped all performers in a 4–3 Yankees win the next afternoon.

As fans left the park, anticipation had replaced scandal. With Opening Day less than twenty-four hours away, the nation's sports pages were filled with predictions and prognostication. Players and sportswriters alike believed the Yankees would fight Philadelphia for the American League crown. Many made the Athletics their favorite. Pittsburgh and Cincinnati were forecast

to duel for the National League pennant. In the five weeks since Ruth's celebrated contract signing, trades, the exhibition games, and Ruth's home runs
had brought to baseball "a million dollars' worth of advertising that was far
less adverse and far more wholesome."[25]

Brushed aside was the winter's scandal. Colonel Jacob Ruppert was confident it would remain that way, largely because of one player—Babe Ruth.
"Watch that boy," Ruppert said. "He may set another home run record this
season."[26]

15

Dawn of a New Day

High above the New Orleans ballpark, the drone of an aircraft engine interrupted eager cheers for the ongoing duel between hitter and pitcher. Fans looked skyward to an airplane circling overhead. Its continuous pattern left one to wonder if the occupants were enjoying their own unique view of this spring-training exhibition game between the Brooklyn Dodgers and Cleveland Indians.[1]

Actually, the plane's two occupants were doing just that. The men had taken off from Kelly Field in San Antonio, Texas, that morning at eleven. Now, four hours later, the pilot circled at the direction of his passenger. What the aviators witnessed was a disconcerting sight below. Despite promotion and even the arrangement of special trains to ferry baseball fans from across the state line in Mississippi, there were only 3,500 spectators in New Orleans' ten thousand-seat ballpark to take in this meeting of big-league ball clubs only eight days before the start of the 1927 season. The smallish crowd was of particular concern to the man seated behind the pilot, a slender man clad from neck to ankles in an aviator jumpsuit, his head covered in a leather aviator cap with goggles protecting his eyes. The passenger, who peered at the game from the skies above, a cigar clenched between his teeth, was the commissioner of baseball, Kenesaw Mountain Landis.

When Landis arrived at the ballpark, sportswriters queried him about his unique mode of travel. The commissioner did not share the opinion of the general public that in 1927 flying was a dangerous, if not risky, proposition. He embraced aviation. It held an important place in the Landis family. The commissioner's son, Reed, returned from World War I a hero with an aerial-combat record worthy of the Distinguished Service Cross and the Silver Star and earned recognition as an ace. Judge Landis saw flying as a practical means for moving about the country quickly. "Everybody will be doing it in a little while," he said.[2]

What the senior Landis was most concerned about in the week leading up to the 1927 season opener was the clash of public opinion. He sought to gauge the pulse of the fans and learn just how much damage the winter of turmoil had caused. Many carried the same question raised by *The Standard Union* in Brooklyn, "Will public attendance be affected adversely by the scandals and near scandals of last winter?"[3]

Opening Day came with its customary exuberant fanfare. The return of baseball almost always had that effect. It was not just a day but an occasion, a spectacle to celebrate an end to winter and a return of the national pastime from its six-month hibernation. Headlines around the country predicted a quarter of a million fans would spin turnstiles in the seven ballparks that were hosts to openers. At none was the lure greater than Yankee Stadium.

On a sunny Tuesday afternoon, the largest Opening-Day crowd in the history of the game poured into the ballpark in the Bronx. The Yankees' business manager put the attendance tally at 72,000 and gushed that another 25,000 were turned away. The draw was not just the hometown Yankees—nor Babe Ruth—but also the opposition. The Philadelphia Athletics were the most talked-about team during the off-season, having added Ty Cobb, Eddie Collins, and Zack Wheat to a team that had finished third, just six games behind the Yankees in 1926. During spring training, one hundred players on American League clubs were asked to pick the eventual pennant winner. Most chose Cobb's Athletics ahead of Ruth's Yankees.[4]

On the turf before the game, music played by the Seventh Regiment band added to the boisterousness. Players paraded to the flagpole in center field, where the 1926 American League pennant was hoisted ceremoniously. Flowers were presented to Miller Huggins. At 3:30 p.m., the mayor of New York, Jimmy Walker, rose from his seat. Ever dapper in a blue suit and blue shirt, Walker raised his right arm and flung the ceremonial first pitch of the 1927 season to the Yankees' starting pitcher, Waite Hoyt.[5] The pomp, the circumstance, all of it cried out to one and all that everything was all right with baseball once again. Even Ruth, in his ghostwritten column the next day, pointed to the Yankee Stadium turnout as a sign the game was in good health. "Anyone who saw those fans packing every corner of the stadium and will still say that the scandal is hurting baseball is crazy."[6]

But twenty-four hours later, it was exactly the question that was raised. Minus the festiveness of Opening Day, the attendance at big-league ballparks crashed back to earth. A day after big-league baseball's seven Opening-Day games drew 232,000 fans, only 19,000 came out to ballparks in American and National League cities.[7]

In Chicago, where over 44,000 fans including the commissioner made up the largest crowd ever to see a game at Wrigley Field, only 7,500 turned up the next afternoon. In Washington, DC, where Tris Speaker's return to prominence from winter vilification was sealed with his selection to receive the ceremonial first pitch from the president Calvin Coolidge, an Opening-Day crowd count of 30,000 plummeted to 4,000 one day later. Around big-league ballparks, the drop represented a stunning 87 percent single-day decline in attendance. It was a drop labeled "unprecedented" by Frank Getty of *United News*.[8] And it was not a one-day aberration.

If the play of star players was expected to reverse the trend and pull fans through the ballpark gates, the theory was wide of the mark. The heralded new-look Philadelphia Athletics were exposed straight from the start as old and slow and whose new stars were over the hill. The team predicted to romp to the American League pennant was swept by the Yankees in the opening series. By late-April, Eddie Collins was hitting just .229, and his defensive play was uncharacteristically shoddy. Ty Cobb appeared to have lost a step. He missed balls in the outfield he'd previously hauled in. Whatever enthusiasm the Washington Senators brought to their fans by signing Tris Speaker was lost before Opening Day. Their star, Walter Johnson, the American League's best pitcher, began the season in bed with a broken ankle, suffered when he was hit by a line drive in an exhibition game.

Poor weather in a few cities kept the crowds down. But an even bigger and potentially longer-lasting damper was thrown by the poor expectations of still other ball clubs. The Boston Red Sox would clearly not be competitive during the 1927 season and would suffer for it at the gate. Dan Howley, the new St. Louis Browns' manager, said the 1927 season would be the first of a three-year building plan, news that would keep fans away throughout much of the summer.

And then there was Babe Ruth. The gallons of ink used to write newspaper stories about his off-season training raised home-run expectations and lured fans to Yankee Stadium in greater numbers than before. But the sellout crowd was not the only first seen on Opening Day in Yankee Stadium. In the sixth inning, Ruth began his walk to home plate to hit when Miller Huggins called him back and replaced his star slugger with a pinch-hitter. Fans were stunned, and sportswriters combed their memory to recall whether it had ever happened before. It had not.

Amid the festiveness of Opening Day, Babe Ruth was the definition of futility. Twice he was set down by strikeouts. The first came in the bottom of the first inning. Just as he was about to step into the batter's box, Ruth became distracted. The mayor vaulted the railing and ran to the slugger to present him with a three-foot silver cup. Once the mayor finished waving to the crowd and left the field, Ruth proceeded to strike out. He popped out to Collins at second base in the fourth inning, then struck out again in the fifth.

Ruth was sharply criticized in print for his Opening-Day failings. The word "flop" was bandied about in many newspapers around the country. Wire-service reporter Henry L. Farrell suggested the Babe had "consumed too many hot dogs during the opening frame and had to retire with a stomachache."[9] It was a charge that made Miller Huggins bristle. The Yankees' manager said his slugger simply had a cold.

In the Yankees' fourth game, Ruth quelled the critics. With his first time at bat, he launched a long home run over the right-field screen, his first of the season. One-half inning later, he was even more impressive. The Athletics had threatened to tie the score. Al Simmons reached base with a single, then was sacrificed to second. Jim Poole sent a base hit to right field, and Simmons was waved around third base to try to score. Ruth charged the ball. He fielded it cleanly, then threw a strike to the Yankees' catcher Pat Collins, who tagged an astonished Simmons out.[10]

In every grandstand or bleacher were the ignorant—those who insisted if Ruth weren't able to hit home runs, he would be in the minor leagues. His throw that cut down Al Simmons confirmed what many managers knew and umpire Billy Evans articulated: "I have always maintained that Babe Ruth aside from his batting, ranks as one of the greatest outfielders the game has ever produced."[11]

While the Yankees won their first six games and eight of their first eleven, Ruth struggled. Over a five-game stretch of games against Boston and Philadelphia, he managed just two hits in sixteen trips to the plate. A particularly embarrassing moment happened against Boston, when Ruth took a mighty swing, stumbled, and fell to the ground, serenaded by laughter.[12] He struck out more than usual, and reporters thought they had an answer—Hollywood. "Perhaps the glare of the winter work has temporarily hurt Ruth's vision," theorized a story distributed by William Randolph Hearst's *International News Service*.[13] More stories with the same claim appeared soon after. Ruth wasn't making contact, they said, because his eyes were damaged by the bright Klieg lights used on the movie set. Christy Walsh brushed aside the notion. "The Babe is just full of a spring cold," he said.[14]

Others in the press speculated Ruth's swing was amiss. It would not have been the first time in his career this had happened. When it did, Ruth had a unique method for correcting bad swing mechanics. He got in a round of golf. Ruth was one of a number of Yankees players who were avid golfers, including their manager, Miller Huggins. Ruth generally shot in the low 90s, but on a good day could shoot 10 strokes lower.[15] Huggins forbid his players to play during the season. He, like many, felt it could damage a batting swing. But in June of 1925,

Ruth experienced just the opposite. Struggling at the plate, Ruth retreated to a golf course for eighteen holes. There he realized why he was topping the baseball and hitting ground balls rather than getting balls in the air. He corrected his batting swing and, over the next eleven days, hit six home runs.

Spring cold aside, there were tactical challenges that stymied Ruth. Given the damage he could do with one swing of the bat, pitchers kept the ball away from him, and opposing managers did not hesitate to order Ruth walked intentionally. Babe Ruth was walked more than any other player in the game. In the 152 games he played during the 1926 season, Ruth drew 144 walks, 28 more than any other player. Particularly egregious was the 1926 World Series. Ruth was walked 11 times. In Game Four he hit 3 home runs, then was walked twice. In the deciding seventh game, Ruth homered to give the Yankees the lead in the bottom of the third inning. In the fifth inning, he walked. Two innings later, with the Yankees trailing and the tying run at second base, Rogers Hornsby ordered Ruth walked intentionally. Then, with two outs in the bottom of the ninth inning, Ruth walked again, though Grover Cleveland Alexander insisted he was just being careful and did not walk Ruth intentionally.

The tactic incensed Ruth. "This intentional pass is getting on my nerves," he said. "It ain't giving the fans a run for their money."[16] It was hardly a new phenomenon; rather, it was one that began almost as soon as he joined the Yankees and began banging out home runs. With the exception of his injury and suspension-plagued season in 1925, Ruth led the American League in walks every year dating back to 1920. His peak came in 1923, when he walked 170 times in 152 games. Few managers ordered Ruth walked intentionally more than Connie Mack of the Athletics. During his time as manager of Cleveland, Tris Speaker had also used the walk as a tool to prevent damage from Ruth. In the wake of the World Series walks, sportswriters and a few club owners offered ideas for rule changes to curb the practice. It was suggested the intentional walk be treated akin to a balk, with base runners allowed to move up one extra base. Another notion called for a batter to receive two bases for a second intentional walk in a game and three for a third. "The passing of Babe Ruth in the World Series has created a feeling among the public that is not good for the game," noted George Daley in the *Commercial Appeal*.[17] Intentional walks, many felt, deprived fans of what they came to the ballpark to see: Babe Ruth hitting home runs. Regardless of its adverse effect, the effort to curtail intentional walks failed to gain traction.

Then there were shifts. More often than not, the left-handed-hitting Ruth would send his hits toward right field. Depending upon the game score and situation, managers would move their fielders around to try to thwart the Yankees' slugger. "Stuffy" McInnis, the Boston Red Sox first baseman, was the first to suggest it. During the 1921 season, McInnis convinced his manager, Hugh Duffy, to position all four infielders beyond the infield dirt and on the outfield grass. The shortstop played directly behind the second-base bag, with the second and first basemen in shallow right field. It became the pitcher's responsibility to cover first base. Twice in the first game when the shift was employed, Ruth hit balls directly to infielders who had been shifted out of their normal position.[18] Other clubs caught on. Some employed a similar tactic, while others were even more drastic and put three infielders on the right side of second base. One club went so far as to put their first baseman in shallow right field. To those who complained, Cardinal's pitcher Grover Cleveland Alexander responded, "Shifting defense is an important part of the game."[19] Ruth became adept at stymying the shift. When Red Sox players were set up to prevent a smash to right field, Ruth hit a drive over the bleachers in left field. In a game against the Senators, a Ruth home run into the center-field bleachers left shifted defenders frustrated. As one writer also noted, Ruth "is excellent at shortening his swing for singles in a pinch."[20]

It was two weeks into the 1927 season when Ruth's fortunes changed. After being held hitless in three of his previous four games, Ruth broke out and went on a tear. He had 3 hits, including a double and a home run in Boston. The next afternoon he had 2 more hits. After leaving Boston for a weekend game with Philadelphia, Ruth thrilled sixty thousand fans by slugging 2 home runs in a 7–2 win over the Athletics. When Ruth had hits in his next three games, his batting average rose 95 points to .328.

An early May road trip that took the Yankees to Chicago, St. Louis, Cleveland, and Washington, DC, saw Ruth hit at a frenetic pace. It helped the Yankees reel off seven consecutive wins. He hit homers in back-to-back games in St. Louis. In Cleveland the ball club's new manager resumed the tactic employed by his predecessor, Tris Speaker. He walked Ruth twice in a tight 4–3 ball game, then two more times the next afternoon in a game that finished 2–1. In the last game of the series in Cleveland, Ruth launched a two-run, sixth-inning home run that helped the Yankees to a 7–2 win. It sparked a torrid power-hitting streak that saw Ruth hit home runs during each of the six days the Yankees played.

On the last day of May, Ruth put an exclamation mark on his sizzling streak. In Philadelphia against the Athletics, he homered in both games of a doubleheader. The second shot out of Shibe Park was as if blown from a cannon. The ball sailed across Twentieth Street and landed on the roof of an apartment building.[21]

Ruth concluded the second month of the season with 16 home runs. It was tops in the American League and almost twice as many as the National League leader, Cy Williams, who had 9. Ruth's tally was achieved in forty-two games. Sportswriters noted that during his record season 1921, when he hit 59, Ruth's 16th came in the Yankees' forty-third game. It was an observation that would initiate preliminary talk of a run at a new record.

Also impressive was the climb of Ruth's batting average. From a paltry .233 in the second week of the season, Ruth was now batting a robust .344. It all went toward helping the Yankees win. Ever since the first game of the season, the ball club held a firm grip on first place in the American League. Heading into the summer months, they showed no signs of faltering. To some club owners, that was a distressing sign. Nothing pumped up attendance like a healthy pennant race. A race was about to break out. It would be one that would impact attendance around the American League and do it in a big way. But this race would have nothing to do with teams and their win-loss records.

16

Move Over, Babe

New York was a city awash in adoration. Confetti and ticker tape rained from high-rise office buildings in a blizzard-like fashion. The shrill sound of whistles and horns filled the air. They were sent out from factories around Manhattan—police sirens and cars on what city streets were passable, the pleasure boats that bobbed on the East and the Hudson Rivers, and the tugs and large commercial ships navigating Upper New York Bay. Each one was an expression of triumph. A mid-June sun basted the two million people who lined a twenty-mile parade route to cheer, shout, wave signs, and pay homage to America's new hero.

This was more than just a celebration. It was a release, an outpouring of adulation far greater than what America's largest city had ever seen before. It was the kind of release reserved for a conqueror, one who had defied long odds to achieve the previously unthinkable and had done so with heroic proportion. That is exactly what Charles Lindbergh had done.

Three weeks earlier, Charles Augustus Lindbergh astounded not only a nation but the world. Motivated by a $25,000 prize from hotel magnate Raymond Ortieg, Lindbergh took off from Roosevelt Field on Long Island on a clear early morning, May 20, 1927, in an attempt to make the first solo transatlantic flight and become the first man to fly from New York to Paris. From tiny hamlets to large metropolises, Americans were riveted to radio updates of Lindbergh's journey. Previous attempts claimed the lives of six aviators. The 3,600-mile journey was almost 2,000 miles farther than anyone had ever flown before.

It was 10:22 p.m., thirty-three hours after he lifted his Ryan monoplane from the Roosevelt Field runway, that Lindbergh's *Spirit of St. Louis* touched down amid great jubilation at Le Bourget Aerodrome outside of Paris. The government escorted Lindbergh home on a navy ship. After a ceremony at the White House, he arrived to great fanfare in New York City, where for four days he was feted with a parade, gave speeches, was toasted at banquets, and received medals from the mayor and governor alike.

On the final day of Lindbergh's stay in New York, the white hands illuminated against the large black clock atop the Yankee Stadium scoreboard showed it was 5:15 p.m. Only moments earlier, Waite Hoyte induced Ken Williams to hit a ground ball to Ray Morehart, playing second base for the Yankees. Morehart's throw to Lou Gehrig secured the final out to seal the home team's 8–1 win over the visiting St. Louis Browns. It was when fans began to gather their things to leave that the sirens were first heard. The sounds grew louder until, finally, the originator—six New York City Police Department motorcycles—made their way down the ramp beyond center field. They escorted a luxury car onto the cinder path that encircled the field. "It's Lindy!" cried a fan. In an instant, those who remained from the twelve thousand that attended the game began a stampede to the field to see their hero.

Lindbergh, a tall, slender, and shy twenty-five-year-old, stood from the back seat. He waved to those still left in the crowd. Lindbergh and his entourage arrived late. Their stop was brief. The motorcade left Yankee Stadium for the Brovoort Hotel. Two minutes after he had arrived at the ballpark, Lindbergh was on his way to meet Raymond Ortieg at a ceremony to receive his $25,000 prize.

In the press area, sportswriters pecked away at their typewriters, chronicling the game that had taken place that afternoon. Their accounts would tell of a furious first inning, of how Earl Combs opened the frame with a single, and how, two batters later, Babe Ruth sent a pitch hurtling deep into the right-field bleachers, giving the Yankees a 2–0 lead. Almost before the fans could cease cheering, the very next batter, Lou Gehrig, sent a ball to almost the exact same spot where Ruth's home run had landed. Ruth's home run was his 22nd of the season, the most in all of baseball. Gehrig's was his 15th, not only second to Ruth in the American League but in the big leagues as well.

As the Yankees players changed from their uniforms after the game, the activity foretold a change. America undeniably had a new hero. Charles Lindbergh was now the country's favorite son. In the days that followed, aviators would become a popular page-one subject for newspapers around the country. But none would grip the attention of the country during the summer months of 1927 like flight of a different kind—the flight of baseballs launched by two men who would begin a duel the likes of which baseball had never seen before. The men were Babe Ruth and a new home-run-hitting challenger, his New York Yankees teammate, Lou Gehrig.

In the days that followed Charles Lindbergh's visit to New York City, a home-run hitting rivalry erupted that would quickly reach epic proportions. Over a ten-game span, Lou Gehrig belted 9 home runs. He hit a pair in the series finale against the Browns. Then in the series finale in Boston, Gehrig hit 3 home runs, the most ever hit in one game at Fenway Park.

Gehrig's three-homer game capped a nine-game win streak by the Yankees that extended their lead over the rest of the American League to ten games. After a couple of hiccups to Philadelphia, they would reel off another nine wins, this time over a ten-game span against Philadelphia, Boston, and Washington, which put them twelve and a half games ahead of their closest pursuer.

During the Boston series, Ruth hit home runs in back-to-back games, giving him 24 for the season. But he was playing injured. In the second game of the St. Louis series, he strained a knee and was removed after just one inning of play. Throughout the games in Boston and when the Yankees returned home to play Philadelphia, Ruth moved with a noticeable limp. It became an injury Miller Huggins could not ignore, and in the second game of the series with the Athletics, he kept Ruth on the bench for the first time all season. It was where Ruth would remain for the next two games.

In Ruth's absence, Gehrig played like a man motivated to fill a void left by his injured teammate. He homered in four consecutive games and five times in seven games. Two home runs in the Philadelphia series gave him 23 for the season. On June 29, in the first game of the series with the Red Sox, Ruth returned to the lineup. He had 4 hits, which lifted his batting average to .354. In the fifth inning of that game, however, Gehrig snatched the limelight. The Yankees' first baseman launched a ball that landed deep in the right-field bleachers. The blast was his 24th of the season, which equaled Ruth's total for the most in either league.

The next afternoon, Gehrig followed a first-inning walk to Ruth by hitting still another home run, one that surpassed Ruth's season tally. Gehrig's lead in the home-run race would be brief. In the bottom of the fourth inning, Ruth walloped one of his own, a blast that landed near the base of the scoreboard behind the bleachers in right center field. At the end of the day, both men were tied with 25 home runs apiece, and a nation was transfixed.

Barely two weeks after his triumphant return to America, Charles Lindbergh vanished from the headlines. He was replaced by Babe Ruth and Lou Gehrig. Large type that blared "GEHRIG TIES RUTH IN HOMERS"[1] or "RUTH FORGES AHEAD OF GEHRIG IN RACE FOR HOME RUN HONORS"[2] became commonplace as the nation shifted its attention to an enthralling home-run-hitting duel. That Babe Ruth suddenly had a challenger was stunning to many. Not since his surgery and suspension-plagued 1925 season had Ruth been challenged for home-run hitting superiority. Questions of whether Ruth could eclipse his record of 59 in a season were replaced by the question of whether Ruth could top the upstart Lou Gehrig.

Like a batting game of leapfrog, the two men swapped home-run hitting supremacy. Gehrig hit 3 home runs in a doubleheader on the Fourth of July to push his total to 28—2 more than Ruth. Four days later, Ruth belted his 27th, then added 2 more the next day to surpass Gehrig with 29. It was two days later during a game in Detroit when Gehrig matched Ruth. The very next afternoon, Ruth took the home-run lead again when he clubbed his 30th in a 7–0 win over Cleveland.

In newspaper newsrooms around the country, greater attention was placed on the ticker each afternoon that the Yankees played. Shouts that "Ruth just hit one! Gehrig just hit another!" became commonplace through-out the summer.[3] Many papers added a home-run tracking feature, a box in which Ruth's and Gehrig's count appeared each day. The *New York Daily News* began the season with a daily box that tracked Ruth's home-run and batting-average figures against that of the Giants' Rogers Hornsby. But Hornsby did not prove to be the box-office attraction the Giants had hoped for, and many of the local newspapers chose to showcase the Yankees and relegate the Giants to the second or third page of the sports section. By the Fourth of July, the *Daily News* removed Hornsby from its comparative box and replaced him with the daily totals of Lou Gehrig.

Gehrig blossomed into both a fan and media favorite. Sportswriters dubbed him Buster or Columbia Lou. When an umpire introduced two young boys to Gehrig, he smiled at their pleadings that he hit a homer for each, then went out and did it.[4]

Gehrig's popularity among a section of Yankees fans had almost as much to do with geography as it did with hitting. While his teammates were from many corners of the country, Lou Gehrig was a native New Yorker. The son of German immigrants, Henry Louis Gehrig was raised first in the Yorkville section of Manhattan before the family moved to the Washington Heights area of the borough. He grew up a Giants fan. As a youth, he saved his money, and every time it reached twenty-five cents, he bought a ticket to sit in the left-field bleachers at the Polo Grounds to watch his favorite team play.

It was while at Commerce High School that Gehrig developed renown as a baseball player. His school team traveled to Chicago for a game with Lane High School in Cubs Park. In what was the highlight of the afternoon, Gehrig hit a home run out of the Chicago Cubs ballpark.

Lou Gehrig was unique among big-league ballplayers—a college man. Gehrig was not just a college man but an Ivy Leaguer. He enrolled at Colum-bia University on a football scholarship and shone as the team's fullback in

1921. In the spring of 1923, Gehrig blossomed into the premier player in college baseball. In a feature story in the *New York Daily News*, Hugh Fullerton praised Gehrig as "a worthy successor to George Sisler. If he can hit major pitching, he may be another 'Babe' Ruth."[5]

Paul Kritchell, one of the Yankees' top scouts, took in Columbia's game with Rutgers and afterward informed his bosses that Gehrig was a player they had to have. On June 11, 1923, Kritchell persuaded Gehrig to leave Columbia after his sophomore year and sign a contract with the Yankees. Four days later, Gehrig made his big-league debut when he replaced Wally Pipp at first base in the ninth inning of the team's 10–0 route over the St. Louis Browns.

In 1925, fate would change Gehrig's role with the Yankees. It happened on July 2. Prior to that afternoon's game, the Yankees were giving a tryout to a young pitcher. They had the teen pitch batting practice. When Wally Pipp stepped into the batter's box, he did so with a purpose. Pipp had been the Yankees' first baseman for ten seasons. Now, however, he was struggling to keep that job. His batting average had fallen to the lowest of his career. Huggins was alternating Pipp with a player ten years his junior in Gehrig. Only the previous afternoon, Gehrig had three hits against the Boston Red Sox. As Pipp took his turn in the batting-practice round, the ball got away from the young pitcher. It struck Pipp above the right ear. He was knocked unconscious. Teammates carried him to the locker room. When Pipp came to, he felt nauseous and was taken to St. Vincent's Hospital for X-rays. Wally Pipp would never start another game for the New York Yankees. First base became Lou Gehrig's position. In the off-season, Pipp was sold to the Cincinnati Reds.

When Gehrig joined the Yankees, he'd followed a "Wee" Willie Keeler hitting approach. Gehrig had read that the former Yankee would adjust his swing to hit the ball inches from where an infielder was positioned. Gehrig witnessed firsthand Ty Cobb do the same. It was Babe Ruth who counseled him to change. "You're big enough to whang that ball a mile. But you'll never do it if you keep trying to poke them to different fields," Ruth said.[6] He urged Gehrig to pull the ball more. The result was impressive. In his first full season with the Yankees (1926), Gehrig hit .313 with 16 home runs and 109 runs batted in.

While shoulder to shoulder as home-run hitting marvels, Babe Ruth and Lou Gehrig couldn't have been more different. Where Ruth was gregarious, Gehrig was quiet, polite, and gentlemanly. He called his home runs "a lot of luck."[7] Ruth reveled in the limelight. Gehrig, on the other hand, liked to escape to the solitude of Lake Oscawanna to fish, or he would hide in a corner of the Yankee locker room to play pinochle with the team's trainer, Doc Woods. While Ruth was a renowned carouser, Gehrig continued to live at home with his mother and father. As different as the men were, they were good for each other. "There is nothing the big fellow likes more than competition," said Ruth's fitness trainer, Artie McGovern. "Gehrig is giving him plenty."[8]

On August 9, twenty thousand fans flocked to Shibe Park in Philadelphia to witness the home-run duel for themselves. Yankees pitchers struggled throughout the afternoon. Ty Cobb had a 3-hit game, and in the bottom of the eighth inning, he singled to extend the Athletics' lead over New York to 8–0. The Yankees were on the verge of being shutout for the first time all season. Lou Gehrig led off the top of the ninth inning and promptly sent a ball deep into the right-field stands for his 38th home run of the season. The blast helped avert a shutout and put Gehrig ahead of Ruth by 3.

For those who expected there to be jealousy between Ruth and Gehrig, they were sorely mistaken. Babe Ruth was Gehrig's biggest cheerleader. "That boy sure can sock 'em," Ruth said. "And more power to him. It helps the Yankees, and it helps me to have a tough hitter coming up right after me."[9]

While Ruth and Gehrig grabbed the headlines in 1927, the Yankee batting order produced with devastating effect. Seventeen times through the first three months of the season, the team put a double-digit score on the scoreboard. Not only was Gehrig flirting with a .400 batting average, but Ruth was close behind in the chase for the batting title. Not far back were Bob Meusel, the Yankees' left fielder who held a .364 batting average; Earle Combs, the center fielder who was hitting .343; and Tony Lazzeri, the second-year second baseman who blossomed into a power-hitting threat while batting .319. So powerful was this Yankee lineup that their nickname around baseball became Murderer's Row.

Fueled by this powerful lineup, the 1927 New York Yankees were a juggernaut. By August 10, they had already won 77 of their 110 games. Their closest pursuer was 12 games back. Though the team had not mathematically clinched the pennant, most felt, as did the syndicated columnist Grantland Rice, that "the battle for the pennant ended about June 10. From that point on main interest has been banked around the Ruth-Gehrig duel."[10] Gehrig and Ruth dispelled the common notion that one needed a fierce pennant race to pull spectators through the turnstiles in summer. The Yankees' July road trip through the Midwest brought large crowds. Seventy-nine thousand came during the four days Gehrig and Ruth visited Detroit. Two of the crowds were near sellouts. Even more—eighty-four thousand—saw the four games the Yankees played in St. Louis. Bigger crowds yet cheered Gehrig and Ruth in Chicago. When ticket sales were tallied after the three-game series, they were just shy of one hundred thousand.

Lou Gehrig's 3-home-run lead over Babe Ruth on August 9 did not last a week. Ruth hit home runs in three games against the Chicago White Sox to pull back into a tie with 38. It was then that the two men began a furious two-week game of home-run hitting leapfrog. On August 19, in Chicago, Gehrig smashed a home run to regain the lead with 39. The very next afternoon in Cleveland, Ruth homered in the first inning to once again equal his teammate. Two days later, in the final game of the series in Cleveland, Ruth hit his 40th. Gehrig hit his in the second game of the ensuing series in Detroit.

Once in St. Louis, the men took the field arm in arm to a standing ovation.[11] Ruth homered in back-to-back games against the Browns to push his season home-run count to 42. Gehrig hit his 41st in the last game of the series.

Over the summer months of July and August, Gehrig and Ruth hit 25 home runs apiece. Four times during that two-month span, Lou Gehrig led baseball in home runs. Twice, Babe Ruth topped the stat sheet. The men spent eleven days tied for the most home runs in both the American and National League. For those ready to crown both an American League and a home-run champion, there was still a great deal of baseball yet to be played.

17

Reviews Are In

The timing couldn't have been better. It was the July Fourth holiday. New York City was alive with activity. People were out by the millions. Traffic jams were monumental. So too was the throng at Coney Island. At Yankee Stadium, a record crowd saw the hometown team stretch its win streak to ten games. Bigger yet, they saw their hero Babe Ruth hit a home run. Interest in the home-run hitting of Ruth and Gehrig was at a bursting point of excitement around the country, which is why the timing employed by the executives at First National Pictures was brilliant. The July Fourth weekend proved an opportune time to release *Babe Comes Home* in New York City.

All, however, had not been rosy for the film project since Ruth left Los Angeles at the end of February. For all the praise she showered on Babe Ruth's work, Anna Q. Nilsson remained an angry woman. She loathed having been made to work with Ruth. Her ire was not about the ballplayer personally but at being forced to costar with an acting novice. Her insistence that it never happen again was met with resistance from studio management. By early May, the two sides negotiated a settlement, and Anna Q. Nilsson left First National Pictures, never to do another film for them again.

Ten days after Nilsson resigned, an even bigger departure shook the studio. This one spread turmoil about First National Pictures. The company had taken on a new investor, an East Coast bank. In exchange for the funding, certain conditions were forced upon First National Pictures. New operational protocols, a different management structure, and new people were put in place. At the company's annual convention in late May, John McCormick, First National Pictures' general manager and the head of West Coast production, erupted indignantly to the changes. McCormick charged the new investor was interfering with his work and abruptly resigned. The move left company management stunned.

Publicly, the outburst was chalked up to McCormick's "Irish temper," and studio executives said they expected him to come back. Rather than heal, things got worse. McCormick was married to Colleen Moore, who, at the time, was the top box-office star in the motion picture industry.[1] Moore had a four-picture deal with First National Pictures that paid her $125,000 a film. Her arrangement was second only to the lucrative contract Gloria Swanson received from United Artists. Reporters who covered the motion picture industry suggested Colleen Moore was worth $6 million a year to First National Pictures.[2] Two days after her husband left, Moore, too, severed her contract with First National Pictures.

Reeling from the departures, First National halted several projects and delayed others. Once studio heads realized McCormick wasn't coming back, they scrambled to replace him. They made a fast hire, but it couldn't get films in editing or final production back on track. Phone calls from Christy Walsh during the first week of June were made to notify reporters in New York City that release of Ruth's film would be delayed. He explained that it was due to problems with the company and not anything to do with Ruth's acting performance.

Defections weren't the only problem to impact *Babe Comes Home*. First National Pictures chose to use the film to introduce a revolutionary new sound system, Vocafilm. Warner Brothers had introduced a rival system, Vitaphone. It was a sound-on-disc system created by an engineer for the Western Electric Company. Warner Brothers released its first film using Vitaphone sound in 1925, and *Don Juan* was a hit at the box office. It was a year and a half later when it reintroduced Vitaphone recording technology on the film *The Jazz Singer*. With Al Jolson starring in the film, *The Jazz Singer* shattered box-office records.

First National Pictures made *Babe Comes Home* its test project for the new recording system from Vocafilm Corporation. When it tested the sixty-minute black-and-white picture before an audience in Los Angeles, the system was a disaster. The film opened with Ruth addressing the audience, a record syncing his sound with his image on film. Audio was inconsistent— faint at times and almost deafening in other spots. An embarrassing moment occurred when an orchestra was shown playing and no sound was heard at all. Critics suggested First National Pictures was rushing out the new technology and that more work had to be done and bugs ironed out. The studio was not deterred and continued with the plan.

For months, First National Pictures had a deal with Mitch and Moe Strand to show *Babe Comes Home* at their highly successful theater on Forty-

Seventh Street and Broadway in New York's Times Square. The deal with the Strand brothers and their partner, Mitchell Mark, also involved their company's entire chain of cinemas. But as the release of *Babe Comes Home* drew near, the Strands backed out. Their commitment had been based upon Anna Q. Nilsson being in the lead role. With Nilsson relegated to a supporting role and a novice Babe Ruth billed in the lead, the Strand brothers were not confident the film would do well and declined to show it.[3]

That left First National Pictures to use New York neighborhood cinemas. An eight-week run at the Longacre on Forty-Eighth Street west of Broadway was arranged. The film was to play twice daily. In Brooklyn, the Oasis agreed to run it. In time *Babe Comes Home* would play at Keeney's on Livingston Street and Hanover Place, as well as at the Savoy.

Large, full-page articles promoted the film. "The Bambino can act, and don't forget it!" screamed the first line.[4] At the direction of Walsh, Ruth hosted several dozen New York writers at a dinner and private screening. But when the film premiered to the public, its initial results were disastrous.

The biggest problem wasn't so much the film or Ruth's acting. It was Vocafilm. In many cities, New York especially, Vocafilm was made a heavily promoted feature of the film. The revolutionary sound technology was advertised in far greater form than even Ruth himself. Newspaper ads screamed, "World Premier!" in type much larger and far bolder than either Ruth's name or the title of the picture.[5] But those who were lured by the promise of something unique and groundbreaking were sorely disappointed.

Far from enticing ticket buyers, Vocafilm had just the opposite effect. It drove customers away. Since the unsuccessful premier, the system had not improved. The *New York Daily News* film critic devoted two-thirds of her review of *Babe Comes Home* to the failings of the sound system. She described a ten-minute series of mini-films designed to showcase Vocafilm that ran prior to *Babe Comes Home*. They included talks and musical interludes. The sound was inconsistent, uncomfortably high in parts while inaudibly low in others. Many in the audience got up and left even before *Babe Comes Home* began.

First National Pictures tried to counter the bad press. In late July the studio took out full-page ads in the industry trade magazine *Variety* to promote the film. It was the only film to use such bold advertising. The studio featured artwork of Babe Ruth swinging the bat. It trumpeted the film as Ruth's starring debut on the big screen. Noticeably absent from the ad was any mention of Vocafilm. But the very next day, in an embarrassing turn, the Longacre in New York City ceased showing the film. Management said it was a temporary pause. It was three weeks before the film resumed at the Longacre. When it did, it featured far less promotion of Vocafilm.

That would not be the only embarrassment for *Babe Comes Home*. *Variety* revealed the film was a box-office flop in Los Angeles. "One of the surprises was the meager interest in Babe Ruth's first starring feature, *Babe Comes Home* at the Uptown for a gross of slightly over $3,000."[6] Critics in Los Angeles did not give it favorable reviews. One chastised it as "frequently vulgar."[7] The *Los Angeles Times* said *Babe Comes Home* "falls lamentably short." It went on to say, "The adaptation is from a story by Gerald Beaumont, late sportswriter, but as it reaches the screen it is little more than a series of loosely connected incidents."[8]

While many critics did not particularly like the movie, their reviews for Babe Ruth, on the other hand, were largely favorable. One from Pensacola, Florida, echoed others in newspapers around the country. "In this picture playing not only a baseball star in diamond and dressing room sequences, but a lover in the novel story, he had a difficult role which he enacted like an experienced film player."[9]

A reporter in Ventura, California, wrote, "Babe Ruth acts as earnestly and skillfully before the camera in *Babe Comes Home*, the current attraction at the Apollo Theatre as he plays baseball."[10]

Across the river from New York, in Paterson, New Jersey, a writer praised, "Ruth has found a new career by virtue of his splendid histrionic performances in the stellar role."[11] Similarly, a newspaper in Wilmington, Delaware, lauded Ruth. "He has proved himself a splendid actor, a whimsical and appealing screen personality."[12]

As summer became fall, additional efforts were made to try to attract paying customers. In some cities, tickets for children were discounted. In others, drawings were held for baseballs signed by Ruth himself.

In the fall First National Pictures' distribution arm brought *Babe Comes Home* to smaller cities around America. The film concluded its run eleven months after its initial release in April in Honolulu, Hawaii. It failed to achieve the goals set forth by First National Pictures. While Ruth would perform a humorous cameo in *Speedy*, which starred his good friend Harold Lloyd, never again would baseball's iconic slugger headline a motion picture.

18

Rewrite the Record Book

It was a single sound that set off the surge, a surge that soon swelled to frightening proportions. The slamming shut of the box-office windows thirty minutes before the game was to start triggered a wave of angry fans. Already, close to thirty-five thousand ticket buyers were squeezed into Boston's Fenway Park. Few were there to see the home team. The Boston Red Sox were in dead last in the American League, fifty games behind the first place Yankees. No, this mob had come, as had fans in Detroit, Chicago, St. Louis, and Philadelphia, to see firsthand the amazing home-run duel taking place between Babe Ruth and Lou Gehrig.

The crowd that purchased tickets was the largest Fenway Park crowd since a game in 1915. They were about to be joined, however, by an unruly mob, angered at being shut out and determined not to be. Soon came word that a horde numbering in the hundreds had broken down the gate on Ipswich Street to force their way in. Shortly after, two more gates were forced open, and hundreds more poured into the ballpark.

Several hundred streamed in beneath the center-field stands and made their way onto the playing field.[1] Even more came onto the field near the left-field corner, while another group massed in front of the Yankees' dugout, anxious to shake hands with Lou Gehrig and Babe Ruth. Blocked by the mob, the Yankees' players were unable to take the field. Such was the level of fervor that the police lost control. Reinforcements were summoned and soon arrived on the field on horseback. They pushed the invaders against the outfield wall and along the wall from the end of both dugouts to each foul pole.[2]

It was forty-five minutes after the scheduled start time before a level of control was gained that allowed play to begin. Local sportswriters estimated fifty thousand fans were crammed into the park. It was like nothing they had ever seen before. Still more, those who didn't want to use force to get in were now atop neighboring houses to watch from rooftops. In the third inning, Gehrig gave the crowd what they wanted to see, his 44th home run. He and Ruth were tied for the most in the majors. By the time the game ended, eighteen innings were played. The Yankees lost, 12–11, and it was only the first game of a doubleheader.

The next day fans were treated to an even more astounding feat. Fireworks began in the fifth inning. Gehrig hit a ball into the center-field bleachers—his 45th home run—to take the league lead. It was a lead he would only hold for one inning, however. That's when Ruth hit what onlookers raved was the longest home run ever hit out of Fenway Park. "The ball was still climbing when it went high over the highest part of the high fence in center field just to the left of the flagpole," described James C. O'Leary in the *Boston Globe*.[3] Some wondered if it was the longest Ruth had ever hit. *Boston Globe* sportswriter Melvin Webb reminded his readers that Ruth's longest-measured home run was hit during a spring-training game in 1920 with the New York Giants in Tampa. That ball landed 551 feet from the point where Ruth's bat smashed it. No one saw just where Ruth's Boston blast landed. James O'Leary wrote, "When it disappeared from view it was headed for the Charles River Basin."[4] The ball traveled so far, sportswriter Webb simply described the blast with one word: "Ruthian."[5]

From Memorial Day to Labor Day, fans across America were captivated by baseball's two-man duel for home-run-hitting superiority. The idea of a home-run record rarely, if ever, escaped anyone's lips. Mathematically, Ruth was so far behind the pace he set in 1921, when he slugged his record 59 home runs, that the idea of breaking that mark now, in 1927, was seldom raised. When the record was spoken of, it wasn't about Ruth but rather the burgeoning sensation, Lou Gehrig, and it was done so as a prediction that one day he would eclipse Ruth's mark.

The focus on the Gehrig-Ruth duel would undergo a dramatic shift by the time the Yankees left Boston, for in the span of seventy-two hours, Babe Ruth produced what, even for him, was the unthinkable. In the seventh inning, Ruth homered for a second time, a line drive that cleared the center-field fence for his 46th home run. Gehrig hit his 45th home run in the fifth inning, but few could know their duel was over.

After a brief respite, the teams took the field again to complete a doubleheader. By the ninth inning, the Yankees trailed Boston, 5–0. Ruth led off the final inning and deposited a pitch from Jack Russell into the bleachers in center field for his 47th home run of the season.

The very next afternoon, the two teams concluded the series. The game would mark the final time Ruth would play in Boston during the 1927 season.

A large crowd for a weekday afternoon, thirteen thousand, turned up. They gave Ruth a noisy ovation when he strode to the plate in the first inning. Their cheers grew moments later when Ruth drove Danny McFayden's pitch over the fence in left field for a home run, his 48th of the season. By the time Ruth came to bat in the eighth inning, the Yankees had fought back from an 8–1 deficit to lead the Red Sox, 10–9. Ruth put an exclamation mark on the comeback with his second home run of the game, a two-run blast.

In the span of forty-eight hours, Babe Ruth had done the unthinkable: hit 5 home runs. His season total was 49, and suddenly, talk shifted from a home-run hitters' duel to serious talk of a new home-run record. Ruth needed 10 to tie his 1921 record of 59. There were twenty-one games left in the season, which meant Ruth would have to hit a home run every other game for a chance at the mark.

As quickly as the record talk began, it stopped or was at least put on hold temporarily. Of all teams, it was quelled by the St. Louis Browns, and not because their pitchers enjoyed any kind of mastery over Ruth. Much to the ire of Yankee Stadium fans, the Browns simply refused to give Ruth anything to hit. Six times Ruth was walked during the first three games of the series. On Sunday afternoon, September 11, in the final game of the series, Ruth finally got a hold of one. He drove Milt Gaston's pitch far into the right-field stands, so far that longtime observers were convinced it was the longest ball he had ever hit in the mammoth ballpark.[6] Ruth stood on 50.

Another binge was about to break out. When Cleveland came to town, Ruth hit homers in both halves of the Tuesday-afternoon doubleheader. His second, number 52, helped the Yankees clinch the American League pennant with a 5–3 victory. Three days later, Ruth almost didn't make it to the ballpark in time for the game in which he hit his 53rd. He spent part of the morning in court, where an assault charge against him was dismissed. Later, his friend, the comedic actor Harold Lloyd (who was in town filming a movie), asked Ruth to take part in a scene. Between the filming and signing autographs, Ruth lost track of the time. With Lloyd driving in a maniacal fashion and exceeding the speed limit while weaving in and out of traffic, Ruth got to Yankee Stadium with little time to spare.

Ruth's 4-homer spree over six games fanned the flames of record talk. Newspapers began running a daily chart that compared the number of games Ruth played and the number of home runs he'd had on that date—when he'd hit 59 home runs in 1921 and now in 1927. The *Arizona Republican* called theirs the "Ruth-O-Meter."[7] The *Miami Herald*; the *Spokesman-Review* in Spokane, Washington; and the *Boston Globe* headlined their tracker with Ruth's accomplishment of the day. As of September 16, that accomplishment showed Ruth as 6 home runs shy of equaling his record of 59. The New York Yankees had twelve games left on the schedule.

Many newspapers around the country continued what had become a summer trend: to run a chart that compared the five top batters in the American League. Still atop the chart was Lou Gehrig, whose batting average was the best in baseball. But since hitting his 45th home run on September 6, Gehrig's play had become perplexing to Yankees fans. Just as Babe Ruth went on a home-run hitting binge, Lou Gehrig slipped into an unexplainable batting slump. For three weeks, his longest drought of the season, Gehrig failed to hit a home run. In five games during that span, he was held without a hit. In seven other games, he managed only a single hit. Gehrig's batting average, which led the league when it was .389 early in September, now slipped. He fell behind Al Simmons and Harry Heilmann in the race for the batting title. Gehrig's average would ultimately fall seventeen points.

None knew the reason for Gehrig's decline. Devoted to his parents, Gehrig's mother was ailing, and surgery was being discussed. September was also the most physically challenging month of the season. Ruth himself admitted that his leg strength faded toward the end of the 1926 season.[8] It was clear by his play that Ruth's work with Artie McGovern was paying dividends. Gehrig met with Christy Walsh and agreed to let the man take on management of his affairs. He also agreed to follow Ruth's example and train with Artie McGovern during the upcoming winter. But first would come a barnstorming tour along with Ruth, one Walsh predicted could be lucrative for the two Yankees stars.

Lou Gehrig's home-run-hitting dry spell would end in the final week of the season. He hit his 46th against the Philadelphia Athletics, but by then, he was well back of Ruth's total. Gehrig would hit another on the last day of the season and finish the campaign with 47.

Two days after hitting his 53rd, Babe Ruth went on another home-run tear. He thrilled fifty thousand fans when he sent a pitch from the White Sox's twenty-one-game-winner Ted Lyons into the right-field bleachers for his 54th home run. It left Ruth 5 away from equaling his record with nine games to go. In the Yankees' next game, Ruth struck again. His 55th left the pitcher in amazement. Sam Gibson was two outs from pitching a shutout. His Detroit Tigers were leading the Yankees, 6–0, when Ruth smashed a pitch to center field. The ball left the bat as a line drive. That's how Heinie Manush read it too. The Tigers' center fielder took two steps in, then suddenly changed course, turned, and ran toward the fence.[9] It was futile. The ball shot over the head of the Detroit outfielder, cleared the fence for a home run, and came to rest thirty rows in front of the Yankee Stadium scoreboard.

When Ruth hit another ninth-inning home run the following afternoon, it not only brought the Yankees from behind to beat Detroit, 8–7, but further heightened thirst for a record, putting the slugger 3 from 59 with six games to play.

Pursuit of the record was the burning subject throughout baseball. Newspapers were rife with headlines about the chase: "RUTH MUST HIT A HOMER A DAY NOW"[10] and "BAMBINO HAS THREE CHANCES."[11]

The final week of the 1927 season began with a visit from the Philadelphia Athletics. Much ballyhooed before the season, Connie Mack's team held down second place, eighteen games behind the Yankees in the standings. Injuries had long since derailed any pennant quest and Ty Cobb (whose .357 batting average was fifth best in the American League) had left the team to get an early start on hunting season.[12]

The game was just a single game, not the usual part of a four-game series. Though the game was a drama-filled, 2–1 pitchers' duel heading into the sixth inning, Mack was churning through his bullpen. Already he had used Rube Walberg, Jack Quinn, and Sam Gray. Now the Athletics' manager summoned his ace, the team's twenty-game-winner, Lefty Grove, to pitch the sixth. The strategy did not work out well.

Joe Dugan opened the inning with a single. Johnny Grabowski walked. Wilcy Moore, the Yankees' pitcher, laid down a sacrifice bunt to move Dugan and Grabowski ninety feet. With Grove struggling with his control, Earle Combs walked, which loaded the bases. That produced a pitcher's worst nightmare. Tossing aside two of the three bats he swung to limber up, Babe Ruth strode to the plate. Like a bullet, Grove's pitch rocketed off Ruth's heavy bat. On a line, the baseball screamed toward the bleachers in right field. A mighty roar accompanied its ascent. Ruth's 57th home run was a grand slam that pushed the Yankees' lead to 6–1 as they won, 7–4.

From small towns to metropolises, the headlines lent a magnetic lure. "RUTH MAY BREAK RECORD" screamed the *Evening Herald* in Pottstown, Pennsylvania.[13] "BABE RUTH IS RECORD BREAKER" read the headline in *The Richmond Item* in Richmond, Indiana.[14] A headline in the *St. Louis Post-Dispatch* pointed out that together, Babe Ruth and Lou Gehrig were responsible for 646 of the Yankees' 938 runs of the season. Accompanying stories were dotted with adjectives such as "remarkable," "amazing," and even "stupendous" to describe Ruth's feat.

A three-game series with the Washington Senators was last on the schedule. When Ruth trotted to right field for the start of the first game, he needed 2 home runs to tie his record, 3 to break it. The crowd may have been small by Yankee Stadium standards, seven thousand, but the fans were boisterous. It was the bottom of the first inning when they got their first chance to cheer their hero, and Ruth did not disappoint. He turned Hod Lisenbee's pitch into a line drive that landed in the right-field bleachers for home run number 58. One inning later, Ruth put fans on the edges of their seats when he sent a ball high into the air toward the stands in right field again. This time the ball banged off the wall inches from clearance, while Ruth raced around the bases for a triple.

The next time Ruth put his bat on the ball, it would not come up short. In the fifth inning, he came to bat with the bases loaded. On the mound, a rookie Paul Hopkins was pitching in his first big-league game. He entered the game when the inning began and promptly surrendered three singles. In a situation worse than any pitcher could imagine, every base was occupied by a base runner, and Babe Ruth was the hitter. When the sound of bat-on-ball contact filled the air, it was quickly replaced by shrieks and yells. Seven thousand pairs of eyes watched in awe as the baseball returned to earth in the right-center-field bleachers. Babe Ruth had equaled his single-season home-run record.

In the seventh inning, Ruth came to bat once more. When the right-handed Hopkins guided a pitch into the strike zone, the Yankee slugger sent it on a trajectory toward the bleacher seats. Red Barnes, another rookie playing in his first big-league game, scampered toward the right-field wall. When he reached up and caught it while up against the fence, groans were heard, and fans were left to wonder what might have been.

Equaling the record set New York abuzz. Babe Ruth had ridden an unparalleled streak of home-run hitting—16 home runs in twenty-six September games—to stand at the precipice of history. After the game Ruth told reporters, "I'll make that sixty yet!"[15]

Friday afternoon, September 30, was particularly warm in the Bronx. Thermometers read eighty-one degrees as game time drew near. It was humid on the east bank of the Harlem River, where eight thousand fans filed into Yankee Stadium, anxious to witness history. Tom Zachary drew the assignment to pitch for the Washington Senators. He was the kind of pitcher who gave Babe Ruth trouble—one who, in the writing of Damon Runyon, "has a way of slopping the ball up at the batters, slow and easy."[16]

In the first inning, Zachary drew the disdain of Yankees fans when he missed with four pitches and walked Ruth.[17] Ruth next came to bat in the bottom of the fourth and sent a single to right field. While his single in the sixth inning ultimately turned into the game-tying run, that was not what the fans bought tickets hoping to see.

Ruth stepped into the batter's box for the fourth and likely last time of the game in the bottom of the eighth inning. The batter prior, Mark Koenig, had tripled and now danced off third base. Zachary got a quick strike on Ruth, then missed with his second pitch to even the count at a ball and a strike. Zachary then tried to fool Ruth. The left-hander threw a screwball, a pitch that was supposed to curve into Ruth's fists. It didn't.[18] When Ruth saw the pitch stray over the plate, he lunged into a mighty swing. The ball shot from his bat down the right-field line. Anticipation rose in the form of voices from the thousands. The umpire Bill Dineen trotted along the line to get a close look at the ball's flight. He stuck out his left arm to indicate the ball was fair, but only by six inches as it landed amid a sea of ravenous souvenir hunters fifteen rows into the bleachers.[19]

Yankee Stadium erupted into a state of delirium. A record many felt could never be broken had been. As Ruth completed his run of the bases, a smiling Lou Gehrig waited at home plate, his right hand extended to congratulate Ruth on his 60th home run. Ruth's blast wasn't just a record, it was also a game winner. With the 4–2 triumph, the Yankees notched their 109th win of the season, an American League record.

As Ruth was congratulated following the game, he was introduced to the fan who caught the historic home run. Joe Ferner asked Ruth if he would autograph the baseball, and he complied. Ruth inscribed, "Sixtieth home run, Babe Ruth, September 30, 1927." Ferner left elated. A day later, he sold the ball to the owner of a chain store for $100.[20]

In the aftermath of the historic game, Christy Walsh was inundated. Telegrams poured in from newspaper editors who wanted a special column from Ruth with his comments about the record. And they wanted it right away, keen for it to run in the next day's editions. Walsh complied, and by nightfall, Walsh had a column with the exclusive reaction from Ruth himself on its way to subscribers. "Of course, I'm mighty pleased," Ruth wrote. "My hopes, my swinging, and my fine were not all in vain. I'm dawgone happy—that's how I'd put it."[21]

The next afternoon the Yankees and Senators met to close out the season. More than twenty thousand came hoping to see Ruth extend his new record. They jeered when he was walked in the first inning; rose in anxious anticipation when his next time up, the ball skied off his bat toward right field only to be caught for an out; and then felt frustration as Ruth's final two at-bats proved futile. He grounded out to the Senators' second baseman and in his final turn, struck out in the eighth inning.

As the Yankees left the field, they were cheered for achieving the remarkable. Not only had Ruth eclipsed perhaps the greatest record in sport but as a team, the Yankees had done what no other had achieved before—110 wins against just 44 losses. Many on the club were in disbelief reading in the papers the words of doubters who questioned their merit. Within a matter of days, they would get their chance to silence those critics. The next stop for Babe Ruth and his Bronx Bombers was Pittsburgh and a date with the National League champions, the Pirates, in the World Series.

19

The Greatest Season

Gray skies cast a pall over the city of Pittsburgh. It represented a stark contrast to the radiance that usually filled a city on the eve of the greatest sporting spectacle in the United States, the World Series. The gloom about Pittsburgh as rain moved ever closer and sweltering heat subsided was, to many, akin to the emergence of the destructive force that stepped from the visitor's dugout and onto the green grass of Forbes Field for practice. But within the New York Yankees, there wasn't just an air of gloominess but a feeling of perplexity, if not outright amazement.

Statistically and by any measure of on-the-field results, the New York Yankees entered the World Series a team of greatness. Not only had the ball club eclipsed the American League record for wins in a single season, but their 110 victories shattered the previous mark. It was one the Yankees had not just amassed; they steamrolled their way to it.

The players Miller Huggins wrote onto his lineup card day in and day out from spring through summer forged into a juggernaut. Babe Ruth's record 60 home runs, while widely celebrated, was just one of many records set by Yankees hitters. While Ruth hit more home runs than any other team in the league, the batting order of Ruth, Gehrig, Lazzeri, Meusel, Collins, Combs, Koenig, and Dugan hit an American League record of 158, almost three times the total hit by the runner-up Philadelphia Athletics. The Yankees set a new American League record for runs scored, 975, which was 100 more than any other team in the game. Their 552 extra-base hits were also a new league record. While Ruth led both leagues in home runs, Gehrig did the same in doubles and Earle Combs in triples. As a team, the Yankees compiled a .307 batting average. Among the six players with the highest batting averages in the American League, three were Yankees. Lou Gehrig finished second

(.373) to Harry Heilmann (.398) for the batting title. Earle Combs and Babe Ruth both posted a .356 batting average, the fifth-best mark in the league. All of it, every single bit of statistical data, is what made it all the more perplexing for the New York Yankees to arrive in Pittsburgh to doubters, naysayers, and out-and-out criticism.

The sharpest of the critics were managers from the rival league, men who would not apply their name to quotes but chided the Yankees. "It's the mediocrity of the rest of the league that makes the New York club stand out so prominent," one said.[1] "Granted the Yankees are a good club, we have about five of them in the National League."[2]

The New York Giants' manager, John McGraw, was not afraid to stand behind his claim that the Yankees were not a smart ball club.[3] Even in light of the Yankees' remarkable accomplishments, Bill Carrigan, manager of the Boston Red Sox, declined to call the team great. "I don't think the Yankees could touch the old Red Sox. I don't think they would be cutting and slashing against Shore, Leonard, Ruth, and Mays," he said.[4]

Of all the criticisms and charges, none was more outrageous than that which reached the ears of Jacob Ruppert. It was a claim that Babe Ruth achieved his home-run record by swinging a bat loaded with buckshot. "What do you mean, buckshot!" the Yankees' owner cried. "There is nothing in his bat but manslaughter."[5]

On the day before the start of the World Series, the Yankees went through a workout in the Pirates' ballpark. When it came Ruth's turn to hit during batting practice, a handful of Pirates players peered with interest from their dugout. For many it was their first glimpse of the big, broad-shouldered man whose peculiar combination of strong upper body offset by thin legs and tiny ankles evoked double takes. Swing after swing sent baseballs careening off benches in the right-field stands. Two managed to reach the second deck. Intrigue among the onlooking Pirates players turned to awe. "Oh boy," Lloyd Waner gasped. "I wish I could do that."[6]

The 1927 season marked the Yankees' fifth American League championship in seven years—the fifth of the seven seasons in which Babe Ruth had been a Yankee. The club won repeat pennants in 1921, 1922, and 1923. Each time, they had faced the Giants in the World Series, winning in 1923 after losing in 1921 and 1922. The World Series of 1926 produced a dramatic showdown with the St. Louis Cardinals, one in which Ruth astounded with the first three-homer game in World Series history. The Yankees ultimately lost the deciding seventh game in a heartbreaking fashion when Ruth was thrown out trying to steal second base. Yet despite all the pennants, trips to the World Series, and records, there were still doubters. There was only one way for the New York Yankees to silence their critics and confirm their greatness. Not only did they have to win the World Series, but they had to do it in a convincing, if not altogether humiliating, fashion.

When the sun rose on Wednesday, October 5, a throng that numbered three thousand snaked from the main box office at Forbes Field. John Green, who worked by day at the Bureau of Engraving in Washington, DC, was at the head of the line. He stroked a lucky rabbit's foot, carried a cowbell in his coat pocket, and said he couldn't wait to see Babe Ruth knock a ball out of the park.[7] A high school student from Indiana hitchhiked his way to Pittsburgh. He arrived at the ticket office that serviced the Forbes Field bleachers twenty-one hours before it was to open and camped overnight to be sure he could purchase the first bleacher ticket sold. Such was the fervor for the World Series. Barney Dreyfuss, who owned the Pirates, told those at a Chamber of Commerce luncheon the demand for World Series tickets was so great, 22,900 unopened envelopes carrying more than $600,000 in purchase orders were returned to senders. Dreyfuss was pressed to construct temporary seating beyond the dugouts and in the outfield to accommodate more fans. He adamantly refused. The man was particularly prickly about the prodding to add outfield bleachers, saying he did not want to shorten the distance from home plate to the fence and make it easier for his opponents' slugging stars, Babe Ruth and Lou Gehrig, to hit home runs.[8]

More than forty-three thousand spilled from the stands when the Pittsburgh Pirates took the field to begin the World Series of 1927. Standing room at Forbes Field was at a premium. Scalpers who clamored for a very few extra tickets commanded more than three times face value for their wares. Under a warm sun that drove many to wear shirtsleeves, a twenty-two-piece band and group of male singers brought festiveness to the occasion with their pregame performance. Outside the offices of *The Pittsburgh Press*, a large electronic scoreboard with speakers amplifying the radio broadcast of the game brought the action to those unable to secure a ticket.

For the hosts, this was their second World Series appearance in three years. The Pirates were a good hitting club, whose right fielder, Paul Waner, won the National League batting title with a .380 average. Much like the Yankees, Pittsburgh finished the season with three players among the top five hitters in the league. Lloyd Waner, Paul's brother and the Pirates' center fielder, hit .355, third best in the league. Pie Traynor, who was the club's third baseman, was fifth in the batting race with a .342 average.

Unlike the Yankees, who clinched the pennant with two weeks still on the schedule and had been in firm command of first place from Opening Day of the season, the Pirates were made to battle to the final weekend before they were able to claim the National League crown. This led some to question whether they were a tired ball club. Their manager, Donie Busch, argued the opposite, that the fierce pennant battle made his players sharp and that the Pirates were primed for these biggest of contests.

The ovation was loud when Babe Ruth stepped to the plate to bat for the first time. The 1927 edition was his eighth World Series, more than any player had played in the history of the game. Cheers echoed as he smashed the first pitch thrown to him. The ball rocketed on the ground past first base and along the foul line for the first hit of the 1927 Series. When Paul Waner made a diving try and failed to catch a ball hit by Lou Gehrig, Ruth never stopped running and scored all the way from first base to put the game's first run on the scoreboard.

In his next turn, Ruth singled again. His hit would spark a rally that would give the Yankees a 4–1 lead. When Ruth came to bat in the fifth inning, the Pirates employed a defensive shift. They moved their first baseman, George Grantham, far off the bag, ignoring Ruth's earlier hits to the right side. Ruth hit the ball directly to Grantham, who suddenly realized no one could cover the bag. An all-out sprint broke out. Ruth raced up the line. Cheers of the crowd grew as Grantham churned the infield dirt. Once he drew closer to the bag, Grantham dropped into a slide. His foot managed to touch first base a split second ahead of Ruth's to record the out. In the seventh inning, Ruth stroked a single to center field for his third hit of the game, a game the Yankees won, 5–4.

The Yankees' 6–2 win a day later was even more decisive. It was achieved without Babe Ruth managing so much as a single hit. Such was the degree of decisiveness, Grantland Rice painted an almost helpless picture of the Pittsburgh Pirates."For the second day in succession, the Yankee steamroller moved sedately across the prostrate forms of the Pittsburgh Pirates and left them flatter than a pancake."[9]

Fans vociferous in their pleading for a home run each time Ruth came to bat were silent as they filed out of Forbes Field. Ruth, in his ghostwritten newspaper column, apologized and predicted the World Series was, for all intents and purposes, over. "I'm sorry I haven't been able to show the Pirate fans a home run in the two games, for I'm afraid it was my last chance. Just between you and me, I don't think we'll come back here again. These three games in our home lot ought to see the thing wound up."[10]

Ruth wasn't alone. Denman Thompson, sports editor of the *Washington Star*, suggested the notion of the Pirates winning four of the remaining five World Series games had "little likelihood of this coming to pass."[11] *United Press* sports editor Frank Getty suggested fans "are beginning to wonder if these Pirates aren't champion Captain Kidders of the game."[12] *The Pittsburgh Press* sports editor Ralph Davis was even more blunt. "Candidly, there are few persons beside Pittsburghers who think they have a chance."[13] Such was the defeatist attitude around Pittsburgh that as sportswriters left for New York, hotel clerks shook their hands and said, "Guess I will not see you again until next year."[14]

Overshadowed by the Yankees' "Murderer's Row" of hitters was the pitching staff. When spring training began, the question many had about the Yankees was about the ability of their pitchers. Few rated the pitching staff on par with the Yankees' hitters, and some went so far as to suggest that poor pitching might cost the team a chance at the pennant. Throughout the 1927 season, however, Waite Hoyt, Herb Pennock, Urban Shocker, Dutch Ruether, and Wilcy Moore exceeded expectations. Hoyt won 22 games to lead all American League pitchers. Moore and Pennock each won 19, while Shocker posted 18 wins. Theirs were not games won on the backs of prolific work by Yankees hitters, either. Only Ruether had an earned run average higher than 3.00. Moore, just a rookie, compiled the lowest earned run average among starting pitchers in the entire American League, 2.28.

For all of the Yankees' remarkable batting accomplishments—particularly those of Babe Ruth—perhaps the greatest individual performance came in Game Three of the World Series and, surprisingly enough, by one of their pitchers—an unlikely one at that, Herb Pennock.

Herb Pennock began his career with the Philadelphia Athletics only for Connie Mack to lose confidence in him and release the left-handed hurler. Pennock was snapped up by the Boston Red Sox, for whom he pitched for the next six seasons. In 1923 the Yankees sought a left-handed starting pitcher. They made a trade with the Red Sox to acquire Pennock. Herb Pennock flourished with the Yankees. He won 19 games in his first season with the club; 21 games the next; and, in 1926, won 23 games. His repertoire consisted of three pitches, a tailing fastball, a change up, and a curveball that he could actually throw from three different angles and at three different speeds.

On Friday afternoon, October 7, Herb Pennock produced the greatest performance of his big-league baseball career and one of the greatest in World Series history. Some were surprised when he was tabbed by Miller Huggins to be the Yankees' starting pitcher that day. Three days earlier, while pitching batting practice in Pittsburgh, Pennock was smacked just above the right knee by a hard-hit line drive. He spent the next several days limping about, and it was suggested the resultant injury would keep him from pitching at all in the World Series.

Pennock easily set down the first three Pirates batters in order in the top of the first. He then replicated the feat in the second inning as well. He completed his first trip through the Pirates' batting order with a third one-two-three inning, recording the nine outs on five ground balls to second base or shortstop, two soft fly balls, and a strikeout. Only one ball was hit hard, a fly ball sent to a somewhat deep region of left field by Hal Ryne in the first inning.

Pennock made it through the fourth and fifth innings with relative ease—particularly in the fifth, when he retired Glenn Wright and Pie Traynor on foul pop-ups, both of which were hauled in by the Yankees' catcher, Johnny Grabowski. Six Pirates went back to the dugout in order in both the sixth and seventh innings, four by groundout, while the other two outs were weak fly balls.

In the seventh inning, both of the Waner brothers were retired on ground balls to Tony Lazzeri at second base. Hal Ryne tried to shake things up by dropping a bunt down the third-base line. The ploy caught Joe Dugan by surprise. The Yankees' third baseman charged the slow-bounding baseball; grabbed it with his bare hand; and, in one motion, fired the sphere across the diamond to Lou Gehrig, who caught it a split second before Ryne's foot hit the bag.

A loud ovation serenaded Pennock on his walk to the dugout. Through seven innings he had yet to surrender a hit. Even more impressively, no Pittsburgh batter had so much as reached first base. Herb Pennock was six outs from tossing a perfect game.

As the Yankees came to bat, the game was still close. While the Pirates had yet to put a digit on the scoreboard, the Yankees were able to post two. Both came in on a triple by Lou Gehrig, who was thrown out trying to stretch it into an inside-the-park home run back in the first inning. In the bottom of the seventh, the Yankees broke the game wide open. They rallied to score three times with the kind of hitting that had seen them blitz through the American League all summer. Then, with two runners on base, Babe Ruth came to bat.

All about the gathering of 60,695 ticket buyers was a ferocious clamoring. From the bleachers through the grandstands, fans implored their hero to hit a home run. At the center of the diamond, Mike Cvengros reared back to unleash a fastball. It was a wicked one that lured Ruth into a mighty swing. A loud groan went up as Ruth whipped his bat around only to miss the relief pitcher's offering. Confidence within the diminutive, left-handed pitcher grew after his first fastball worked successfully. Cvengros tried another. It was a decision the relief pitcher would soon regret. The contact was loud. In a flash, Ruth turned Cvengros's fastball into a bullet, one that screamed toward the right-field bleachers. The ball never rose higher than fifteen feet above the ground. When it landed, the baseball was smothered by fans. An ear-piercing roar rose from Yankee Stadium as Ruth trotted from base to base, and three more runs were put on the scoreboard. In the dugout Yankees players were ecstatic. They had been pulling for a Ruth home run in the Series.[15] Fans shredded their scorecards, then tossed the torn paper, which filled the air as celebratory confetti.[16] Once Ruth crossed home plate, the Yankees held a commanding 8–0 lead.

The mood around Yankee Stadium was not the kind usually associated with such a one-sided game, especially in the press area. There, sportswriters consulted record books. They exchanged notes about previous pitching gems. Never had either a no-hitter or a perfect game been thrown in a World Series, which led Regis Welsh, the sports editor of the *Pittsburgh Post-Gazette*, to call this "the most gripping of all World Series contests."[17]

As Ruth trotted to his position to begin the eighth inning, fans in the bleachers rose in a loud standing ovation. They waved handkerchiefs and newspapers. Ruth tipped his cap in return. But as play resumed, the attentions of the collective horde shifted to the work of Herb Pennock. Glenn Wright, the Pirates' cleanup hitter, led off the eighth inning. Through the first six innings, the Pirates had been aggressive, swinging at Pennock's first offering and early in the count. Now Wright exhibited patience. Pennock worked the corners but failed to entice Wright to swing. For the first time all afternoon, Pennock went to three balls on a hitter. On a three-ball, one-strike count, Wright hit a smash that appeared headed to left field. Koenig, however, went to his right—a long way to his right. On the edge of the outfield grass, he gloved the smash, pivoted, and unleashed a strong throw that barely managed to smack Gehrig's glove ahead of the Pirates' shortstop for the twenty-second consecutive out in the game.[18]

Mixing up locations and changing the speed of his pitches served Pennock well all afternoon. His first offering to Pie Traynor was swung on and missed to cheers from the crowd. Pennock then threw a curveball. It came in low and over the outside corner of the plate. Traynor swung, got the meat part of the bat on the ball, and lined a clean single into left field to puncture the bubble of drama and give the Pirates their first base runner of the game. Clyde Barnhart followed Traynor with a double to left field. It brought Traynor home to end Pennock's shutout. The Yankee pitcher induced the next two batters to groundout and escape further damage.

The futility of Pirates hitters to produce much of anything all afternoon against Pennock sent hundreds of fans to the exits when the ninth inning began. True to their belief, Pennock gave up only a lone single to Lloyd Waner before he completed the 8–1, three-hit win. In the clubhouse after the game, Pennock chided Ruth. "I thought for a while you were going to let me down," Pennock laughed. "No homer, no 'nothing' then 'bam' right down the middle and the game was in!"[19] "Shoosh, I had to hit a homer," Ruth replied. "No hits yesterday. Three foozles today. Now I'm satisfied. I wouldn't be surprised if I got another tomorrow."[20]

The Yankees were confident. It was a confidence that bordered on cockiness. Many cringed at the idea of a four-game World Series sweep. Most of all, men at the top of baseball shuddered at the notion. Their eye was on the till, with a motivation for this or any World Series to go a full seven games and generate maximum income from ticket sales. Surprisingly, Jacob Ruppert was not of that vein. "I want them to win just as soon as they can. Four straight will suit me perfectly."[21]

To the Yankees' owner, prestige trumped money. Only three times since the American and National League winners had begun an annual fall matchup for baseball supremacy had the World Series been decided in a sweep. The 1907 Chicago Cubs were the first to do it, blanking the Detroit Tigers. The Boston Braves did it in 1914, when they beat the Philadelphia Athletics in four straight games. Ruppert's own Yankees were on the losing side of the third World Series sweep in 1922, when they lost to the Giants.

For a time, it appeared the World Series would not be decided on that Saturday after all. Morning rain muddied the Yankee Stadium infield and soaked the grass. It was just after 11:00 a.m. when the rain stopped and the ground crew began frenzied work to make the field playable. The morning storm and continuing dark skies lowered the crowd count to just under fifty-eight thousand. Those who stayed away missed one of the more dramatic struggles of the season.

From the outset Babe Ruth set out to decide the outcome almost single handedly. After Pittsburgh had taken a 1–0 lead in the top of the first inning, Ruth's single drove in Earle Combs in the bottom of the first to tie the game. When the Yankees' slugger came up in the fifth inning, the game was still tied. He fulfilled his earlier prediction when he stroked a curveball from Carmen Hill into the right-field bleachers to give the Yankees a 3–1 lead. They held onto that lead until the seventh inning. That's when two Yankee errors, a single, and a sacrifice fly, allowed the Pirates to tie the score.

Once the tie game went to the bottom of the ninth, tension all around Yankee Stadium was thick. It was made so by the batter scheduled to hit third in the inning, Babe Ruth. Johnny Miljus was pitching his third inning in relief. After setting down the Yankees with relative ease in the seventh and eighth innings, he quickly ran into trouble. Miljus walked the leadoff batter, Earle Combs. Mark Koenig laid down a bunt that Pie Traynor failed to handle, and, just like that, the Yankees had two runners on with nobody out and Ruth coming to bat.

Miljus's first pitch to Ruth got away from the catcher and allowed Combs and Koenig to advance to third and second base, respectively. It was then the Pirates' manager, Donie Bush, evoked the wrath of Yankees fans. He trekked to the mound and ordered Miljus to walk Ruth intentionally. Ruth was furious. He barked at Bush, yelling that he would pay the manager $1,000 if he would let Miljus pitch to him.[22] The Pirates' skipper laughed out loud.[23] As the Yankee slugger trotted to first base, fans jeered the Pirates' pitcher and manager. The spotlight then shifted to Lou Gehrig, but the budding Yankee star struck out. Up next was Bob Meusel, but he, too, struck out.

Fans grinned at the sight of Jacob Ruppert in his box with fingers crossed. Many felt the same way. The Yankees were down to their last hope, Tony Lazzeri. In the Yankees' dugout, Miller Huggins barked at his players to be alert. He predicted Miljus "is going to wild pitch. He's trying too hard."[24] With the winning run ninety feet away, Miljus let loose with a pitch that went awry. The ball grazed off the glove of his catcher, Johnny Gooch. Seeing Gooch spring from his crouch and scramble toward the Yankees' dugout in pursuit of the baseball, Combs began a dash toward home plate, one that succeeded to score an improbable game-winning run.

Yankee Stadium erupted into a state of delirium. Fans leaped over the railing and ran to celebrate with their heroes. Miljus swung his glove to forge a path to the Pirates' dugout. Several Yankees players had to do the same thing. Thousands reveled to the thrilling 4–3 win and the rare World Series sweep. As the celebration heightened, doubt was dissolved. The greatness of the 1927 New York Yankees could no longer be questioned. "There is no use trying to deprive the Yankees of their laurels. They are a great ball club," wrote *The Pittsburgh Press* sports editor Ralph Davis.[25] In a glum Pirates club house, their manager, Donie Bush, praised, "That is the best club I ever saw. I don't know of another National League team that could have done better than we did."[26] Ruth told of being approached by Rogers Hornsby. "Babe," he said, "I underestimated your club. The Yankees this year are 100 percent stronger than the club the Cardinals met in the series last year."[27]

As he celebrated, Miller Huggins capsulized just what many Yankees fans were thinking. "We've proved to the public the thing that I've known for a long time—the Yankees are real champions."[28]

20

From Disdain to Acclaim

The game's final out had been recorded when the unimaginable began. A surge, frightening in scope and voracious in intensity, spilled from the wooden stands of Dexter Park in the New York borough of Queens. A local club—an independent ball club called the Bushwick—had packed the house with a special ball game, one against a barnstorming club that had formed following the conclusion of the World Series just three days prior.

On the field the jockeying among fans turned to pushing and shoving. Some were knocked to the ground, two were trampled by the swell. Soon a punch was thrown and then another before full-scale fights ensued. More than a few of those involved would show up for work the next morning with a black eye.[1] Police reserves scurried to control the mob, but only one man could—the man the mob was after.

Though angry in nature, the quest emanated not from ire, but rather adulation and had just one objective: to touch, speak with, or receive an autograph from one player—not just any player but one in particular. The bigger-than-usual crowd came because of him, the bigger-than-life talent and personality. Now they pushed, trampled, and even fought in a display of lost self-control, all to try to reach their hero. In the aftermath of his 1927-season heroics, everyone (or so it seemed) wanted a piece of that hero, Babe Ruth.

Baseball exited its 1927 season in a far different place from where it had begun. The change of calendar year saw the game labeled crooked, with two of its biggest stars hit by insidious charges that left the faith of fans shaken and the integrity of the sport impugned. In the months that followed, the scandal was swept aside by a scintillating summertime home-run duel, a remarkable late-season surge to an improbable home-run record, and then a World Series triumph by what sportswriter Damon Runyon said was, "one of the greatest baseball clubs of all time."[2] Marvel returned to the forefront. Shame was washed away, while disdain gave way to acclaim.

Home runs were proof the games were indeed on the up-and-up. That the World Series was decided in four games—and not manipulated to go longer to generate more money for owners—was proof all was right once again with baseball.

No one was more responsible for the restoration of baseball's good name than Babe Ruth. "Ruth comes in a class by himself," wrote *The Pittsburgh Press* sports editor Ralph Davis, following the World Series.[3] Ruth's teammate Lou Gehrig went even further. "The Babe is a freak. He's the greatest player, the greatest hitter in the history of the game, but he's a freak just the same."[4]

The fall of 1927 was not the first time Ruth had come to the rescue of a troubled game. When he'd joined the New York Yankees in 1920, it was mere months after the 1919 Black Sox scandal, the charge the Chicago White Sox had thrown the World Series. Then Ruth's remarkable home-run-hitting exploits shifted conversation from scandal to sensation and pulled fans back to baseball.

Throughout the summer of 1927, scant mention of the winter gambling scandal that involved Ty Cobb and Tris Speaker was made. Instead, headlines and countless column inches in newspaper sports pages from Carolina to California were filled with tales of the remarkable slugging of Ruth and Gehrig. But Ruth contributed much more than just media coverage that brightened the reputation of the game.

Babe Ruth's home-run-hitting barrage helped several American League teams avert financial catastrophe. Over the course of the 1927 season, home attendance for five of the eight American League clubs fell from the 1926 season. None fell more than in Cleveland. Competitiveness (or a lack thereof) was certainly to blame. In 1926, the team under its player-manager, Tris Speaker, finished in second place, just three games behind the pennant-winning Yankees. Over the course of the season, the team drew 627,426 fans to Dunn Field. But amid the scandal that followed the 1926 season, Speaker resigned. Even after he was cleared of wrongdoing, the ball club announced it would not have him back.

In 1927, with a new manager who had largely the same cast of players to work with but minus Speaker, the club fell to sixth place. Out of pennant contention from practically the first day of the season, attendance plummeted to the team's lowest total in ten years. Were it not for Ruth and the Yankees, things might have turned out much worse.

So riveting was the Gehrig-Ruth home-run duel during June, July, and August and then Ruth's September race to a new home-run record, that games with the Yankees accounted for a large percentage of the home attendance total of not just the Cleveland Indians but that of several other American League teams. Thirty percent of Cleveland's total attendance from its seventy-seven home games came from just the team's eleven home games with the Yankees.

Ruth and the Yankees had an even more positive impact on the revenues of the Boston Red Sox. In 1927 the team endured a third consecutive last-place finish. Only 305,275 fans attended the club's home games. But of that total, 47 percent was generated from the eleven games the Red Sox played in Fenway Park against the Yankees.

In St. Louis the Browns drew a paltry 247,897 to Sportsman's Park. The total represented a decline of almost 40,000 from what the club drew during the 1926 season. Forty-one percent of the Browns' home attendance was generated from home games in May, July, and August with the Yankees.

Home attendance at Chicago White Sox games fell by almost one hundred thousand from the team's 1926 season. The White Sox turnstile counts, though, were buoyed by visits from the Yankees. Those games produced a sellout in May, two near-sellouts in July, and four large crowds in August. The Yankees played to two sellouts and four near sellouts in Detroit during the 1927 season. Similarly, they played before two overflow crowds and three that were close to capacity at Griffith Stadium in a season in which the Washington Senators' home attendance fell by 20 percent.

Most perplexing throughout the season was the turnstile spinning in Philadelphia. The Athletics began the 1927 season with high hopes. Sportswriters predicted the additions of Ty Cobb, Eddie Collins, and Zak Wheat would propel the club to the American League pennant. They didn't. After losing the first four games of the season to the Yankees, the Athletics were never a threat. While they did manage to finish in second place, they were a distant second, nineteen games behind the Yankees in the standings. Despite the promise and the new stars, the Athletics' home attendance fell by almost 109,000 from 1926. Yet whenever the Yankees came to town, Shibe Park was often filled beyond capacity. The schedule maker helped too. The Yankees were the opposition for the Athletics' home opener, a game which drew thirty-five thousand. When the team played its first Saturday game, normally a good drawing date, it was against the Yankees and again drew thirty-five thousand. The Memorial Day holiday saw the Athletics at home to play a doubleheader against Ruth and his teammates. That game pulled forty thousand to Shibe Park. In all, games with their New York rivals accounted for 34 percent of the Athletics' 1927 crowd count.

It was Ruth and the New York Yankees that were responsible for the biggest home crowd each American League team enjoyed during the 1927 season. In Chicago, 52,000 came to the White Sox's May 8 game with the Yankees. The Boston Red Sox drew 36,000 to their Labor Day doubleheader against the Yankees. The 33,000 who came to Navin Field for the Tigers' game with the Yankees was equaled only by the Tigers' Opening-Day turn-out. Unfortunately for the St. Louis Browns, the majority of their home dates with the Yankees fell on midweek afternoons, historically bad days to pull in a big crowd. A Monday afternoon game with the Yankees in July was made a lady's day and brought the largest turnout of the season—22,427— to Sportsman's Park. Cleveland's largest home crowds came from a pair of Sunday games with the Yankees—May 22 (which drew 23,000) and August 21 (which pulled 19,000). Aside from their Opening-Day game, Washington's largest turnout of the season was from a game with the Yankees at the height of the Gehrig-Ruth home-run duel. The July 3 game was witnessed by 30,000.

Not only were the New York Yankees the American League's biggest box-office draw on the road, they set attendance records at home. Their seventy-seven 1927 home games drew an American League record of 1,164,015 fans. The Yankees were the only American League club to top 1 million in attendance. Runners-up were the Detroit Tigers, who were a distant second, drawing 773,716. Only once prior to the 1927 season had the Yankees drawn a crowd larger than 70,000. That occurred in 1923 at the very first game ever played in Yankee Stadium. In 1927 the drama of a home-run record chase and a pennant-pursuing ball club helped the Yankees draw 70,000 or more to their stadium three times. The first came on Opening Day of the season. The second was on May 1, against the Athletics, and the third happened on the Fourth of July. On two other occasions, crowd counts at Yankee Stadium exceeded 60,000.

While once again Babe Ruth was responsible for the resuscitation of baseball, this time was different from 1921. The restoration of baseball's integrity, the replenishment of depleted box-office tills, and the inflated financial health of the New York Yankees came about from a metamorphosis—the transformation of an aging ballplayer whose career was thought to be on the decline. The differ-ence between the Babe Ruth of 1921 and 1927's Babe Ruth was Christy Walsh.

For years the influencers in Ruth's life had tried to their wits' end to evoke change in the ballplayer. Jacob Ruppert coaxed, Miller Huggins disciplined, and even the mayor of New York, Jimmy Walker, became involved and tried to persuade. The men employed paternalism, fines, suspensions, even humiliation—all to no avail. But throughout the summer of 1927, Ruth's outrageous gambling habits were excised, his excessive spending reined in, and the cavorting curtailed. Even the oft-argumentative and cantankerous Ruth was quiet on the field. Artie McGovern said he had never once heard Ruth complain. Most of all, Ruth's gluttony stopped. His improved health, heightened level of fitness, and increase in strength all contributed significantly to a history-making season.

The genesis of Ruth's transformation was one man's work. "It was Christy Walsh more than fines or the threat of his job that brought Ruth to the realization that no candle will burn long from both ends, and it was Walsh who chained him up and tossed him into a gymnasium for a winter season of the hardest work Babe ever did," acknowledged wire service reporter Henry Farrell.[5] Where others failed, Walsh succeeded. From the very beginning with their ghostwriting project, Christy Walsh had engendered the trust of Babe Ruth. He came to understand Ruth, what motivated him, what brought out reluctance, and what he did and didn't like. Over time, their relationship grew. It was Walsh who shielded Ruth from the unscrupulous and put him together with reputable businessmen to endorse their products for a fee. Walsh created for Ruth lucrative barnstorming, vaudeville, and motion picture opportunities. From a burgeoning confidence built through successes, Christy Walsh achieved what Ruppert, Huggins, and Walker could not, the development of self-control in Babe Ruth. It was Christy Walsh, reported the *San Francisco Examiner*, "who has as much to do with the rejuvenation of Ruth as any other force."[6]

Christy Walsh made Ruth understand the value of investing. Where once Ruth was free-spending and wary of banks, by October of 1927, Ruth had almost $80,000 in investment accounts. Even during the World Series, Ruth made time to accompany Walsh to the Bank of Manhattan, where he deposited another $30,000 into a trust fund.

Following the disastrous season of 1925, Walsh was able to convince Ruth of the importance of being healthy and fit. He introduced him to Artie McGovern, then insisted Ruth hire the trainer and pay him out of his own pocket. McGovern's work brought about improved play during the 1926 season. It made Ruth willing to undertake even more a year later, which produced the improbable record-setting summer. All the miles Ruth ran during the winter of 1927 in Los Angeles; the pounds and pounds of weight he vigorously pushed, pulled, and threw; and the exertion and contortion all done to generate greater strength and produce more flexibility created the season of the extraordinary.

A player who had been declared washed up at the age of thirty, mocked in the press for being uncaring and overweight, and chided by fans as a hot dog gorger enjoyed not only his greatest season but the greatest season in the history of baseball. Babe Ruth did so at the age of thirty-three. It was a transformation both spectacular and astounding. Not only did Ruth break the greatest record in the history of the game, hitting 60 home runs in a season, he led the American League in runs scored, was second to his teammate Lou Gehrig in runs batted in (173 to 165), and finished the season fifth in the batting race with a .356 average, two percentage points behind the third-place finisher, Bob Fothergill of Detroit.

Most astounding and perhaps the greatest measure of McGovern's work was Ruth's play during the final month of the season. September is when most players tire and their performance falters, but not the 1927-edition Babe Ruth. He hit more home runs during the month of September games—seventeen in twenty-seven—than in any other month of the season. Equally impressive, Ruth's already lofty batting average actually rose over the final month.

For all of his transformative contributions to baseball, *The Sporting News* felt Ruth's dedication to fitness training was the most impactful yet.

> The name of Babe Ruth will live long in baseball because of his sensational home-run records, because of his dramatic appeal to the crowds. But far more does he deserve to be known to baseball history as the player who had the "guts" to forego the indulgences he had practiced since boyhood, the courage to substitute the practice of self-denial in the matter of his previous excesses of his own volition when the liberties permitted in the game did not demand it, and the one who blazed the trail for the physical conditioning of the greater baseball teams of the future.[7]

The publication strongly urged every ball club to employ a fitness trainer and for players to follow Ruth's example. The first who did was Ruth's teammate. In the final weeks of the 1927 season, Lou Gehrig hired Christy Walsh to manage his affairs. As part of the agreement, Gehrig would train under the direction of Artie McGovern.

Baseball as a whole was a sport on the brink of change. Soon Christy Walsh would not be alone working phones or lurking in hallways on behalf of a ballplayer. His work for Babe Ruth was widely publicized and, thus, well-known throughout the game. Predictions abounded that other creative and entrepreneurial men would soon follow in Walsh's path. "The magnates will probably cause the introduction of the vogue of private managers for ball players."[8] Some would focus on loosening the tight fists of club owners to get better pay for ballplayers. Others would unleash business savvy to generate more money away from the game for players they represented. But few would or even could replicate what Christy Walsh meant to Babe Ruth or, for that matter, to professional baseball.

As Christy Walsh boarded a train to begin a winter barnstorming tour, he did so with a confidence that he had saved Babe Ruth. Walsh's trust saved Ruth from the unscrupulous. His business acumen saved Ruth from himself. The creative brilliance Christy Walsh employed during his years in the advertising industry were used to make Babe Ruth exceedingly wealthy and to build a nest egg for the slugger's family. But the innovative talent didn't benefit Ruth alone.

Baseball was an even bigger benefactor from the work of Christy Walsh. It was Walsh who brought the game's greatest star to the masses and to areas of the country that were devoid of big-league ball. The work of Walsh illuminated a personality, one that the previously disconnected found to be both likeable and good. When baseball lost its way, when its biggest stars neglected their legions of supporters and fell into the morass of gambling and game-fixing, it was Babe Ruth who was there to save it, to restore the game to its rightful place on the highest of sports pedestals. But behind Ruth was Christy Walsh, who constructed, then executed the programs that generated the publicity that sent a reinvigorated slugger into a season that rescued baseball from the abyss.

Notes

INTRODUCTION

1. "Old Doc Rain Casts Pall Over Stadium," *New York Daily News*, October 8, 1927, 98.
2. Mooney, Bill, "Babe Ruth Hitting Mechanics," YouTube.com, June 20, 2009, https://www.youtube.com/watch?v=wBmB—g0_U8.
3. Alexander, Grover Cleveland, "Hero of World Series Is not Afraid of Babe," *The Tampa Times*, March 30, 1927, 12.
4. "Babe Ruth Highlights," YouTube.com, September 20, 2020, https://www.youtube.com/watch?v=6-4Z2rMcFo8.
5. Newkirk, Susan A., "Baseball Legend Carmen Hill Dies," *The Indianapolis Star*, January 3, 1990, 44.
6. "Baseball History," https://www.facebook.com/groups/1050532598627699, March 1, 2014.
7. "Baseball History," https://www.facebook.com/groups/1050532598627699.

CHAPTER 1

1. "Judge Landis in Fresno Visit for Single Day," *The Fresno Morning Republican*, October 30, 1926, 18.
2. "Baseball Czar Visits Dutch Leonard Here," *The Fresno Bee*, October 29, 1926, 19.
3. Murnane, Tim, "Tim Murnane Pays a Visit to Dutch Leonard's Vineyards," *The Boston Sunday Globe*, January 9, 1916, 15.
4. "Dutch Leonard Home Again after Season with Detroit," *The Fresno Morning Republican*, October 12, 1919, 1.

5. Murnane, Tim, "Leonard, Carrigan Almost Whole Show in Boston's 6–0 Win," *The Boston Globe*, August 6, 1914, 7.

6. Evans, Billy, "Leonard Promises to Annex Five Games and American League Flag for Cobb's Tigers," *The Tuscaloosa News and Times-Gazette,* August 24, 1924, 6.

7. Greene, Sam, "Revival of Tigers Reveals Big Punch," *The Sporting News*, June 4, 1926, 1.

8. Bullion, Harry, "Bengals Are Buried under an Avalanche of Runs by Athletics," *Detroit Free Press*, July 15, 1925, 16.

9. Bullion, "Bengals Are Buried under an Avalanche of Runs," 16.

10. "Lively Ball Is Blamed by Leonard for His Tired Arm," *Muscatine Journal and News-Tribune*, August 24, 1925, 6.

11. Walsh, Davis J., "Heilmann Is Credited with Forcing Expose," *The Minneapolis Morning Tribune*, December 23, 1926, 25.

12. "This Is What They Wrote," *Detroit Free Press*, December 22, 1926, 16.

13. "Landis Names Ty Cobb in Scandal," *The Border Cities Star*, December 21, 1926, 1.

14. "This Is What They Wrote."

15. "Navin Field Curtain Rung on Thursday," *Detroit Free Press*, September 26, 1919.

CHAPTER 2

1. McGeehan, W. O., "Ruth Breaks Home Run Record," *New York Tribune*, July 20, 1920, 12.

2. "Yanks Buy Babe Ruth for $125,000," *The New York Times,* January 6, 1920, 16.

3. "Hub City's Fans Upset by News of Babe Ruth's Sale," *New York Daily News*, January 7, 1920, 19.

4. "Hub City's Fans Upset by News of Babe Ruth's Sale," 19.

5. O'Leary, James C., "Red Sox Sell Ruth for $100,000 Cash," *The Boston Daily Globe*, January 6, 1920, 1.

6. "Scribbled by Scribe," *The Sporting News*, August 5, 1920, 4.

7. "Babe Draws Crowd but Ping Does Work," *The Sporting News*, June 24, 1920, 1.

8. "Ruth Is Hero Where Once Cobb Reigned," *The Sporting News*, August 12, 1920, 3.

9. "Ruth Is Hero Where Once Cobb Reigned."

10. "Scribbled by Scribe."

11. McGeehan, W. O., "Ping Bodie's Homer Wins for Yankees—Giants Take Two and Dodgers Blank Phillies," *New York Tribune*, June 4, 1920, 12.

12. Hunt, Marshall A., "Records Topple in Giant-Yank Series," *New York Daily News,* October 16, 1921, 76.

13. Rice, Grantland, "The SportLight," *New York Tribune*, August 11, 1920, 18.

14. Walsh, Christy, "Ruth's Ghost Closed in Wave of 1936," *Birmingham News*, October 4, 1937, 11.

15. Walsh, Christy, "Babe Ruth Scrapbook," Volume 1, Part 3, National Baseball Library, Giamatti Research Center.

16. Ruth, "Babe," "Ruth Says Crooked Players Should Be Barred Forever," *The Times Dispatch*, August 7, 1921, 14.

17. Ruth, "Ruth Says Crooked Players Should Be Barred Forever."

18. Ruth, Babe, "Babe Ruth Has No Special Tricks for Specific Hurler," *Richmond Times-Dispatch,* September 22, 1921, 9.

19. Ruth, "Babe," "All Pitchers Look Alike to the King of Batters," *Times Leader*, September 22, 1921, 14.

20. Macbeth, W. J., "Can Babe Ruth Make It Sixty?," *New York Tribune,* September 19, 1921, 13.

21. Lowery, Frank, "Ruth, Gehrig Play Here Monday," *Stockton Independent*, October 19, 1928, 8.

CHAPTER 3

1. "Landis Tossed Baseball Scandal Bomb for Sake of the Game," *The Dayton Herald*, December 22, 1926, 29.

2. Corbett, James J., "Ban, 'Czar of Baseball,' Once Loved and Revered, Now Stands Amid Foes," *The San Antonio Evening News*, October 14, 1919, 8.

3. Daniel, Dan, "High Lights and Shadows in All Spheres of Sports," *New York Sun*, October 11, 1919, 19.

4. "We Threw World Series, Cicotte, Jackson Admit," *Chicago Daily Tribune*, September 29, 1920, 1.

5. "We Threw World Series, Cicotte, Jackson Admit."

6. Klein, Frank O., "Baseball Scandal Grows," *Collyer's Eye*, January 8, 1927, 1.

7. Sanborn, I. E., "New Power Soon Rules Baseball with an Iron Hand," *Chicago Tribune*, October 1, 1920, 19.

8. Kilgallen, James L., "Court Attack on Organized Baseball May Follow Trial," *The Pittsburgh Post*, August 4, 1921, 1.

9. "Baseball Safe in Hands of Judge Landis," *New York Tribune*, August 8, 1921, 9.

10. "Judge Landis Is Right," *Detroit Free Press*, August 6, 1921, 6.

11. Ruth, Babe, "Ruth Says Crooked Players Should Be Barred Forever," *The Times Dispatch*, August 7, 1921, 14.

12. Peet, William, "Sport Flashes," *Honolulu Advertiser*, January 12, 1927, 8.

13. Kelsey, Clark B., "Landis Evades Questions about Cobb and Speaker," *Oakland Tribune*, January 13, 1927, 25.

14. Maxwell, Don, "Ban Johnson Blows Lid off Scandal," *Chicago Daily Tribune*, January 17, 1927, 1.

15. Maxwell, "Ban Johnson Blows Lid off Scandal," 1.

16. "West Clears Cobb, Speaker," *Daily News*, December 30, 1926, 28.

17. "Charges Game Was Fixed," *Chicago Daily Tribune*, December 23, 1926, 13.

18. Maxwell, Don, "Rumors Fly of Major League Investigation," *Chicago Tribune*, December 21, 1926, 21.

19. Maxwell, Don, "Landis Silent on New Ball Scandal," *Chicago Tribune*, December 21, 1926, 1.

20. "Tris Speaker and Cobb in Baseball Scandal," *Los Angeles Times,* December 22, 1926, 1.

21. "Cobb, Speaker, Leonard, and Wood under Investigation," *Boston Evening Globe,* December 21, 1926, 1.

22. "Landis Links Ty Cobb and Tris Speaker in a Scandal," *St. Louis Post-Dispatch,* December 21, 1926, 1.

23. "Ty and Tris Scandal Rocks Sports World to Its Foundations," *Oakland Tribune,* December 22, 1926, 17.

24. Hunt, Marshall, "Baseball in 1919 Not Lilly White," *New York Daily News*, December 24, 1926, 24.

25. Welsh, Regis M., "Violators of Public Confidence, Two Greats Pay Penalty," *The Pittsburgh Post*, December 23, 1926, 1.

26. Finke, M. Carl, "Finke Thinks," *Dayton Daily News*, December 24, 1926, 14.

27. Rice, Grantland, "Ball Fandom Turns Ear to Ban Johnson," *The Windsor Star*, December 23, 1926, 1.

28. Davis, Ralph, "Baseballs Newest Black Eye Shakes Confidence of Public," *The Pittsburgh Press*, December 22, 1926, 32.

29. Gallico, Paul, "Still Retaining the Shirt," *New York Daily News*, December 24, 1926, 24.

30. Runyon, Damon, "Runyon Says," *Intelligencer Journal*, December 23, 1926, 14.

31. Bennett, Carle H., "What Happened in Chicago Not My Concern: Leonard," *The Fresno Bee*, December 23, 1926, 1.

32. Vila, Joe, "Ruppert Answers Scandal Mongers," *The Sporting News*, January 20, 1927, 1.

CHAPTER 4

1. Kemp, Abe, "Babe Ruth in S.F. Lauds Accused Trio," *San Francisco Examiner*, December 25, 1926, 23.

2. "George Herman Ruth Not Worrying about Trouble," *The Bulletin*, December 25, 1926, 5.

3. "Vaudeville," *Minneapolis Daily Star*, November 1, 1926, 6.

4. "Home Run King Pleases Crowds," *The Spokesman-Review,* November 15, 1926, 5.

5. "Cured by Home Runs," *The Lexington Leader*, October 12, 1926, 5.

6. Kellogg, Elenore, "Bambino Lets Fans Wait as He Sees Boy on the Fly," *New York Daily News*, October 12, 1926, 33.

7. Kellogg, Elenore, "Bambino Lets Fans Wait."

8. "How Are You Johnny?" *The Evening Star*, October 13, 1926, 8.

9. "Ruth in the Sickroom," *The Pittsburgh Post*, October 13, 1926, 6.

10. "Ruth Twice a Hero," *Port Chester Daily Item*, October 13, 1926, 6.

11. Kemp, Abe, "Ruth to Arrive in SF Tomorrow," *San Francisco Examiner*, December 23, 1926, 24.

12. Gallico, Paul, "A Most Important Hero," *New York Daily News*, October 13, 1926, 32.

CHAPTER 5

1. "Senate May Seek Baseball Truth," *El Paso Herald*, December 29, 1926, 5.

2. "Ty Cobb Becomes Ill at Asheville," *Atlanta Journal Constitution*, December 6, 1926, 7.

3. Davis, Ralph, "Ralph Davis Says," *The Pittsburgh Press*, December 27, 1926, 20.

4. Vaughan, Irving, "Cobb, Speaker Will Fight Charges," *New York Daily News*, December 23, 1926, 32.

5. Vaughan, "Cobb, Speaker Will Fight Charges."

6. "'I Am Not Done with Leonard,' says Cobb," *The Philadelphia Inquirer*, December 24, 1926, 17.

7. "Ty Says American Heads Are Guilty," *The Philadelphia Inquirer*, December 24, 1926, 17.

8. "'My Conscience Clear,' Ty Says to Home Folk," *Chicago Daily Tribune*, December 24, 1926, 13.

9. "'My Conscience Clear.'"

10. Wadhams, Phil, "The Price of Honor," *Lincoln State Journal*, December 24, 1926, 7.

11. "Leonard Says Landis Broke Faith," *Modesto News-Herald*, December 29, 1926, 1.

12. Vore, F. H., "Leonard's Statement," *The Fresno Bee*, December 29, 1926, 10.

13. Vore, "Leonard's Statement."

14. Kelsey, Clark B., "Comiskey Says Cobb and Speaker Should Have Lingered if Innocent," *The Sacramento Bee*, December 27, 1926, 14.

15. Horn, Blinkey, "Detroit Plans Airing of Scandal Charges," *The Tennessean*, December 30, 1926, 11.

16. "Cobb Opens Fight in Detroit Today to Clear Name," *Detroit Free Press*, December 29, 1926, 1.

17. "Fire Dies Down in New Scandal of Big Leagues," *The Eugene Guard*, December 24, 1926, 2.

18. "Jacksonville for Ty," *The Times Dispatch*, December 30, 1926, 13.

19. "Many Cleveland Fans Are Skeptical about Speaker," *Philadelphia Inquirer*, December 23, 1926, 24.

20. Welsh, Regis M., "Called 'Rat' by Old Friend," *The Pittsburgh Daily Post*, December 24, 1926, 11.

21. Rippingille, Frank, "14 Year Flyer Defends Cobb," *The Plain Speaker*, December 23, 1926, 13.

22. "'Impossible to Believe,' Billy Sunday Avers in Defense of Cobb and Speaker," *The Minneapolis Star*, December 23, 1926, 11.

23. Bentley, John, "Taking a Sight," *Lincoln State Journal*, December 23, 1926, 9.

24. Jenkins, Burris, Jr., "Cobb and Speaker Muff Chance?" *Lincoln Journal Star*, December 27, 1926, 6.

25. Williams, Joe, "The Nut Cracker," *Muncie Evening Press*, December 28, 1926, 7.

26. "Many American Fans Hold Confidence in Cobb and Speaker," *Arizona Republic*, December 27, 1926, 11.

27. Evans, Billy, "Leonard's Charges Prompted by Grudge against Tiger Boss," *The Times Herald*, December 24, 1926, 7.

28. O'Malley, Austin, "Leonard Says Landis Broke Faith," *Modesto News Herald*, December 29, 1926, 1.

29. O'Malley, Austin, "Dutch Hints Cobb Dragged Tris into It," *Minneapolis Daily Star*, December 23, 1926, 11.

30. O'Malley, "Dutch Hints Cobb Dragged Tris into It."

31. O'Malley, Austin, "Baseball Is Not on the Level, Says Former Twirler," *Wisconsin State Journal*, December 22, 1926, 15.

32. O'Malley, "Baseball Is Not on the Level."

33. Jones, David, "Dutch Leonard," Society for American Baseball Research, SABR Biography project, http://sabr.org. Accessed September 17, 2021.

34. O'Malley, "Baseball Is Not on the Level."

35. O'Malley, "Baseball Is Not on the Level."

36. "Ty Cobb Demands That Judge Landis Give Decision in Baseball's Latest Scandal," *The Dayton Herald*, December 24, 1926, 12.

CHAPTER 6

1. "Baseball Scandal Grows," *Chester Times*, January 4, 1927, 12.

2. "More Baseball Crookedness Uncovered," *Chattanooga Times*, January 2, 1927, 22.

3. "Three Ball Clubs Are Charged in Two Deals," *Coshocton Tribune*, January 3, 1927, 3.

4. "Deposed Player Was Reluctant Reporter Says," *The Fresno Bee*, January 10, 1926, 8.

5. Kelsey, Clark B., "More on Throwing Baseball Games," *The Brainerd Daily Dispatch*, December 30, 1926, 6.

6. Hoffman, Gene, "Donie Bush Believes Two Pitchers Got Money," *Minneapolis Daily Star*, January 3, 1927, 10.

7. "'Risberg Should Be Boiled in Oil,' Ruth," *Los Angeles Daily News*, January 3, 1927, 16.

8. Maxwell, Don, "Accused Roar Hot Denials to Risberg," *Chicago Tribune*, January 3, 1927, 29.

9. "Attack Hurts Cobb," *The Fresno Bee*, January 12, 1927, 14.

10. "Fresno Southpaw Refuses to Give Statement," *The Fresno Daily Republican*, December 22, 1926, 16.

11. Maxwell, Don, "26 Deny Charges of 'Thrown' Games," *Chicago Daily Tribune*, January 6, 1927, 15.

12. "Score Stands 35–2 against Them after Risberg, Gandil Go to Bat," *The Sporting News*, January 13, 1927, 5.

13. Kelsey, Clark B., "Risberg, Despite Player Denials, Holds On," *The News Herald*, January 6, 1927, 8.

14. "Accused Men Call Risberg Story Lie," *The Boston Globe*, January 6, 1927, 1.

15. Kelsey, Clark B., "Risberg, Despite Player Denials."

16. Kelsey, Clark B., "Risberg, Despite Player Denials."

17. "Sox Games Framed—Gandil," *Chicago Tribune*, January 7, 1927, 19.

18. "What Chick Gandil and Bill James Told Landis," *Chicago Tribune*, January 8, 1927, 20.

19. "What Chick Gandil and Bill James Told Landis."

20. "What Chick Gandil and Bill James Told Landis."

21. "What Chick Gandil and Bill James Told Landis."

22. Shand, Bob, "Grist from the Sports Mill," *Oakland Tribune*, October 7, 2021, 25.

23. Gallico, Paul, "A Longing for Goats," *New York Daily News*, January 14, 1927, 140.

24. "A Question of Affrontery," *Detroit Free Press*, January 14, 1927, 6.

25. "Gandil and Risberg Leave for Home, Saying They Told No Lies," *Nashville Banner*, January 9, 1927, 11.

26. McGill, Ralph, "The Sport Aerial," *Nashville Banner*, January 9, 1927, 11.

27. "Landis Faced with Biggest Job of His Regime," *Arizona Daily Star*, January 9, 1927.

CHAPTER 7

1. "Baseball Awaits Landis' Decision," *Lancaster New Era*, January 10, 1927, 14.

2. "Landis Tossed Baseball Scandal Bomb for Sake of the Game," *Dayton Herald*, December 22, 1926, 29.

3. "Judge Landis Clears Accused," *New York Daily News*, January 13, 1927, 32.

4. "Gandil Says Cobb Should Be Cleared," *The Boston Globe*, January 14, 1927, 27.

5. Maxwell, Don, "American League Door Still Shut on Cobb, Speaker," *Chicago Tribune,* January 13, 1927, 15.

6. "Landis Tossed Baseball Scandal Bomb for Sake of the Game," *Dayton Herald*, December 22, 1926, 29.

7. Gallico, Paul, "That Longing for Goats," *New York Daily News*, January 14, 1927, 140.

8. "A Question of Effrontery," *Detroit Free Press*, January 14, 1927, 6.

9. Rice, Grantland, "The Sportlight," *The Baltimore Sun,* January 11, 1927, 12.

10. "Same Case Retried Says Ban Johnson," *The Des Moines Register*, January 13, 1927, 16.

11. "Ban Johnson Says Landis 'Tarred' Cobb and Speaker," *St. Louis Star*, January 17, 1927, 14.

12. Murphy, Will, "Another Battle Looms Between Landis, Johnson," *New York Daily News*, January 16, 1927, 45.

13. Hawkins, Dick, "Hawk-Eye-ing Sports," *The Atlanta Constitution*, January 12, 1927, 7.

14. Maxwell, Don, "American League Door Shut on Cobb, Speaker."

15. Foster, John B., "C. Comiskey of Chicago on Warpath," *Des Moines Tribune*, January 20, 1927, 19.

16. "Johnson Gives New Angles in Ball Scandal," *The Chattanooga News*, January 19, 1927, 20.

17. Hoffman, Gene, "Landis and Johnson Marshal Forces for Showdown in Chicago," *The Bee*, January 19, 1927, 8.

18. Evans, Billy, "The Passing of Ban Johnson Removes Great Ball Man," *The Post Crescent*, January 27, 1927, 14.

19. Vaughn, Irving, "Landis Meeting with American League Is Off," *Chicago Tribune*, January 24, 1927, 23.

20. Greene, Sam, "Never Doubted Ty's Honesty Says Navin," *The Sporting News*, February 3, 1927, 1.

21. "Indians to Drop Speaker in Spite of Exoneration," *The Dayton Herald*, January 27, 1927, 1.

22. "Cobb and Speaker Turned Away from Old Homes," *The Hartford Courant*, January 28, 1927, 12.

23. Hunt, Marshall, "Not Guilty Verdict for Ty, Tris," *New York Daily News*, January 28, 1927, 44.

24. "Leonard Ill Will Make No Comment," *The Boston Globe*, January 28, 1927, 24.

25. "Ban Johnson Has No Comment on Decision," *The Commercial Appeal*, January 28, 1927, 17.

26. "Idols of Baseball Given Clean Bill," *The Billings Gazette*, January 28, 1927, 8.

27. Walsh, Davis J., "Stampede for Stars Starts," *Port Chester Daily Item*, January 28, 1927, 6.

28. "New Manager to Lead Browns in Pennant Chase," *The Selma Times Journal*, February 2, 1927, 5.

29. "Mack Wants Cobb," *Stevens Point Journal*, February 1, 1927, 7.

30. Gallico, Paul, "The Enemy Was Not Fit," *Daily News*, January 25, 1927, 28.

31. McGill, Ralph, "The Sport Aerial," *Nashville Banner*, January 17, 1927, 11.

32. "Chicago Welcomes Scandal Fade Out," *The Sporting News*, February 3, 1927, 2.

CHAPTER 8

1. "Send Hornsby Back, St. Louis Plea to Landis," *Chicago Tribune*, December 22, 1926, 25.

2. "Hornsby Gets OK to Do Training," *The Brooklyn Daily Times*, February 14, 1927, 14.

3. Savage, C. J., "Moore Terms Hornsby One of the Heaviest Gamblers He Has Served," *The Courier-Journal*, January 12, 1927, 13.

4. "Hornsby's Attorney Asks Itemized Statement of $92,800 Debt Claim," *St. Louis Post Dispatch*, January 11, 1927, 27.

5. Staff Correspondent, "Hornsby Trial Ready," *Collyer's Eye*, October 29, 1927, 1.

6. "Hornsby's Love for Betting on Horse Races Caused Rift between Player and Breadon," *The Bridgeport Telegram*, January 12, 1927, 18.

7. "'Hornsby Left No Alternative' Says Breadon Discussing Trade," *The Sporting News*, December 23, 1926, 1.

8. "Scribbled by Scribe," *The Sporting News*, December 30, 1926, 4.

9. Staff Correspondent, "Hornsby Trial Ready," *Collyer's Eye,* October 29, 1927, 1.

10. Klein, Frank, "Like Card's with Wagering Coup," *Collyer's Eye*, October 9, 1926, 1.

11. "McGraw 'Calls' Hornsby," *Collyer's Eye*, November 20, 1926, 1.

12. "Hornsby's Attorney Seeks Itemized Statement of $92,800 Debt Claim," *St. Louis Post Dispatch*, January 10, 1927, 27.

13. "Another Baseball Scandal Uncovered," *The Springfield Leader*, January 9, 1927, 27.

14. "Cobb and Hornsby Parked in Center of Baseball Stage," *Memphis Commercial Appeal*, February 6, 1927, 18.

15. Small, Robert T., "Ruth Remains One of Few Baseball Heroes in Eyes of Boys," *Los Angeles Evening Express*, December 25, 1926, 19.

16. Farrell, Henry L., "Ruth, Landis Saved Baseball Once; Can They Do It Again?" *Wisconsin State Journal*, December 22, 1926, 16.

17. Farrell, Henry, "Great Players Leave Game under Cloud," *United Press*, December 22, 1926, 16.

CHAPTER 9

1. Campbell, Dan, "Ruth Movie Star Talks of Screen Career," *Whittier News*, February 12, 1927, 4.

2. "Babe to Act in Earnest," *Eastern Star*, February 27, 1927, 64.

3. Landy, George, "Anna from Ystad," *Filmplay Journal*, August 1921, 35.

4. Landy, George, "Anna from Ystad," *Filmplay Journal*, August 1921, 34.

5. "Bambino Special Idol of Boys of U.S.," *The Yonkers Herald*, October 13, 1927, 4.

6. Fife, George Buchanan, "Ruth's Own Story," *Los Angeles Evening Express*, April 11, 1927, 1.

7. Gehrig, Lou, "Following the Babe," *The Pittsburgh Press*, September 24, 1927, 10.

8. "Harding Urges Labor to Exert Babe Ruth Zeal," *The New York Herald*, September 7, 1920, 1.

9. "Caruso Admits He Never Heard Babe Ruth Sing," *Daily News*, October 9, 1920, 23.

10. Hunt, Marshall, "Movie Natural—That's Mr. Ruth!" *New York Daily News*, February 24, 1927, 35.

11. Hunt, Marshall, "Laughter Gagman's Bestest Gag," *New York Daily News*, February 26, 1927, 41.

12. Hunt, "Movie Natural—That's Mr. Ruth!"

13. Hunt, "Movie Natural—That's Mr. Ruth!"

14. Hunt, "Movie Natural—That's Mr. Ruth!"

15. Campbell, Dan, "Ruth Movie Star Talks of Screen Career," *Whittier News*, February 12, 1927, 4.

16. Hunt, Marshall, "Meet G. Herman Ruth, Actor," *New York Daily News*, February 11, 1927, 44.

17. "Babe Ruth Has Busy Day Arranging Finances," *Democrat and Chronicle*, March 4, 1927, 32.

18. Ripley, Robert, "Believe It or Not," *The Akron Beacon Journal*, March 11, 1927, 34.

19. Ripley, Robert, "Believe It or Not."

20. Hunt, Marshall, "Yes Sir, Babe Tells Extras What's What," *New York Daily News*, February 12, 1927, 25.

21. Hunt, "Yes Sir, Babe Tells Extras What's What."

22. Hunt, "Yes Sir, Babe Tells Extras What's What."

23. Hunt, "Yes Sir, Babe Tells Extras What's What."

24. "Ruth Comes Back to Baseball for Period," *The Palm Beach Post,* February 26, 1927, 9.

25. "Ruth Comes Back to Baseball for Period."

CHAPTER 10

1. Williams, Joe, "Another Good Man Goes Wrong," *Knoxville News-Sentinel,* December 10, 1927, 17.

2. Rice, Thomas S., "Ruth Sacrificed Himself as Martyr of Baseball: Now Works for the Team," *Brooklyn Daily Eagle,* April 8, 1925, 24.

3. "The Bambino, Year's Big Drama Fizzles Out to Childish Comedy," *The Sporting News,* September 10, 1925, 1.

4. Hunt, Marshall, "Ruthless Bosses Drive Babe Ruth Back to Work," *New York Daily News,* March 12, 1925, 103.

5. "Ruth Will Be Fit for Seasons Opening, Appetite Laid Him Low," *The Brooklyn Standard Union,* April 8, 1925, 16.

6. "Bambino Digging Grave with Teeth," *New York Daily News,* April 9, 1925, 34.

7. Hunt, Marshall, "Babe Ruth under Knife Today," *New York Daily News,* April 17, 1925, 34.

8. Evans, Billy, "Yankees Great Slugger Not Taking Care of Stomach," *The Brooklyn Citizen,* April 15, 1925, 9.

9. Evans, "Yankees Great Slugger Not Taking Care."

10. "Babe Ruth Warning Given to Dentists," *The Evening Sun,* May 8, 1925, 11.

11. Brown, Norman E., "The Biggest 'Busts' of 1925," *The Bulletin*, October 22, 1925, 3.

12. Winkworth, Joe, "I've Been Sappiest of Saps—Ruth," *Buffalo Labor Journal,* November 12, 1925, 2.

13. Brown, Warren, "Babe Ruth Big Show as Yanks Work at Park," *St. Petersburg Times,* March 5, 1926, 13.

14. Pusey, Otis, "McGovern to Train 'Big Bam,'" *The Deseret News*, January 29, 1927, 9.

15. Nasium, Jim, "Fitting Ruth for the Part Nature Meant Him to Play," *The Sporting News,* December 29, 1927, 5.

16. "Fans Speculating on Future of 'Babe' Ruth," *The Fresno Bee,* January 17, 1926, 22.

17. Rice, Grantland, "The Sportlight," *The Miami Herald,* March 6, 1927, 25.

18. "Ruth in Fine Shape," *The Berkshire Evening Eagle,* February 18, 1927, 22.

19. Ray, Bob, "Bambino Wants Salary Raised," *Los Angeles Times,* February 10, 1927, 41.

CHAPTER 11

1. "Cobb Signs with Mack's at $60,000 Salary," *Los Angeles Times*, February 9, 1927, 41.

2. "Babe Spurning Former Salary," *The Bulletin,* February 11, 1927, 6.

3. "Babe Ruth Demands $100,000 Contract," *The Minneapolis Star*, February 10, 1927, 10.

4. Holmes, Thomas, "Babe Ruth Indignant, Ed Barrow Smiles, and All Pro Bono Publicity," *The Brooklyn Daily Eagle,* February 11, 1927, 26.

5. "Baseball Done Brown," *The San Bernardino Daily Sun*, October 21, 1926, 24.

6. Evans, Billy, "Babe Ruth's Salary, in Reality, Is a Matter for Every Club in the American League," *Brooklyn Citizen,* February 22, 1927, 9.

7. "The Inquiring Reporter," *Chicago Tribune*, February 20, 1927, 31.

8. "One Minute Interviews," *The Daily News,* February 11, 1927, 11.

9. Pegler, Westbrook, "Babe Sneers at Mere $52,000 for His Services Next Season," *The Commercial Appeal*, February 11, 1927, 17.

10. "One of Yankees' Big Problems Is Getting Babe under Contract," *Associated Press*, October 12, 1926.

11. Pegler, "Babe Sneers at Mere $52,000."

12. Holmes, "Babe Ruth Indignant, Ed Barrow Smiles."

13. Brantlinger, Jimmy, "Looking 'Em Over," *Altoona Tribune*, February 22, 1927, 10.

14. "Ruth Sends Letter to Yanks But No Contract," *St. Louis Star and Times*, February 22, 1927, 12.

15. Kelly, Mark, "Ruth Offered Huge Salary to Stay in Movies," *Tampa Bay Times*, February 21, 1927, 14.

16. Pegler, Westbrook, "Year of Keen Competition Seen between Gotham Nines," *Atlanta Constitution*, February 22, 1927, 9.

17. Gallico, Paul, "Getting Straightened Out," *New York Daily News*, March 1, 1927, 30.

18. Ruth, Babe, "Letter to Colonel Jacob Ruppert," *New York Daily News*, February 27, 1927, 167.

19. "Ruth's Demand Is Too High Says Colonel," *Los Angeles Record*, February 28, 1927, 9.

20. Grayson, Harry, "The Second Guess," *Los Angeles Record*, February 28, 1927, 9.

21. Gallico, "Getting Straightened Out."

22. Gallico, Paul, "And Then Came Christmas," *New York Daily News,* March 4, 1927, 68.

23. Farrell, Dave, "Christy Walsh, Boss of Babe to Guide Lou Gehrig's Course," *The Yonkers Herald*, August 18, 1927, 14.

24. Campbell, Dan, "Babe Ruth Has Blossomed Out into Real Movie Star; Baseball Still First Love," *Visalia Daily Times*, February 12, 1927, 6.

CHAPTER 12

1. Hunt, Marshall, "'Gosh, I'm Funny,' Says Bam," *New York Daily News*, February 13, 1927, 44.

2. Hunt, "'Gosh, I'm Funny,' Says Bam."

3. Hunt, Marshall, "Babe Gets in Shape with an Ethiopian," *New York Daily News*, February 23, 1927, 37.

4. "Local Lad Gets Babe Ruth Ball," *Times-Advocate*, January 17, 1927, 4.

5. "Babe Ruth Arrested in Long Beach," *Los Angeles Times*, January 23, 1927, 12.

6. "Babe Ruth Rushes to Plane after He Over Fishes," *The San Bernardino County Sun*, January 23, 1927, 23.

7. "Babe Ruth Rushes to Plane."

8. "Babe Ruth to Be Placed on Trial Today," *Stockton Daily Independent*, January 24, 1927, 5.

9. "Babe Ruth Sought on Bench Warrant," *Los Angeles Daily News,* January 25, 1927, 3.

10. "Road Grind for Babe Ruth," *Associated Press*, February 4, 1927, 27.

11. Kelly, Mark, "Bambino Can Have Contract at Any Time," *San Francisco Examiner*, February 21, 1927, 26.

12. Hunt, Marshall, "G. Ruth, Umpire Murderer Goes Goo Goo," *New York Daily News*, February 18, 1927, 45.

13. McGeehan, W. O., "Down the Line," *Oakland Tribune*, March 1, 1927, 34.

14. Hunt, Marshall, "Hands Up Col.! Babe Nigh," *New York Daily News*, March 2, 1927, 2.

15. "Ruppert Silent Awaits Salary Talk with Ruth," *Chicago Tribune*, March 1, 1927, 23.

CHAPTER 13

1. "Ruppert Brewery Multiplies Stock," *New York Times*, November 28, 1922, 1.

2. Gregory, L. H., "Here's Why and How Babe Ruth Will Get $60,000 Yearly for Life," *The Morning Call*, February 2, 1929, 19.

3. Winkworth, Joe, "Home Run King Insists He'll Rise to Greatest Heights in 1926," *Buffalo Labor Journal*, November 12, 1925, 2.

4. Gregory, "Here's Why and How Babe Ruth Will Get $60,000."

5. Tosetti, Linda Ruth, Presentation to New York Giants Preservation Society, September 9, 2021.

6. Ruth, George Herman, and Helen Ruth, Separation Agreement, August 1925, National Baseball Hall of Fame Giamatti Research Library.

7. "Havana Bookies Take Babe Ruth for Much Coin," *San Francisco Chronicle*, January 2, 1921, 10.

8. Vila, Joe, "Not Conscious Alone That Caused Ruth to Change Tack," *The Sporting News*, October 27, 1921, 1.

9. Francis, C. Philip, "The Babe and Brother Matthias," *UCatholic* (blog), April 4, 2016, https://ucatholic.com/blog/the-babe-and-brother-matthias/.

10. "The Caper Who Taught Babe Ruth to Hit Homeruns," *CapeBretonToday.com*, 2019, https://capebreton.lokol.me/the-man-who-taught-babe-ruth-to-hit-home-runs.

11. Zucco, Tom, "Babe Ruth Put on a Show to Remember," *St. Petersburg Times*, February 6, 1995, 1.

12. Francis, "The Babe and Brother Matthias."

13. Ruth, Babe, "Babe Ruth's Own Story," *The Evening Sun*, August 10, 1920, 15.

14. Francis, "The Babe and Brother Matthias."

15. O'Leary, J. C., "Three New Men for Red Sox," *Boston Daily Globe*, July 10, 1914, 1.

16. "To Accompany Babe Ruth," *The Evening Sun*, September 2, 1920, 16.

17. Winkworth, Joe, "'I've Been the Sappiest of Saps'—Ruth," *The Sporting News*, November 5, 1926, 2.

18. Winkworth, "'I've Been the Sappiest of Saps.'"

19. Genovese, George, conversation with the author, October 11, 2010.

20. "Ruth Plays Role of Innocent Abroad on His Visit to Cuba," *The Sporting News*, January 13, 1921, 6.

21. Hunt, Marshall, "Bet on Ponies? Nay, Nay, Says Bam; Dogs? Yes," *New York Daily News*, February 10, 1926, 117.

22. Ray, Bob, "Babe Ruth, Home-Run Clouter and Actor Arrives Here for Week's Theatrical Sojourn," *The Los Angeles Times*, January 3, 1927, 10.

23. Ray, "Babe Ruth, Home-Run Clouter."

24. Winkworth, "'I've Been the Sappiest of Saps.'"

25. "Babe Waits Huggins Reinstatement Order," *New York Daily News*, September 2, 1925, 31.

26. Hershey, Scott, "All Baseball Mourns Death of 'Col. Jake,'" *Memphis Commercial Appeal*, January 14, 1939, 10.

27. Caldera, Pete, "Visit NYC Baseball Landmarks: Yorkville Was Home to Yankees Legends and an Iconic Brewery," *NorthJersey.com*, June 18, 2020.

28. "Babe Ruth to Get $70,000 a Year to Play for Ruppert's Yanks," *The Orlando Sentinel*, March 3, 1927, 13.

29. "Ruth Signs Three-Year Contract for $210,000," *Los Angeles Times*, March 3, 1927, 41.

30. Pegler, Westbrook, "Offer of $100,000 to Jimmy Walker Arouses Wrath of Babe Ruth's Boss," *Sioux City Journal*, April 25, 1927, 9.

31. Pegler, "Offer of $100,000 to Jimmy Walker."

32. Hunt, Marshall, "Babe Belts Homeric $210,000 Hit," *New York Daily News*, March 3, 1927, 3.

CHAPTER 14

1. Hunt, Marshall, "Babe Shows Yanks How to Hit 'Em," *New York Daily News*, March 8, 1927, 34.

2. "Babe Ruth Knocks Ball Out of Lot in First Workout," *Press and Sun-Bulletin*, March 8, 1927, 17.

3. "Thomas Alva Edison Slams Ty's Curve," *Florida State News*, March 8, 1927, 5.

4. "Efficiency," *The Miami News*, March 20, 1927, 6.

5. "Babe Ruth Knocks Ball Out of Lot."

6. Bell, Brian, "Bambino Is Taking Baseball Seriously," *The Tampa Tribune*, March 16, 1927, 14.

7. McGowen, Roscoe, "Hugmen Will Toss First Balls Today," *New York Daily News*, February 28, 1927, 93.

8. Hunt, Marshall, "Bam Twists Ankle in Exhibition Tilt," *New York Daily News*, March 11, 1927, 221.

9. "Baseball Committee Reports on Exhibition," *The Orlando Sentinel*, March 15, 1927, 13.

10. "Babe Ruth Day," *The Orlando Sentinel*, March 10, 1927, 1.

11. "The Town Slouch," *The Orlando Sentinel*, March 11, 1927, 4.

12. Ryder, Jack, "Bank-Roll Babe Injured in Game," *The Enquirer*, March 11, 1927, 14.

13. "Baseball Committee Reports on Exhibition Games," *The Orlando Sentinel*, March 15, 1927, 5.

14. Hunt, "Bam Twists Ankle in Exhibition Tilt."

15. Hunt, Marshall, "Babe Shows Lazzeri Defects in His Swing," *New York Daily News*, March 21, 1927, 30.

16. Huggins, "Doc," "Al Lang Heads Up Stadium Club," *Tampa Bay Tribune,* December 30, 1926, 1.

17. Huggins, "Doc," "Sport Pills," *St. Petersburg Times*, March 20, 1927, 1.

18. Harris, Bill, "Low Down on Some High Up's of Some Champion Baseball Clubs Stopping Here," *The Knoxville Journal*, April 6, 1927, 8.

19. McCusker, Herb, "Babe Tells How It Feels to Earn $350 a Pound," *Atlanta Constitution*, April 5, 1927, 15.

20. "Game Cancelled," *The Knoxville Journal*, April 6, 1927, 8.

21. Wilson, Bob, "Talk Sport," *Knoxville News Sentinel*, April 6, 1927, 13.

22. Horn, Blinkey, "Cardinals Win Slugging Battle from Yankees," *The Tennessean*, April 8, 1927, 11.

23. McGill, Ralph, "The Sport Aerial," *Nashville Banner*, April 8, 1927, 16.

24. "Babe, Picture of Health, Eager for Start of American Race," *Pittsburgh Daily Post*, April 9, 1927, 11.

25. Walsh, Davis J., "More Interest Manifested in Baseball Than at Any Time in Past Years," *The Dayton Herald*, April 11, 1927, 16.

26. "Ruppert Says Yanks Sure of Repeat," *The Boston Globe*, April 4, 1927, 10.

CHAPTER 15

1. Meany, Thomas W., "Dodgers Rally in Ninth to Beat Out Cleveland 8–3," *The Brooklyn Daily Times*, April 3, 1927, 21.

2. "Landis Flies," *Lexington Herald-Leader*, April 9, 1927, 5.

3. "Major League Baseball Opening Tuesday Will Be of More Than Usual Interest," *The Standard Union*, April 10, 1927, 14.

4. "Mack's Picked to Win by Players," *Austin American-Statesman*, April 10, 1927, 9.

5. Isaminger, James C., "Uncertain Fielding Fatal to Athletics," *The Philadelphia Inquirer*, April 13, 1927, 25.

6. Ruth, Babe, "Babe Ruth's Own Story; Crowds Prove Scandal Hasn't Hurt Baseball," *The Press and Sun Bulletin*, April 13, 1927, 24.

7. "232,000 Witness Opening Games," *New York Daily News*, April 13, 1927, 39.

8. Getty, Frank, "Baseball Attendance Figures Drop Sharply on Second Day," *Buffalo Evening News*, April 14, 1927, 34.

9. Farrell, Henry L., "Yanks Seen as Improved Club," *The Progress Bulletin*, April 16, 1927, 12.

10. Isaminger, James C., "Yankee Bats Again Fell Elephant Herd," *The Philadelphia Inquirer*, April 16, 1927, 24.

11. Evans, Billy, "According to Billy Evans," *The Sporting News*, February 10, 1927, 7.

12. "Suppose Babe Had Not Missed That Swing," *The Standard Union*, April 20, 1927, 10.

13. "Did Movies Affect Babe's Eyes?," *Pensacola News Journal*, May 16, 1927, 2.

14. Farrell, Henry L., "What Is Wrong with Bambino?," *The Pomona Progress*, April 27, 1927, 13.

15. "Famous Guys Who Golf," *The Journal Times*, January 15, 1925, 17.

16. Vaughn, Jim, "Baseball By-Plays," *The Sporting News*, August 18, 1927, 4.

17. Daley, George, "The Intentional Walk Is Again under Barrage," New York World, *The Commercial Appeal*, October 19, 1926, 16.

18. "Found a Way to Stop Babe Ruth," *Brooklyn Daily Eagle*, May 3, 1921, 20.

19. Alexander, Grover Cleveland, "Successful Pitching," *Des Moines Tribune*, April 2, 1927, 12.

20. Rice, Thomas S., "Ruth's True Skill Isn't Appreciated," *The Sporting News*, October 14, 1926, 1.

21. Hunt, Marshall, "Nos. 15 and 16 for Bam as Yanks Cop!," *New York Daily News*, June 1, 1927, 32.

CHAPTER 16

1. "Gehrig Ties Ruth in Homers," *Stockton Daily Independent*, July 12, 1927, 7.

2. "Ruth Forges Ahead of Gehrig in Race for Home Run Honors," *The Brooklyn Standard Union*, July 10, 1927, 14.

3. Gallico, Paul, "A Great Moral Lesson," *New York Daily News*, September 3, 1927, 20.

4. Evans, Billy, "You'd Be Surprised," *Santa Ana Register*, July 7, 1927, 16.

5. Fullerton, Hugh, "Gehrig Biggest Star in College Baseball," *New York Daily News*, May 6, 1923, 61.

6. Kofoed, J. C., "The New Home Run King," *Dayton Daily News*, September 11, 1927, 74.

7. Daley, G. W., "Gehrig, Yankees Star, Says Luck Plays an Important Part in Home Runs," *St. Louis Post-Dispatch*, July 3, 1927, 4.

8. Gould, Alan J., "Gehrig Proves Help to Babe," *The Times Herald*, June 14, 1927, 13.

9. Murphy, Will, "Babe Jealous of Lou! Chorus—No!" *New York Daily News*, July 26, 1927, 28.

10. Rice, Grantland, "The Sportlight," *The Boston Globe*, September 1, 1927, 19.

11. Van Pelt, Jack, "Stewart Knocked from the Mound," *St. Louis Star*, July 19, 1927, 15.

CHAPTER 17

1. Jackson, Denny, "Colleen Moore Biography," IMDb, https://www.imdb.com
/name/nm0601067/bio?ref_=nm_ov_bio_sm.
2. "On an Executive," *The Record*, June 11, 1927, 7.
3. Thirer, Irene, "Babe Ruth as Film Star Won't Get Broadway Run," *New York Daily News*, June 8, 1927, 152.
4. "Swats His Way into Screen Stardom," *St. Albans Daily Messenger*, May 16, 1927, 5.
5. Longacre Theatre, "Amusements," advertisement, *New York Daily News*, July 25, 1927, 49.
6. "Little Interest in Waiters or Babe Ruth on LA Screens," *Variety*, July 6, 1927, 7.
7. "Cinematic Fare," *Los Angeles Times*, July 31, 1927, 48.
8. "Babe Ruth Goes to Bat," *Los Angeles Times*, June 27, 1927, 25.
9. "Babe Ruth Real Actor on Screen," *Pensacola News Journal*, July 12, 1927, 8.
10. "News of the Theatres," *The Ventura Free Press*, June 27, 1927, 3.
11. "Babe Ruth Film at the Garden," *The Morning Call*, June 4, 1927, 12.
12. "The Screen," *The Evening Journal*, June 24, 1927, 25.

CHAPTER 18

1. "Sporting," *The Berkshire Eagle*, September 6, 1927, 4.
2. O'Leary, James, "More Than 34,000 Jammed Fenway Park," *Boston Globe*, September 6, 1927, 1.
3. O'Leary, James, "Ruth Reels Off Three Home Runs," *Boston Globe*, September 7, 1927, 1.
4. O'Leary, "Ruth Reels Off Three Home Runs."
5. Webb, Melvin, "He May Slump Occasionally But He's the Same Old 'Batting Babe' After All," *Boston Globe*, September 7, 1927, 12.
6. Hunt, Marshall, "Browns Take Yanks after 21 Beatings," *New York Daily News*, September 12, 1927, 24.
7. "Ruth-O-Meter," *Arizona Republic*, July 9, 1927, 11.
8. "Baseball Notes," *Brown County Democrat*, September 17, 1926, 2.
9. Wilk, Woody, conversation with the author, July 18, 2022.
10. "Ruth Must Hit a Homer a Day Now," *The Yonkers Herald*, September 28, 1927, 13.
11. "Ruth Has Three Chances," *Times Union*, September 28, 1927, 57.
12. "Cobb Starts Out for Hunt in Wyoming," *Casper Star-Tribune*, September 22, 1927, 7.
13. Babe Ruth May Break Record This Season," *Evening Herald*, September 28, 1927, 7.
14. "Ruth Is Record Breaker," *The Richmond Item*, September 28, 1927, 9.

15. Hunt, Marshall, "Babe Carpenters No. 60!," *New York Daily News*, October 1, 1927, 28.

16. Runyon, Damon, "Goslin and Harris Hit Homers, Scoring 3 Runs," *The Morning Herald*, October 6, 1924, 10.

17. Hereford, Robert A., "10,000 Fans in Stadium Go Wild When Ruth Crashes His 60th Homer," *The Morning Call*, October 1, 1927, 11.

18. "Babe's 60th Homer Vicious Line Drive," *The Boston Globe*, October 1, 1927, 6.

19. "Babe's 60th Homer Vicious Line Drive."

20. "Caught Babe's 60th Clout," *Times Union*, October 3, 1927, 43.

21. Ruth, Babe, "Don't Quit Too Soon Is Word from Babe Ruth," *Minneapolis Star*, October 1, 1927, 14.

CHAPTER 19

1. Evans, Billy, "Waner Brothers of Pirates Exceedingly Fast on Bases," *The Plain Speaker*, September 1, 1927, 12.

2. Evans, "Waner Brothers of Pirates."

3. Farrell, Henry J., "Brawn against Brain Argument in Impending World Series," *The Brooklyn Daily Times*, September 28, 1927, 1.

4. "Calls Old Red Sox Better Than Yankees," *The Morning Call*, September 27, 1927, 19.

5. "Manslaughter!," *Cincinnati Enquirer*, October 3, 1927, 15.

6. Davis, Ralph, "Ruth Stands in Class All Alone as Idol of Fans," *The Pittsburgh Press*, October 9, 1927, 46.

7. "First in Line," *The Pittsburgh Press*, October 7, 1927, 50.

8. Davis, Ralph, "Ralph Davis Says," *The Pittsburgh Press*, October 5, 1927, 26.

9. Rice, Grantland, "Dull Game as Yanks Win Again," *The Pittsburgh Press*, October 7, 1927, 41.

10. Ruth, Babe, "We Won't Have to Return to Pittsburgh Says Bambino," *San Francisco Examiner*, October 7, 1927, 6.

11. Thompson, Denman, "Pirates Face Nearly Hopeless Task," *Washington Star*, October 7, 1927, 34.

12. Getty, Frank, "'We're Not Licked Yet,' Claim Pirates," *The News-Herald*, October 7, 1927, 10.

13. Davis, Ralph, "Ralph Davis Says," *The Pittsburgh Press*, October 7, 1927, 38.

14. McGeehan, W. O., "McGeehan Offers Proof That Fans Concede Yanks Series," *Baltimore Sun*, October 7, 1927, 16.

15. Hoyt, Waite, "Pennock Is Star of Series," *New York Telegram*, October 8, 1927, 8.

16. Hunt, Marshall, "Meet Our Mr. Pennock!" *New York Daily News*, October 8, 1927, 28.

17. Welsh, Regis M., "Pennock's Hurling Enables Yanks to Win," *Pittsburgh Post-Gazette*, October 8, 1927, 1.

18. Gould, Alan J., "Yankee Tornado Is Still Gathering Force," *The Billings Gazette*, October 8, 1927, 6.

19. Neil, Edward J., "Star Southpaw and Babe Are Satisfied," *The Billings Gazette*, October 8, 1927, 6.

20. Neil, "Star Southpaw and Babe Are Satisfied."

21. Murphy, Will, "Ruppert Craves Four in a Row," *New York Daily News*, October 8, 1927, 27.

22. "Ruth Tells Story of the Big Series," *The Lima News*, October 16, 1927, 25.

23. McGeehan, W. O., "Down the Line," *The Pittsburgh Press*, October 11, 1927, 31.

24. "The World Series Put to Bed," *The Morning Call*, October 11, 1927, 18.

25. Davis, Ralph, "Yanks Win Baseball Championship," *The Pittsburgh Press*, October 9, 1927, 1.

26. White, Paul W., "Yanks Run Riot in Celebration of Triumph," *The Standard Union*, October 9, 1927, 18.

27. Ruth, Babe, "No Series Hero Ruth Thinks," *The Courier-Journal*, October 10, 1927, 6.

28. Huggins, Miller, "Huggins Praises Pirates," *The Pittsburgh Press*, October 10, 1927, 25.

CHAPTER 20

1. "Fans Riot to Get Close Up of Babe; Many Are Hurt," *New York Daily News*, October 13, 1927, 40.

2. Runyan, Damon, "Runyon Says," *The Evening News*, October 13, 1927, 22.

3. Davis, Ralph, "Ralph Davis Says," *The Pittsburgh Press*, October 13, 1927, 30.

4. "Players Award Thrills Gehrig," *The Spokesman-Review*, October 15, 1927, 15.

5. Farrell, Henry L., "Christy Walsh, Boss of Babe, to Guide Lou Gehrig's Course," *The Yonkers Herald*, August 18, 1927, 14.

6. "S.F. Baseball Fans Await Ruth, Gehrig," *San Francisco Examiner*, October 9, 1927, 36.

7. Nasium, Jim, "What Physical Culture Training Would Do for Game," *The Sporting News*, October 27, 1927, 3.

8. Farrell, Henry L., "Christy Walsh, Boss of Babe, to Guide Lou Gehrig's Course," *The Yonkers Herald*, August 18, 1927, 14.

Bibliography

All baseball statistics are from Baseball-Reference.com.
Attendance data, unless otherwise noted, is from Baseball-Reference.com.
Baseball game information is from BackToBaseball.com and Retrosheet.org.

"232,000 Witness Opening Games," *New York Daily News*, April 13, 1927, 39.

"A Question of Affrontery," *Detroit Free Press*, January 14, 1927, 6.

"Absolute Secrecy Maintained in Cobb-Speaker Case," *The Chippewa Herald Telegram*, January 14, 1927, 7.

"Accuse Cobb and Speaker," *New York Daily News*, December 22, 1926, 1.

"Acting While He Trains Babe Ruth's Role Now," *Los Angeles Times*, February 27, 1927, 74.

Alexander, Grover Cleveland, "Hero of World Series Is Not Afraid of Babe," *The Tampa Times*, March 30, 1927, 12.

"Anna Q. Nilsson," *Los Angeles Evening Express,* March 17, 1920, 27.

"Another Baseball Scandal Uncovered," *The Springfield Leader*, January 9, 1927, 27.

"Another Showdown Expected Previous to League Session," *The Scranton Republican*, January 21, 1927, 18.

"Attack Hurts Cobb," *The Fresno Bee*, January 12, 1927, 14.

"Babe Draws Crowd but Ping Does Work," *The Sporting News*, June 24, 1920, 1.

"Babe Getting Wise about Money," *Pensacola News Journal*, February 23, 1927, 9.

"Babe Ruth Among Stars to Shine at Wampas Ball," *The Record*, February 7, 1927, 1.

"Babe Ruth Arrested in Long Beach," *Los Angeles Times*, January 23, 1927, 12.

"Babe Ruth Cleared in Child Labor Case," *San Francisco Examiner*, February 26, 1927, 26.

"Babe Ruth Day," *Orlando Sentinel*, March 10, 1927, 1.

"Babe Ruth Demands $100,000 Contract," *The Minneapolis Star*, February 10, 1927, 10.

"Babe Ruth Film at the Garden," *The Morning Call,* June 4, 1927, 12.

"Babe Ruth Gets Plenty Doesn't Need Benefit, Declares Ed Barrow," *Brooklyn Times Union*, March 12, 1925, 18.

"Babe Ruth Goes to Bat," *Los Angeles Times*, June 27, 1927, 25.

"Babe Ruth Has Busy Day Arranging Finances," *Democrat and Chronicle*, March 4, 1927, 32.

"Babe Ruth Highlights," YouTube.com, September 20, 2020, https://www.youtube.com /watch?v=6-4Z2rMcFo8.

"Babe Ruth in the Hospital after Fainting Spell on Way Home; Fake Report of Death Circulated," *The Ithaca Journal*, April 9, 1925, 1.

"Babe Ruth Knocks Ball Out of Lot in First Workout," *Press and Sun-Bulletin*, March 8, 1927, 17.

"Babe Ruth May Break Record This Season," *Evening Herald*, September 28, 1927, 7.

"Babe Ruth Out of Game," *St. Louis Post-Dispatch*, August 30, 1925, 1.

"Babe Ruth Pays $1,000 to His Trainer; Now Weighs 212," *The San Francisco Examiner*, January 30, 1926, 25.

"Babe Ruth Raises Ire of Hotel Inmates When Storm Wrecks His Training Hour," *Stockton Daily Independent*, February 17, 1927, 12.

"Babe Ruth Real Actor on Screen," *Pensacola News Journal*, July 12, 1927, 8.

"Babe Ruth Rushes to Plane after He Over Fishes," *The San Bernardino County Sun*, January 23, 1927, 23.

"Babe Ruth to Be Placed on Trial Today," *Stockton Daily Independent*, January 24, 1927, 5.

"Babe Ruth to Get $70,000 a Year to Play for Ruppert's Yanks," *The Orlando Sentinel*, March 3, 1927, 13.

"Babe Ruth Warning Given to Dentists," *The Evening Sun*, May 8, 1925, 11.

"Babe Ruth Will be Seen on Silver Screen," *The Dayton Herald*, January 22, 1927, 16.

"Babe Ruth, Once 'Broke' Has No Worry over Money Now," *The Kansas City Star*, October 22, 1929, 9.

"Babe Ruth's Popularity Costly," *Los Angeles Times*, June 26, 1927, 21.

"Babe Ruth's Visit Cheers Boy, 11, Who Is Fighting His Way Back to Health," *The Des Moines Register*, October 12, 1926, 11.

"Babe Ruth's Visit to Tax Collector Draws Crowd," *The Brooklyn Eagle*, March 6, 1927, 42.

"Babe Spurning Former Salary," *The Bulletin*, February 11, 1927, 6.

"Babe to Act in Earnest," *Eastern Star*, February 27, 1927, 64.

"Babe Waits Huggins Reinstatement Order," *New York Daily News*, September 2, 1925, 31.

"Babe, Picture of Health, Eager for Start of American Race," *Pittsburgh Daily Post*, April 9, 1927, 11.

"Babe Ruth Fans Go into Frenzy," *The Sun and New York Herald*, July 26, 1920, 1.

"Babe's 60th Homer Vicious Line Drive," *The Boston Globe*, October 1, 1927, 6.

"Babe's Doctor Denies Brain Injury," *New York Daily News*, April 10, 1925, 34.

"Ball Fandom Turns Ear to Ban Johnson," *The Windsor Star*, December 23, 1926, 1.

"Bambino Digging Grave with Teeth," *New York Daily News*, April 9, 1925, 34.

"Bambino Special Idol of Boys of U.S.," *The Yonkers Herald*, October 13, 1927, 4.

"Ban Johnson Has No Comment on Decision," *The Commercial Appeal*, January 28, 1927, 17.

"Ban Johnson in Explanation of Scandal Origin," *Fresno Daily Republican*, January 18, 1927, 12.

"Ban Johnson Says Landis 'Tarred' Cobb and Speaker," *St. Louis Star*, January 17, 1927, 14.

"Bargain—And How," *The Pittsburgh Press*, October 3, 1927, 1.

"Baseball Awaits Landis' Decision," *Lancaster New Era*, January 10, 1927, 14.

"Baseball Committee Reports on Exhibition Games," *Orlando Sentinel*, March 15, 1927, 5.

"Baseball Czar Visits Dutch Leonard Here," *The Fresno Bee*, October 29, 1926, 19.

"Baseball Done Brown," *The San Bernardino Daily Sun*, October 21, 1926, 24.

"Baseball History," Facebook.com, March 1, 2014.

"Baseball Notes," *Brown County Democrat*, September 17, 1926, 2.

"Baseball Quiz on Today before Grand Jurymen," *Chicago Tribune*, September 22, 1920, 17.

"Baseball Safe in Hands of Judge Landis," *New York Tribune*, August 8, 1921, 9.

"Baseball Scandal Grows," *Chester Times*, January 4, 1927, 12.

"Baseball War Is On," *New York Tribune*, November 9, 1920, 1.

"Batting Poses of Babe Ruth," *The Bristol Daily Courier*, September 29, 1921, 1.

"Believe It or Not—by Ripley," *The Akron Beacon Journal*, March 11, 1927, 34.

Bell, Brian, "Bambino Is Taking Baseball Seriously," *The Tampa Tribune*, March 16, 1927, 14.

Bennett, Carle H., "What Happened in Chicago Not My Concern: Leonard," *The Fresno Bee*, December 23, 1926, 1.

Bentley, John, "Taking a Sight," *Lincoln State Journal*, December 23, 1926, 9.

Brantlinger, Jimmy, "Looking 'Em Over," *Altoona Tribune,* February 22, 1927, 10.

Brown, Norman E., "The Biggest 'Busts' of 1925," *The Bulletin*, October 22, 1925, 3.

Brown, Warren, "Babe Ruth Big Show as Yanks Work at Park," *St. Petersburg Times*, March 5, 1926, 13.

Bullion, Harry, "Bengals Are Buried under an Avalanche of Runs by Athletics," *Detroit Free Press*, July 15, 1925, 16.

Bullion, Harry, "Georgian Ends Brilliant Career," *Detroit Free Press*, November 4, 1926, 20.

———, "Hurlers Pounded Hard as Teams Split Twin Bill," *Detroit Free Press*, July 10, 1927, 12.

———, "Ty Cobb Resigns as Tiger Manager and George Moriarty Succeeds Him," *Detroit Free Press*, November 4, 1926, 20.

Burg, Copeland, "Accused Stars in Chicago to Fight Risberg," *Minneapolis Daily Star*, January 3, 1927, 10.

Caldera, Pete, "Visit NYC Baseball Landmarks: Yorkville Was Home to Yankees Legends and an Iconic Brewery," *NorthJersey.com*, June 18, 2020.

"Calls Old Red Sox Better Thank Yankees," *The Morning Call*, September 27, 1927, 19.

Campbell, Dan, "Babe Ruth Has Blossomed Out into Real Movie Star; Baseball Still First Love," *Visalia Daily Times*, February 12, 1927, 6.

———, "Ruth Movie Star Talks of Screen Career," *Whittier News*, February 12, 1927, 4.

"Caruso Admits He Never Heard Babe Ruth Sing," *Daily News*, October 9, 1920, 23.

"Caught Babe's 60th Clout," *Times Union*, October 3, 1927, 43.

"Charges Game Was Fixed," *Chicago Daily Tribune*, December 23, 1926, 13.

"Chicago Welcomes Scandal Fade Out," *The Sporting News*, February 3, 1927, 2.

"Christy Walsh Dies at Home," *Oakland Tribune*, December 30, 1955, 34.

"Christy Walsh Still Smiling," *Los Angeles Times*, December 14, 1919, 132.

"Cinematic Fare," *Los Angeles Times*, July 31, 1927, 48.

"Coast President Waits for Facts in Scandal Case," *The Fresno Bee*, December 27, 1926, 8.

"Cobb and Hornsby Parked in Center of Baseball Stage," *Memphis Commercial Appeal*, February 6, 1927, 18.

"Cobb and Speaker Turned Away from Old Homes," *The Hartford Courant*, January 28, 1927, 12.

"Cobb Is Not Wanted," *New York Daily News*, January 28, 1927, 92.

"Cobb Opens Fight in Detroit Today to Clear Name," *Detroit Free Press*, December 29, 1926, 1.

"Cobb Passes from Baseball as Games First Millionaire," *The Sacramento Bee*, November 13, 1926, 39.

"Cobb Signs with Mack's at $60,000 Salary," *Los Angeles Times*, February 9, 1927, 41.

"Cobb, Speaker, Leonard, and Wood under Investigation," *Boston Evening Globe*, December 21, 1926, 1.

"Cobb Starts Out for Hunt in Wyoming," *Casper Star-Tribune*, September 22, 1927, 7.

"Cobb Sure He Can Prove Innocence," *The Pittsburgh Post*, December 24, 1926, 11.

"Cobb, Speaker Out for Good Says Official," *St. Louis Globe-Democrat*, January 14, 1927, 13.

"Cobb's $60,000 Agitates Babe Ruth," *The Omaha Daily News*, February 15, 1927, 11.

Cobb, Ty, "Ty Cobb Answers Accusers and Declares He's Innocent," *Intelligencer Journal*, December 23, 1926, 14.

"Comiskey Hard Hit by Perfidy of His Players," *Chicago Tribune*, September 29, 1920, 3.

"Commission to Hear Story of Ousted Player," *The Minneapolis Star*, December 30, 1926, 14.

Corbett, James J., "Ban, 'Czar of Baseball,' Once Loved and Revered, Now Stands Amid Foes," *The San Antonio Evening News*, October 14, 1919, 8.

Correspondent, "Hornsby Trial Ready," *Collyer's Eye*, October 29, 1927, 1.

"Crippled Kiddies Cheered by Ruth," *The San Francisco Examiner*, December 25, 1926, 23.

Crissey, George, "Judge Landis, 78, Dies; Was Baseball Czar 24 Years," *New York Daily News*, November 26, 1944, 338.

Cuddy, Jack, "Art McGovern Buried Today," *The Amarillo Globe-Times*, November 4, 1942, 10.

"Cured by Home Runs," *The Lexington Leader*, October 12, 1926, 5.

Daley, G. W., "Gehrig, Yankees Star, Says Luck Plays an Important Part in Home Runs," *St. Louis Post-Dispatch*, July 3, 1927, 4.

————, "The Intentional Walk Is Again under Barrage," New York World, *The Commercial Appeal*, October 19, 1926, 16.

Daniel, Dan, "High Lights and Shadows in All Spheres of Sport," *The New York Sun*, October 11, 1919, 19.

Davis, Ralph, "Ralph Davis Says," *The Pittsburgh Press*, December 27, 1926, 20.

————, "Ralph Davis Says," *The Pittsburgh Press*, October 13, 1927, 30.

————, "Ralph Davis Says," *The Pittsburgh Press*, October 5, 1927, 26.

————, "Ralph Davis Says," *The Pittsburgh Press*, October 7, 1927, 38.

————, "Ruth Stands in Class All Alone as Idol of Fans," *The Pittsburgh Press*, October 9, 1927, 46.

————, "Yanks Win Baseball Championship," *The Pittsburgh Press*, October 9, 1927, 1.

"Demon Cartoonist Goes to New York," *Los Angeles Times*, October 7, 1917, 87.

"Deposed Player Was Reluctant Reporter Says," *The Fresno Bee*, January 10, 1926, 8.

"Detroit Star Forced Dutch to Tell Story," *Minneapolis Daily Star*, December 22, 1926, 10.

"Did Landis Try to Hold Back Scandal Story?," *Oakland Tribune*, December 29, 1926, 22.

"Did Movies Affect Babe's Eyes?," *Pensacola News Journal*, May 16, 1927, 2.

"Doctor Sues Hornsby for $387," *St. Louis Post-Dispatch*, January 14, 1927, 3.

"Double Header for 'Ruth Day' Saturday," *The Boston Globe*, September 18, 1919, 10.

"Dutch Hints Cobb Dragged Tris into It," *The Minneapolis Star*, December 23, 1926, 11.

"Dutch Leonard Home Again after Season with Detroit," *The Fresno Morning Republican*, October 12, 1919, 1.

"Dutch Leonard Leaves to Join the Red Sox," *The Fresno Morning Republican*, March 7, 1912, 16.

"Dutch Leonard Is on Hospital List with Broken Hand," *Detroit Free Press*, September 5, 1914, 10.

"Dutch Leonard Keeps Sox in Flag Race," *The Washington Times*, August 10, 1914, 10.

"Dutch Leonard Still Mourns Wrong Dog Answers Lost Ad," *The Fresno Morning Republican*, October 24, 1925, 7.

"Dutch Leonard Is Denied Reinstatement by Landis," *The Fresno Morning Republican*, January 8, 1924, 12.

"Efficiency," *The Miami News*, March 20, 1927, 6.

Evans Billy, "According to Billy Evans," *The Sporting News*, February 10, 1927, 7.

———, "Babe Ruth's Salary, in Reality, Is a Matter for Every Club in the American League," *Brooklyn Citizen*, February 22, 1927, 9.

———, "Billy Evans," *The Los Angeles Record*, February 17, 1925, 7.

———, "Billy Evans Says," *Florida State News*, March 10, 1927, 5.

———, "Billy Evans Says," *The Bradenton Herald*, February 7, 1927, 6.

———, "Leonard Promises to Annex Five Games and American League Flag for Cobb's Tigers," *The Tuscaloosa News-and Times Gazette*, August 24, 1924, 6.

———, "Leonard's Charges Prompted by Grudge against Tiger Boss," *The Times Herald*, December 24, 1926, 7.

———, "The Passing of Ban Johnson Removes Great Ball Man," *The Post Crescent*, January 27, 1927, 14.

———, "Waner Brothers of Pirates Exceedingly Fast on Bases," *The Plain Speaker*, September 1, 1927, 12.

———, "Yankees Great Slugger Not Taking Care of Stomach," *The Brooklyn Citizen*, April 15, 1925, 9.

———, "You'd Be Surprised," *Santa Ana Register*, July 7, 1927, 16.

"Famous Guys Who Golf," *The Journal Times*, January 15, 1925, 17.

"Fans Riot to Get Close Up of Babe; Many Are Hurt," *New York Daily News*, October 13, 1927, 40.

"Fans Speculating on Future of 'Babe' Ruth," *The Fresno Bee*, January 17, 1926, 22.

"Fans Wondering How Vaudie Tour Will Effect Ruth," *Shamokin News-Dispatch*, January 31, 1927, 6.

Farrell, Henry L., "Base on Balls in Pinch Hard Rule to Change," *Oakland Tribune*, November 4, 1926, 26.

———, "Brawn against Brain Argument in Impending World Series," *The Brooklyn Daily Times*, September 28, 1927, 1.

———, "Christy Walsh, Boss of Babe, to Guide Lou Gehrig's Course," *The Yonkers Herald*, August 18, 1927, 14.

———, "Gotham Begins Wondering as Babe in Slump," *Santa Ana Register*, April 27, 1927, 17.

———, "Great Players Leave Game under Cloud," *United Press*, December 22, 1926, 16.

———, "What About Gehrig's Pay Next Year? Yank Sensation under Walsh's Wing," *Santa Ana Register*, September 7, 1927, 17.

———, "What Is Wrong with Bambino?" *The Pomona Progress*, April 27, 1927, 13.

———, "Yanks Seen as Improved Club," *The Progress Bulletin*, April 16, 1927, 12.

Fife, George Buchanan, "Ruth's Own Story," *Los Angeles Evening Express*, April 11, 1927, 1.

Finke, M. Carl, "Finke Thinks," *Dayton Daily News*, December 24, 1926, 14.

"Fire Dies Down in New Scandal of Big Leagues," *The Eugene Guard*, December 24, 1926, 2.

"First Exhibition Here Since Exhibition Game in 1924," *The Dunsmuir News*, December 10, 1926, 10.

"First in Line," *The Pittsburgh Press*, October 7, 1927, 50.

Foster, John B., "C. Comiskey of Chicago on Warpath," *Des Moines Tribune*, January 20, 1927, 19.

———, "Risberg's Accusations Denied," *Oakland Tribune*, January 6, 1927, 13.

"Found a Way to Stop Babe Ruth," *Brooklyn Daily Eagle*, May 3, 1921, 20.

Francis, C. Philip, "The Babe and Brother Matthias," *UCatholic.com*, April 4, 2016.

"Fresno Southpaw Refuses to Give Statement," *The Fresno Daily Republican*," December 22, 1926, 16.

Fullerton, Hugh, "Gehrig Biggest Star in College Baseball," *New York Daily News*, May 6, 1923, 61.

———, "Scientists Test Home Run King," *The Lexington Herald*, September 23, 1921, 4.

Gallico, Paul, "A Great Moral Lesson," *New York Daily News*, September 3, 1927, 20.

———, "A Great Moral Lesson," *New York Daily News*, September 3, 1927, 20.

———, "A Longing for Goats," *New York Daily News*, January 14, 1927, 140.

———, "A Most Important Hero," *New York Daily News*, October 13, 1926, 32.

———, "And Then Came Christmas," *New York Daily News*, March 4, 1927, 68.

———, "Getting Straightened Out," *New York Daily News*, March 1, 1927, 30.

———, "Hey, Hold That Shirt!," *New York Daily News*, December 23, 1926, 24.

———, "Still Retaining the Shirt," *New York Daily News*, December 24, 1926, 24.

———, "That Longing for Goats," *New York Daily News*, January 14, 1927, 140.

———, "The Enemy Was Not Fit," *New York Daily News*, January 25, 1927, 28.

———, "This Fat Gloomy World," *New York Daily News*, February 7, 1925, 70.

"Gambling Losses Not Collectable, Hornsby's Reply," *The St. Louis Star and Times*, May 20, 1927, 23.

"Game Cancelled," *The Knoxville Journal*, April 6, 1927, 8.

"Gandil and Risberg Leave for Home, Saying They Told No Lies," *Nashville Banner*, January 9, 1927, 11.

"Gandil Confirms Risberg's Story of Paying Detroit," *Chicago Tribune*, January 3, 1927, 29.

"Gandil Disappears on Eve of Ball Quiz," *Chicago Tribune*, January 4, 1927, 15.

"Gandil Says Cobb Should Be Cleared," *The Boston Globe*, January 14, 1927, 27.

Gehrig, Lou, "Following the Babe," *The Pittsburgh Press*, September 24, 1927, 10.

Genovese, George, conversation with the author, October 11, 2010.

"George Herman Ruth Not Worrying about Trouble," *The Bulletin*, December 25, 1926, 5.

Getty, Frank, "Baseball Attendance Figures Drop Sharply on Second Day," *Buffalo Evening News*, April 14, 1927, 34.

———, "'We're Not Licked Yet,' Claim Pirates." *The News-Herald*, October 7, 1927, 10.

Gould, Alan J., "Gehrig Proves Help to Babe," *The Times Herald*, June 14, 1927, 13.

———, "Yankee Tornado Is Still Gathering Force," *The Billings Gazette*, October 8, 1927, 6.

Grayson, Harry, "The Second Guess," *Los Angeles Record,* February 28, 1927, 9.

Greene, Sam, "Never Doubted Ty's Honesty Says Navin," *The Sporting News*, February 3, 1927, 1.

———, "Revival of Tigers Reveals Big Punch," *The Sporting News*, June 4, 1926, 1.

Gregory, L. H., "Here's Why and How Babe Ruth Will Get $60,000 Yearly for Rest of Life," *The Morning Call*, February 2, 1929, 19.

"Growers Vote to Halt Picking on Every Week-end," *The Fresno Bee*, September 30, 1926, 5.

Haley, Martin J., "Hornsby No 'Welcher' on Gambling Debts Statement Points Out," *St. Louis Globe-Democrat*, January 14, 1927, 17.

———, "Moore to Carry $92,800 Claim against Hornsby to Landis and Courts," *St. Louis Globe-Democrat,*" January 11, 1927, 12.

"Halts Sox Inquiry," *Chicago Tribune*, September 30, 1920, 1.

"Harding Urges Labor to Exert Babe Ruth Zeal," *The New York Herald*, September 7, 1920, 1.

Harris, Bill, "Low Down on Some High Up's of Some Champion Baseball Clubs Stopping Here," *The Knoxville Journal*, April 6, 1927, 8.

"Havana Bookies Take Babe Ruth for Much Coin," *San Francisco Chronicle*, January 2, 1921, 10.

Hawkins, Dick, "Hawk-eyeing Sports," *Atlanta Journal Constitution*, January 12, 1927, 7.

"Hearst Offers Trial," *San Francisco Examiner*, December 26, 1926, 71.

"Heilmann Signs Ruth for $50,000 Policy," *New York Daily News*, October 17, 1923, 26.

Hereford, Robert A., "10,000 Fans in Stadium Go Wild When Ruth Crashes His 60th Homer," *The Morning Call*, October 1, 1927, 11.

"Here Is What Swede Risberg and Accused Players Told Judge Landis," *Oakland Tribune*, January 6, 1927, 13.

Hershey, Scott, "All Baseball Mourns Death of 'Col. Jake,'" *Memphis Commercial Appeal*, January 14, 1939, 10.

Hickey, Rudy, "Babe Says That Sacramento Is a Sunday, Big Time Stop Should He Again Tour Coast," *The Sacramento Bee*, October 26, 1927, 26.

Highfill, Paul, "Sold Nothing, Signed Nothing, Leonard Says," *The Fresno Morning Republican,* December 24, 1926, 11.

Hoffman, Gene, "Donie Bush Believes Two Pitchers Got Money," *Minneapolis Daily Star*, January 3, 1927, 10.

———, "Landis and Johnson Marshal Forces for Showdown in Chicago," *The Bee,* January 19, 1927, 8.

Holmes, Thomas, "Babe Ruth Indignant, Ed Barrow Smiles, and All Pro Bono Publicity," *The Brooklyn Daily Eagle,* February 11, 1927, 26.

———, "Opinions Differ as to Effect of 'Scandal' on Fan," *The Brooklyn Daily Eagle*, January 5, 1927, 24.

———, "Ruth Indignant, Ed Barrow Smiles and All Pro Bono Publicity," *The Brooklyn Daily Eagle*, February 11, 1927, 26

"Home Run King Pleases Crowds," *The Spokesman-Review*, November 15, 1926, 5.

Horn, Blinkey, "Cardinals Win Slugging Battle from Yankees," *The Tennessean*, April 8, 1927, 11.

———, "Detroit Plans Airing of Scandal Charges," *The Tennessean*, December 30, 1926, 11.

"Hornsby Bet $1,000 a Day, Moore Avers," *New York Daily News*, October 22, 1927, 27.

"Hornsby Gets OK to Do Training," *The Brooklyn Daily Times*, February 14, 1927, 14.

"Hornsby Had 3 Phones to Handle Bets, Says Bookmaker," *St. Louis Globe-Democrat*, October 22, 1927, 3.

"'Hornsby Left No Alternative' Says Breadon Discussing Trade," *The Sporting News*, December 23, 1926, 1.

"Hornsby Lost Years Salary in Month on Races," *St. Louis Post-Dispatch*, May 21, 1927, 12.

"Hornsby Will Get $116,700 for Stock," *St. Louis Post-Dispatch*, April 9, 1927, 9.

"Hornsby's Attorney Asks Itemized Statement of $92,800 Debt Claim," *St. Louis Post Dispatch*, January 11, 1927, 27.

"Hornsby's Love for Betting on Horse Races Caused Rift between Player and Breadon," *The Bridgeport Telegram*, January 12, 1927, 18.

"Hornsby-Breadon Split Up Started over Frank Moore," *St. Louis Globe-Democrat*, January 11, 1927, 12.

"Hot Water Replaces Coffee on Ruthian Dietary," *New York Daily News*, January 12, 1926, 78.

"Hot-Stove Leaguers Busy," *Los Angeles Times*, February 20, 1927, 20.

"How Are You Johnny?," *The Evening Star*, October 13, 1926, 8.

Hoyt, Waite, "Pennock Is Star of Series," *New York Telegram*, October 8, 1927, 8.

"Hub City's Fans Upset by News of Babe Ruth's Sale," *New York Daily News,* January 7, 1920, 19.

Huggins, Doc,"Al Lang Heads Up Stadium Club," *Tampa Bay Tribune*, December 30, 1926, 1.

———, "Sport Pills," *St. Petersburg Times*, March 20, 1927, 1.

Huggins, Miller, "Huggins Praises Pirates," *The Pittsburgh Press*, October 10, 1927, 25.

"Huggins Suspends Babe Ruth; 'Unbecoming Conduct' Charged," *New York Daily News*, August 30, 1925, 140.

Hunt Marshall, "Babe Shows Lazzeri Defects in His Swing," *New York Daily News*, March 21, 1927, 30.

———, "Babe Belts Homeric $210,000 Hit," *New York Daily News*, March 3, 1927, 3.

———, "Babe Carpenters No. 60!," *New York Daily News*, October 1, 1927, 28.

———, "Babe Gets in Shape with an Ethiopian," *New York Daily News*, February 23, 1927, 37.

———, "Babe Ruth under Knife Today," *New York Daily News*, April 17, 1925, 34.

———, "Babe Shows Yanks How to Hit 'Em," *New York Daily News*, March 8, 1927, 34.

————, "Bet on Ponies? Nay, Nay, Says Bam; Dogs? Yes," *New York Daily News*, February 10, 1926, 117.

————, "Babe Carpenters No. 60!," *New York Daily News*, October 1, 1927, 28.

————, "Babe Wallops Three, Gehrig One," *New York Daily News*, September 7, 1927, 32.

————, "Bam Twists Ankle in Exhibition Tilt," *New York Daily News*, March 11, 1927, 53.

————, "Bambino Digging Grave with Teeth," *New York Daily News,* April 9, 1925, 86.

————, "Ban Johnson Eased Out," *Daily News*, January 24, 1927, 2.

————, "Baseball in 1919 Not Lilly White," *New York Daily News*, December 24, 1926, 24.

————, "Browns Take Yanks after 21 Beatings," *New York Daily News*, September 12, 1927, 24.

————, "Cobb, Speaker, to Seek U.S. Aid," *New York Daily News*, December 27, 1926, 110.

————, "G. Ruth, Umpire Murderer Goes Goo Goo," *New York Daily News*, February 18, 1927, 45.

————, "Gehrig Explodes 27, 28," *New York Daily News*, July 5, 1927, 26.

————, "'Gosh I'm Funny,' Says Bam," *New York Daily News*, February 13, 1927, 44.

————, "Hands Up Col.! Babe Nigh," *New York Daily News*, March 2, 1927, 2.

————, "Laughter Gagman's Bestest Gag," *New York Daily News*, February 26, 1927, 41.

————, "Lou Busts 34, 35; Yanks Cop Two!," *New York Daily News*, July 31, 1927, 52.

————, "Lou Gehrig's Homers Come Home," *New York Daily News*, August 15, 1927, 28.

————, "Meet G. Herman Ruth, Actor," *New York Daily News*, February 11, 1927, 44.

————, "Meet Our Mr. Pennock!," *New York Daily News*, October 8, 1927, 28.

————, "Movie Natural—That's Mr. Ruth!," *New York Daily News*, February 24, 1927, 35.

————, "Moviedom Bids Bambino Farewell," *New York Daily News*, February 27, 1927, 108.

————, "Nos. 15 and 16 for Bam as Yanks Cop!," *New York Daily News*, June 1, 1927, 32.

————, "Not Guilty Verdict for Ty, Tris," *New York Daily News*, January 28, 1927, 44.

————, "One–Two–Three for the Babe," *New York Daily News*, October 7, 1926, 40.

————, "Records Topple in Giant-Yank Series," *New York Daily News*, October 16, 1921, 76.

————, "Ruth Demands $200,000," *New York Daily News*, February 27, 1927, 167.

————, "Ruth Shows Yanks How to Hit 'Em," *New York Daily News*, March 8, 1927, 34.

———, "Ruth Socks No. 56 to Win from Tigers in Ninth, 8–7," *New York Daily News*, September 23, 1927, 376.

———, "Ruth Surgery Today," *New York Daily News*, April 18, 1925, 52.

———, "Ruthless Bosses Drive Babe Ruth Back to Work," *New York Daily News*, March 12, 1925, 103.

———, "Ty, Tris, to Sue for $1,000,000," *New York Daily News*, December 29, 1926, 92.

———, "World Series Tour Washed Out as South Goes Wet," *New York Daily News*, April 6, 1927, 333.

———, "Yank Pennant Hinges on Calorie," *New York Daily News*, February 25, 1927, 52.

———, "Yanks Tuck Red Sox Away, 12–10, in Hitting Orgy," *New York Daily News*, September 8, 1927, 283.

———, "Yes Sir, Babe Tells Extras What's What," *New York Daily News*, February 12, 1927, 25.

Husted, Bob, "The Referee," *The Dayton Herald*, December 23, 1926, 22.

"'I Am Not Done with Leonard,' says Cobb." *The Philadelphia Inquirer*, December 24, 1926, 17.

"Idols of Baseball Given Clean Bill," *The Billings Gazette*, January 28, 1927, 8.

"'Impossible to Believe,' Billy Sunday Avers in Defense of Cobb and Speaker," *The Minneapolis Star*, December 23, 1926, 11.

"Indians to Drop Speaker in Spite of Exoneration," *The Dayton Herald*, January 27, 1927, 1.

"Inside Story of Plot to Buy World Series," *Chicago Tribune*, September 25, 1920, 1.

"Insist 'Dutch' Won't Relent," *Detroit Free Press*, March 12, 1922, 24.

Isaminger, James C., "Uncertain Fielding Fatal to Athletics," *The Philadelphia Inquirer*, April 13, 1927, 25.

———, "Yankee Bats Again Fell Elephant Herd," *The Philadelphia Inquirer*, April 16, 1927, 24.

Jackson, Denny, "Colleen Moore Biography," IMDb, https://www.imdb.com/name/nm0601067/bio?ref_=nm_ov_bio_sm.

"Jacksonville for Ty," *The Times Dispatch*, December 30, 1926, 13.

Johnson, Charles, "The Lowdown on Sports," *The Minneapolis Star*, December 24, 1926, 8.

"Johnson Gives New Angles in Ball Scandal," *The Chattanooga News*, January 19, 1927, 20.

"Johnson Reiterates Open Hearing Stand," *The Sporting News*, January 20, 1927, 1.

"Johnson Trains New Fire on Landis," *Chicago Tribune*, January 10, 1927, 19.

"Judge Landis Clears Accused," *New York Daily News*, January 13, 1927, 32.

"Judge Landis Fines Ruth Share of World Series Money and Suspends Slugger until May 20," *New York Tribune*, December 6, 1921, 14.

"Judge Landis in Fresno Visit for Single Day," *The Fresno Morning Republican*, October 30, 1926, 18.

"Judge Landis Is Right," *Detroit Free Press*, August 6, 1921, 6.

"Judge Landis Signs as Baseball Chief," *Chicago Tribune*, November 13, 1920, 3.

Kellogg, Elenore, "Bambino Lets Fans Wait as He Sees Boy on the Fly," *New York Daily News*, October 12, 1926, 33.

Kelly, Mark, "Ruth Offered Huge Salary to Stay in Movies," *Tampa Bay Times*, February 21, 1927, 14.

Kelsey, Clark B., "Comiskey Says Cobb and Speaker Should Have Lingered if Innocent," *The Sacramento Bee*, December 27, 1926, 14.

———, "Landis Evades Questions about Cobb and Speaker," *Oakland Tribune*, January 13, 1927, 25.

———, "More on Throwing Baseball Games," *The Brainerd Daily Dispatch*, December 30, 1926, 6.

———, "Risberg, Despite Player Denials, Holds On," *The News Herald*, January 6, 1927, 8.

Kemp, Abe, "Babe Ruth in S.F. Lauds Accused Trip," *San Francisco Examiner*, December 25, 1926, 23.

———, "Ruth to Arrive in SF Tomorrow," *San Francisco Examiner*, December 23, 1926, 24.

Kilgallen, James L., "Court Attack on Organized Baseball May Follow Trial," *The Pittsburgh Post*, August 4, 1921, 1.

Klein, Frank G., "Baseball Scandal Grows," *Collyer's Eye*, January 8, 1927, 1.

———, "Like Card's with Wagering Coup," *Collyer's Eye*, October 9, 1926, 1.

———, "New Evidence Exposes Landis Baseball Farce," *Collyer's Eye*, January 15, 1927, 11.

Kofoed, J. C., "The New Home Run King," *Dayton Daily News*, September 11, 1927, 74.

"Landis Bars Acquitted Players Forever from Leagues," *The Brooklyn Citizen*, August 1, 1921, 1.

"Landis Faces Greatest Task of His Baseball Regime," *St. Louis Globe-Democrat*, January 9, 1927, 11.

"Landis Flies from Texas to Louisiana," *The San Francisco Examiner*, April 2, 1927, 30.

"Landis Flies," *Lexington Herald-Leader*, April 9, 1927, 5.

"Landis Links Ty Cobb and Tris Speaker in a Scandal," *St. Louis Post-Dispatch*, December 21, 1926, 1.

"Landis Names Ty Cobb in Scandal," *The Border Cities Star*, December 21, 1926, 1.

"Landis Ponders on Motives of Risberg, Gandil," *Chicago Tribune*, January 10, 1927, 19.

"Landis Refuses to Act as Collector in Hornsby-Moore Case," *St. Louis Globe-Democrat*, January 13, 1928, 15.

"Landis Refuses to Discuss Case," *The News and Observer*, December 29, 1926, 8.

"Landis to Hear New Scandal Charges," *Chicago Tribune*, December 30, 1926, 15.

"Landis Tossed Baseball Scandal Bomb for Sake of the Game," *Dayton Herald*, December 22, 1926, 29.

"Landis's Secret Service Digs up Dirt on Players," *New York Daily News*, December 23, 1926, 104.

Landy, George, "Anna from Ystad," *Filmplay Journal*, August 1921, 35.

LeBlanc, Joe, "Clever Coup by Ban Johnson Upsets Plans of Opponents," *Collyer's Eye*, January 29, 1921, 4.

Lee, John, "Dutch Leonard Seeking Retirement," *The Fresno Morning Republican*, February 1, 1926, 7.

"Leonard Denies Sale of Scandal Notes," *Chicago Tribune*, December 29, 1926, 19.

"Leonard Denies Signing Anything," *The Tacoma Daily Ledger*, December 24, 1926, 8.

"Leonard Ill Will Make No Comment," *The Boston Globe*, January 28, 1927, 24.

"Leonard Out Until Aug. 6 Says Landis," *Detroit Free Press*, August 2, 1924, 12.

"Leonard Says Landis Broke Faith," *Modesto News-Herald*, December 29, 1926, 1.

"Leonard to Talk at 'Proper Time,' His Wife Asserts," *The Fresno Bee*, December 22, 1926, 1.

"Leonard's Refusal to Face Cobb and Speaker Stressed by Landis," *The Sporting News*, February 3, 1927, 3.

Linthicum, Jesse A., "Commenting on Sports," *The Baltimore Sun*, January 8, 1927, 10.

"Little Interest in Waiters or Babe Ruth on LA Screens," *Variety*, July 6, 1927, 7.

"Lively Ball Is Blamed by Leonard for His Tired Arm," *Muscatine Journal and News-Tribune*, August 24, 1925. 6.

"Local Lad Gets Babe Ruth Ball," *Times-Advocate*, January 17, 1927, 4.

Longacre Theatre, "Amusements," advertisement, *New York Daily News*, July 25, 1927, 49.

"Lost and Found," *The Fresno Bee*, October 22, 1925, 16.

Macbeth, W. J., "Can Babe Ruth Make It Sixty?," *New York Tribune*, September 19, 1921, 13.

"Mack Wants Cobb," *Stevens Point Journal*, February 1, 1927, 7.

"Mack's Picked to Win by Players," *Austin American-Statesman*, April 10, 1927, 9.

"Mainly about People," *New York Daily News*, October 8, 1921, 11.

"Major League Baseball Opening Tuesday Will Be of More Than Usual Interest," *The Standard Union,* April 10, 1927, 14.

"Manslaughter!," *Cincinnati Enquirer*, October 3, 1927, 15.

"Many American Fans Hold Confidence in Cobb and Speaker," *Arizona Republic*, December 27, 1926, 11.

"Many Cleveland Fans Are Skeptical about Speaker," *Philadelphia Inquirer*, December 23, 1926, 24.

"Market for Hornsby Stock Looms as Court Dissolves Attachment," *St. Louis Globe-Democrat*, February 12, 1927, 20.

Mathewson, Christy, "Mathewson Wants All Home Runs to Count," *The Boston Globe*, January 8, 1920, 6.

Maxwell, Don, "26 Deny Charges of 'Thrown' Games," *Chicago Tribune*, January 6, 1927, 15.

———, "Accused Roar Hot Denials to Risberg," *Chicago Tribune*, January 3, 1927, 29.

———, "American League Door Shut on Cobb, Speaker," *Chicago Tribune*, January 13, 1927, 15.

————, "Ban Johnson Blows Lid off Scandal," *Chicago Tribune*, January 17, 1927, 25.

————, "Cobb and Speaker Claim Charge of 'Throwing Baseball Game' Frame Up on Part of Leonard," *Atlanta Journal Constitution*, December 22, 1926, 1.

————, "Cobb and Speaker Deny Plot Charges," *Chicago Tribune*, December 22, 1926, 22.

————, "Gandil to Aid Risberg; Quiz on Today," *Chicago Tribune*, January 5, 1927, 19.

————, "Landis Silent on New Ball Scandal," *Chicago Tribune*, December 21, 1926, 1.

————, "Landis Wires Thirty to Come to Bribe Trial," *Chicago Tribune*, January 3, 1927, 29.

————, "Leonard Names Baseball Idols in Conspiracy," *Chicago Tribune*, December 22, 1926, 22.

————, "Rumors Fly of Major League Investigation," *Chicago Tribune*, December 21, 1926, 21.

————, "Sox Games Framed—Gandil," *Chicago Tribune*, January 7, 1927, 19.

————, "Ban Johnson Blows Lid off Scandal," *Chicago Daily Tribune*, January 17, 1927, 1.

McCusker, Herb, "Babe Tells How It Feels to Earn $350 a Pound," *Atlanta Constitution*, April 5, 1927, 15.

McGeehan, W. O., "Down the Line," *Oakland Tribune*, March 1, 1927, 34.

————, "Down the Line," *The Pittsburgh Press*, October 11, 1927. 31.

————, "In All Fairness," *New York Tribune*, May 17, 1920, 13.

————, "Judge Landis the Benevolent Despot of Baseball: To Keep the Game 'What the Fans Want It to Be,'" *New York Tribune*, November 21, 1920, 67.

————, "McGeehan Offers Proof That Fans Concede Yanks Series," *Baltimore Sun*, October 7, 1927, 16.

————, "Ping Bodie's Homer Wins for Yankees—Giants Take Two and Dodgers Blank Phillies," *New York Tribune,* June 4, 1920, 12.

————, "Ruth Breaks Home Run Record," *New York Tribune*, July 20, 1920, 1.

McGill, Ralph, "The Sport Aerial," *Nashville Banner*, January 9, 1927, 11.

————, "The Sport Aerial," *Nashville Banner*, January 17, 1927, 11.

————, "The Sport Aerial," *Nashville Banner*, April 8, 1927, 16.

McGowen, Roscoe, "Hugmen Will Toss First Balls Today," *New York Daily News*, February 28, 1927, 93.

"McGraw "Calls" Hornsby," *Collyer's Eye*, November 20, 1926, 1.

Meany, Thomas W., "Dodgers Rally in Ninth to Beat Out Cleveland 8–3," *The Brooklyn Daily Times*, April 3, 1927, 21.

Menke, Frank G., "Pair Cannot Hold Position as Manager," *Montgomery Advertiser*, January 10, 1927, 6.

"Messenger West Admits Toting Sealed Envelope," *New York Daily News*, December 23, 1926, 40.

Mooney, Bill, "Babe Ruth Hitting Mechanics," YouTube.com, June 20, 2009, https://www.youtube.com/watch?v=wBmB--g0_U8.

Moore, Colleen, Imdb.com, Jackson, Denny. Minibiography. https://www.imdb.com/name/nm0601067/bio.

"More Baseball Crookedness Uncovered," *Chattanooga Times*, January 2, 1927, 22.

Morgenstern, W. V., "Cobb-Speaker 'Framed' Game, Says Leonard," *The Shreveport Times*, December 22, 1926, 9.

"Mrs. Ruth and Baby Leave to Join the Babe," *New York Daily News*, September 26, 1922, 3.

Murnane, T. H., "Leonard, Carrigan Almost Whole Show in Boston's 6–0 Win," *The Boston Globe*, August 6, 1914, 7.

———, "Tim Murnane Pays a Visit to Dutch Leonard's Vineyards," *The Boston Globe*, January 9, 1916, 15.

———, "Tim Murnane Pays a Visit to Dutch Leonard's Vineyards," *The Boston Sunday Globe*, January 9, 1916, 15.

Murphy, Will, "Another Battle Looms between Landis, Johnson," *New York Daily News*, January 16, 1927, 45.

———, "Babe Jealous of Lou! Chorus—No!," *New York Daily News*, July 26, 1927, 28.

———, "Ruppert Craves Four in a Row," *New York Daily News*, October 8, 1927, 27.

"'My Conscience Clear,' Ty Says to Home Folk," *Chicago Daily Tribune*, December 24, 1926, 13.

Nasium, Jim, "Fitting Ruth for the Part Nature Meant Him to Play," *The Sporting News*, December 29, 1927, 5.

———, "What Physical Culture Training Would Do for Game," *The Sporting News*, October 27, 1927, 3.

"Navin Denies Cobb Charges in Ball Fight," *Detroit Free Press*, December 24, 1926, 1.

"Navin Field Curtain Rung on Thursday," *Detroit Free Press*, September 26, 1919, 15.

Neil, Edward J., "Star Southpaw and Babe Are Satisfied," *The Billings Gazette*, October 8, 1927, 6.

"Never Doubted Ty's Honesty Says Navin," *The Sporting News*, February 3, 1927, 1.

Newkirk, Susan A., "Baseball Legend Carmen Hill Dies," *The Indianapolis Star*, January 3, 1990, 44.

"New Manager to Lead Browns in Pennant Chase," *The Selma Times Journal*, February 2, 1927, 5.

"New Star Baffles Director," *Los Angeles Times*, February 23, 1927, 23.

"News of the Theatres," *The Ventura Free Press*, June 27, 1927, 3.

"Not So Clear That West Has Been Help," *The Sporting News*, January 6, 1927, 3.

"Old Alex Admits He Didn't Walk Babe on Purpose," *The Tampa Tribune*, April 5, 1927, 15.

"Old Doc Rain Casts Pall over Stadium," *New York Daily News*, October 8, 1927, 98.

O'Leary, J. C., "Three New Men for Red Sox," *The Boston Globe*, July 10, 1914, 1.

———, "Red Sox Sell Ruth for $100,000 Cash," *The Boston Globe*, January 6, 1920, 1.

————, "More Than 34,000 Jammed Fenway Park," *The Boston Globe*, September 6, 1927, 1.

————, "Ruth Reels off Three Home Runs," *The Boston Globe*, September 7, 1927, 1.

————, "Red Sox Sell Ruth for $100,000 Cash," *The Boston Globe*, January 6, 1920, 1.

O'Malley, Austin, "Baseball Is Not on the Level, Says Former Twirler," *Wisconsin State Journal*, December 22, 1926, 15.

————, "Baseball Is Not on the Level, Says Former Twirler," *Wisconsin State Journal*, December 22, 1926, 15.

————, "Dutch Hints Cobb Dragged Tris into It," *Minneapolis Daily Star*, December 23, 1926, 11.

————, "Leonard Says Landis Broke Faith," *Modesto News Herald*, December 29, 1926. 1.

"On an Executive," *The Record*, June 11, 1927, 7.

"One Minute Interviews," *The Daily News*, February 11, 1927. 11.

"One of Yankees' Big Problems Is Getting Babe under Contract," *Associated Press*, October 12, 1926.

Peete, William, "Sport Flashes," *The Honolulu Advertiser*, January 12, 1927, 8.

Pegler, Westbrook, "Babe Sneers at Mere $52,000 for His Services Next Season," *The Commercial Appeal*, February 11, 1927, 17.

————, "Fans Criticize Landis, but Cobb and Speaker Demand No Hearing," *Sioux City Journal,* January 14, 1927, 13.

————, "Offer of $100,000 to Jimmy Walker Arouses Wrath of Babe Ruth's Boss," *Sioux City Journal*, April 25, 1927, 9.

————, "Physician Hopes to Have Slugger Ready for Tuesday's Game," *The Daily Times,* April 10, 1925, 28.

————, "Year of Keen Competition Seen Between Gotham Nines," *Atlanta Constitution*, February 22, 1927, 9.

"P.G.A. Champion Will Appear at Sunnyside Club," *The Fresno Morning Republican*, December 14, 1926, 13.

"Pitchers Must Throw Ball Faster to Fool Bambino," *Courier-Post*, September 20, 1921, 15.

Pittsburghbaseballhistory.com, Carmen Hill, October 1, 2020.

"Place in Sun Most Pleasing to Burly Babe," *Fall River Daily Globe*, March 26, 1919, 6.

"Players Award Thrills Gehrig," *The Spokesman-Review*, October 15, 1927, 15.

"Playing Truant Babe Ruth Sent to St. Mary's," *Buffalo Express*, February 4, 1923, 44.

Pusey, Otis, "McGovern to Train 'Big Bam,'" *The Deseret News*, January 29, 1927, 9.

Ray, Bob, "Babe Ruth, Home-Run Clouter and Actor Arrives Here for Week's Theatrical Sojourn," *Los Angeles Times*, January 3, 1927, 10.

————, "Bambino Wants Salary Raised," *Los Angeles Times*, February 10, 1927, 41.

"Red Sox Get Away to Great Start," *The Boston Globe*, April 24, 1919, 11.

Rice, Grantland, "Dull Game as Yanks Win Again," *The Pittsburgh Press*, October 7, 1927, 41.

———, "It Has Been Upon Higher Plan of Honesty Than Most Professional Sport," *Des Moines Tribune*, January 20, 1927, 19.

———, "The Sportlight," *The Baltimore Sun*, January 11, 1927, 12.

———, "The Sportlight," *The Boston Globe*, September 1, 1927, 19.

———, "The Sportlight," *The Miami Herald*, March 6, 1927, 25.

———, "The SportLight," *New York Tribune*, August 11, 1920, 18.

———, "Ball Fandom Turns Ear to Ban Johnson," *The Windsor Star*, December 23, 1926, 1.

Rice, Thomas S., "Ruth Sacrificed Himself as Martyr of Baseball: Now Works for the Team," *Brooklyn Daily Eagle*, April 8, 1925, 24.

———, "Ruth's True Skill Isn't Appreciated," *The Sporting News*, October 14, 1926. 1.

Ripley, Robert, "Believe It or Not," *The Akron Beacon Journal*, March 11, 1927, 34.

Rippingille, Frank, "14 Year Flyer Defends Cobb," *The Plain Speaker*, December 23, 1926, 13.

"'Risberg Should Be Boiled in Oil,' Ruth," *Los Angeles Daily News*, January 3, 1927, 16.

"Road Grind for Babe Ruth," *Press-Telegram*, February 4, 1927, 27.

Rohn, Harland, "Fans of Chicago Doubt Charges Laid to Idols," *Detroit Free Press*, December 24, 1926, 10.

"Royal Giants Beat Babe Ruth's Team," *Brooklyn Times Union*, October 12, 1926, 10.

Runyan, Damon, "Baseball Scandal Hits Cobb, Speaker," *The San Francisco Examiner*, December 22, 1926, 31.

———, "'Dutch' Leonard Pitches Brilliant Baseball in Decisive Fracas," *San Francisco Examiner*, October 12, 1915, 13.

———, "Goslin and Harris Hit Homers, Scoring 3 Runs," *The Morning Herald*, October 6, 1924, 10.

———, "Runyon Says," *Intelligencer Journal*, December 23, 1926, 14.

———, "Runyon Says," *The Evening News*, October 13, 1927, 22.

"Ruppert and Huston to Support Landis in Dealing with Ruth's Violation of League Rule," *New York Tribune*, October 18, 1921, 14.

"Ruppert Answers Scandal Mongers," *The Sporting News*, January 20, 1927, 1.

"Ruppert Brewery Multiplies Stock," *New York Times*, November 28, 1922, 1.

"Ruppert Says Yanks Sure of Repeat," *The Boston Globe*, April 4, 1927, 10.

"Ruppert Silent Awaits Salary Talk with Ruth," *Chicago Tribune*, March 1, 1927, 23.

"Ruth Arrested Gives Bail," *Petaluma Argus-Courier*, February 3, 1927, 7.

Ruth, "Babe," "All Pitchers Look Alike to the King of Batters," *Times Leader*, September 22, 1921, 14.

———, "Babe Ruth Explains How He Makes Home Runs; Uses Free Easy Swing," *The Evening World*, August 16, 1920, 3.

———, "Babe Ruth Has No Special Tricks for Specific Hurler," *Richmond Times-Dispatch*, September 22, 1921, 9.

————, "Babe Ruth's Own Story," *The Evening Sun*, August 10, 1920, 15.

————, "Babe Ruth's Own Story; Crowds Prove Scandal Hasn't Hurt Baseball," *The Press and Sun Bulletin*, April 13, 1927, 24.

————, "Babe Ruth Struck a Homer in First League Game," *The Evening World*, August 11, 1920, 3.

————, "Babe Ruth Tells How He Came Back," *The Courier-Journal*, December 12, 1926, 84.

————, "Babe Ruth Tells of Year He Lost the 'Batting Eye'; Didn't Keep Optic on Ball," *The Evening World,* August 13, 1920, 3.

————, "Babe Ruth Tells the Inside Story of His Come-Back," *Tacoma Daily Ledger*, January 16, 1927, 19

————, "Big League for Babe Ruth Achieved in First Year," *The Evening World*, August 12, 1920, 3.

————, "Don't Quit Too Soon Is Word from Babe Ruth," *Minneapolis Star*, October 1, 1927, 14.

————, "Got Chance on School Nine, Made Good with Home Run," *The Evening World*, August 9, 1920, 3.

————, "Letter to Colonel Jacob Ruppert," *New York Daily News*, February 27, 1927, 167.

————, "No Series Hero Ruth Thinks," *The Courier-Journal*, October 10, 1927, 6.

————, "Ruth Says Crooked Players Should Be Barred Forever," *The Times Dispatch*, August 7, 1921, 14.

————, "'There Goes Our Team,' Boy Said of Babe," *The Evening World*, August 10, 1920, 3.

————, "We Won't Have to Return to Pittsburgh Says Bambino," *San Francisco Examiner*, October 7, 1927, 6.

"Ruth Comes Back to Baseball for Period," *The Palm Beach Post*, February 26, 1927, 9.

"Ruth Flops from King to Jester," *The Sporting News*, September 10, 1925, 1.

Ruth, George Herman, and Helen Ruth, Separation Agreement, August 1925, Babe Ruth Archives, National Baseball Library, Giamatti Research Center.

"Ruth in Fine Shape," *The Berkshire Evening Eagle*, February 18, 1927, 22.

"Ruth in the Sickroom," *The Pittsburgh Post*, October 13, 1926, 6.

"Ruth Is Hero Where Once Cobb Reigned," *The Sporting News*, August 12, 1920, 3.

"Ruth Is Record Breaker," *The Richmond Item*, September 28, 1927, 9.

"Ruth Passes Lou! Hits 28 and 29! Yanks Win First," *New York Daily News*, July 10, 1927, 54.

"Ruth Plays Role of Innocent Abroad on His Visit to Cuba," *The Sporting News*, January 13, 1921, 6.

"Ruth Sends Letter to Yanks but No Contract," *St. Louis Star and Times*, February 22, 1927, 12.

"Ruth Sets Record Heydler Declares," *The Boston Globe*, September 9, 1919, 8.

"Ruth Signs Three-Year Contract for $210,000," *Los Angeles Times*, March 3, 1927, 41.

"Ruth Tells Story of the Big Series," *The Lima News*, October 16, 1927, 25.

"Ruth Twice a Hero," *Port Chester Daily Item*, October 13, 1926, 6.

"Ruth Visits Sick Boy," *Lexington Leader*, October 12, 1926, 5.

"Ruth Will Be Fit for Seasons Opening, Appetite Laid Him Low," *The Brooklyn Standard Union*, April 8, 1925, 16.

"Ruth-O-Meter," *Arizona Republican*, July 27, 1927, 6.

"Ruth's Demand Is too High Says Colonel," *Los Angeles Record*, February 28, 1927, 9.

Ryder, Jack, "Bank-Roll Babe Injured in Game," *The Enquirer*, March 11, 1927, 14.

"Same Case Retried Says Ban Johnson," *The Des Moines Register*, January 13, 1927, 16.

Sanborn, I. E., "New Power Soon Rules Baseball with an Iron Hand," *Chicago Tribune*, October 1, 1920, 19.

Savage, C. J., "Moore Terms Hornsby One of the Heaviest Gamblers He Has Served," *The Courier-Journal*, January 12, 1927, 13.

"Says Hornsby Bet $70,000 on Races in Two Months," *St. Louis Post-Dispatch*, January 22, 1927, 1.

"Scandal Evidence Not Revealed until Last Summer, Navis Says," *Pittsburgh Daily Post*, December 22, 1926,13.

"Science Explains 'Babe' Ruth's Home Runs," *San Francisco Examiner*, July 25, 1920, 68.

"Scribbled by Scribe," *The Sporting News*, August 5, 1920, 4.

"Scribbled by Scribe," *The Sporting News*, August 23, 1920, 4.

"Scribbled by Scribe," *The Sporting News*, December 30, 1926, 4.

"Senate May Seek Baseball Truth," *El Paso Herald*, December 29, 1926, 5.

"Send Hornsby Back, St. Louis Plea to Landis," *Chicago Tribune,* December 22, 1926, 25.

"Send Hornsby Back, St. Louis Plea to Landis," *Chicago Tribune*, December 22, 1926, 22.

"S.F. Baseball Fans Await Ruth, Gehrig," *San Francisco Examiner*, October 9, 1927, 36.

Shaffer, Rosalind, "Babe Ruth's Film Venture Recalls Other Hits and Flops," *New York Daily News,* March 6, 1927, 70.

Shand, Bob, "Grist from the Sports Mill," *Oakland Tribune*, October 7, 2021, 25.

"Sluggers Ego Causes Sale, Frazee Says," *The Washington Post*, January 7, 1920, 9.

Small, Robert T., "Ruth Remains One of Few Baseball Heroes in Eyes of Boys," *Los Angeles Evening Express*, December 25, 1926, 19.

"Sore with Barrow," *Boston Post*, July 4, 1918, 7.

"Sox Games Framed—Gandil," *Chicago Tribune*, January 7, 1927, 19.

"Speaker Will Appeal to Courts in Scandal," *The Pittsburgh Daily Post,* December 23, 1926, 13.

"Sporting," *The Berkshire Eagle*, September 6, 1927, 4.

"Statement by West," *The Boston Globe*, December 30, 1926, 21.

"Statements of Players in New Baseball Scandal," *Chicago Tribune*, December 22, 1926, 26.

"Sues Mrs. Hornsby for $505," *St. Louis Post-Dispatch*, February 5, 1927, 2.

"Sunnyside," *The Fresno Bee*, October 6, 1924, 9.

"Suppose Babe Had Not Missed That Swing," *The Standard Union*, April 20, 1927, 10.

"Swats His Way into Screen Stardom," *St. Albans Daily Messenger*, May 16, 1927, 5.

"Syndicate Is Organized by Christy Walsh," *Oakland Tribune*, April 24, 1921, 10.

"The Bambino, Year's Big Drama Fizzles Out to Childish Comedy," *The Sporting News*, September 10, 1925, 1.

"The Caper Who Taught Babe Ruth to Hit Homeruns," *CapeBretonToday.com*, 2019. https://capebreton.lokol.me/the-man-who-taught-babe-ruth-to-hit-home-runs. Accessed July 8, 2022.

"The Day on the Circuit," *The Brooklyn Daily Eagle*, September 24, 1925, 24.

"The Inquiring Reporter," *Chicago Tribune,* February 20, 1927, 31.

"The Old Sports Musings," *The Philadelphia Inquirer*, February 14, 1927, 14.

"The Screen," *The Evening Journal*, June 24, 1927, 25.

"The Town Slouch," *The Orlando Sentinel*, March 11, 1927, 4.

"The World Series Put to Bed," *The Morning Call*, October 11, 1927, 18.

Thirer, Irene, "Babe Ruth as Film Star Won't Get Broadway Run," *New York Daily News*, June 8, 1927, 152.

"This Is What They Wrote," *Detroit Free Press*, December 22, 1926, 16.

"Thomas Alva Edison Slams Ty's Curve," *Florida State News*, March 8, 1927, 5.

Thompson, Denman, "Pirates Face Nearly Hopeless Task," *Washington Star*, October 7, 1927, 34.

"Three Ball Clubs Are Charged in Two Deals," *Coshocton Tribune*, January 3, 1927, 3.

"To Accompany Babe Ruth," *The Evening Sun,* September 2, 1920, 16.

Tosetti, Linda Ruth, Presentation to New York Giants Preservation Society, September 9, 2021.

"Tris Speaker and Cobb in Baseball Scandal," *Los Angeles Times*, December 22, 1926, 1.

"Tris Speaker Resigns as Manager of Cleveland Team," *The Baltimore Sun*, November 30, 1926, 14.

"Two Sox Confess," *Chicago Tribune*, September 29, 1920, 1.

"Ty and Tris Scandal Rocks Sports World to Its Foundations," *Oakland Tribune*, December 22, 1926, 17.

"Ty Cobb Becomes Ill at Asheville," *Atlanta Journal Constitution*, December 6, 1926, 7.

"Ty Cobb Demands That Judge Landis Give Decision in Baseball's Latest Scandal," *The Dayton Herald*, December 24, 1926, 12.

"Ty Cobb Flop as Manager—Navin," *New York Daily News*, December 24, 1926, 24.

"Ty Cobb, Speaker Plan Defense to Dutch's Attack," *Modesto News-Herald*, December 29, 1926, 10.

"Ty Says American Heads Are Guilty," *The Philadelphia Inquirer*, December 24, 1926, 17.

"U.S. Senators Defend Cobb and Speaker," *Chicago Tribune*, December 25, 1926, 15.

Van Pelt, Jack, "Stewart Knocked from the Mound," *St. Louis Star*, July 19, 1927, 15.

"Vaudeville," *Minneapolis Daily Star*, November 1, 1926, 6.

Vaughan Irving, "Babe Ruth, Mad, Denies Orgies; Here to Fight," *Chicago Tribune*, August 31, 1925, 1.

————, "Cobb, Speaker Will Fight Charges," *New York Daily News*, December 23, 1926, 32.

————, "Hearing Ends, Landis Rules Wednesday," *Chicago Tribune*, January 8, 1927, 19.

————, "Landis Meeting with American League Is Off," *Chicago Tribune*, January 24, 1927, 23.

————, "Ruppert Seeks Showdown on Johnson," *Chicago Tribune*, January 20, 1927, 15.

————, "Vaughn Believes Johnson Will Tender Resignation," *The Sporting News*, January 27, 1927, 1.

Vila, Joe, "Not Conscious Alone That Caused Ruth to Change Tack," *The Sporting News*, October 27, 1921, 1.

————, "Ruppert Answers Scandal Mongers," *The Sporting News*, January 20, 1927, 1.

Vore, F. H., "Leonard's Statement," *The Fresno Bee*, December 29, 1926, 10.

Wadhams, Phil, "The Price of Honor," *Lincoln State Journal*, December 24, 1926, 7.

Walsh, Christy, "Babe Ruth Scrapbook," Volume 1, Part 3, National Baseball Library, Giamatti Research Center.

————, "Carry Pencil When Writing Christy Says," *The Birmingham News*, September 7, 1937, 20.

————, "Ruth's Ghost Era Closed in Wane of 1936," *The Birmingham News*, October 4, 1937, 11.

————, "Walsh Tells of His First Feature Job," *The Birmingham News*, October 2, 1937, 9.

Walsh, Davis J., "Heilmann Is Credited with Forcing Expose," *Minneapolis Star Tribune*, December 23, 1926, 25.

————, "Heilmann Is Credited with Forcing Expose," *The Minneapolis Morning Tribune*, December 23, 1926. 25.

————, "More Interest Manifested in Baseball than at Any Time in Past Years," *The Dayton Herald*, April 11, 1927, 16.

————, "N.Y. Sports Editor Understands Rog Bet Way Out of St. Louis," *The St. Louis Star and Times*, January 11, 1927, 12.

————, "Stampede for Stars Starts," *Port Chester Daily Item*, January 28, 1927, 6.

"Walsh Publicity Man for Greer-Robbins," *Los Angeles Express*, May 2, 1914, 5.

"Walsh to Visit Parents," *Los Angeles Times*, November 21, 1926, 51.

Ward, Arch, "In the Wake of the News," *Chicago Tribune*, November 27, 1944, 19.

"Warrant for Bambino Is Served in Bathtub," *New York Tribune,* May 4, 1921, 12.

Webb, Melvin, "He May Slump Occasionally but He's the Same Old "Batting Babe" After All," *Boston Globe*, September 7, 1927, 12.

Welsh, Regis M., "Called 'Rat' by Old Friend," *The Pittsburgh Daily Post*, December 24, 1926, 11.

————,"Pennock's Hurling Enables Yanks to Win," *Pittsburgh Post-Gazette*, October 8, 1927, 1.

————, "Violators of Public Confidence, Two Greats Pay Penalty," *The Pittsburgh Post*, December 23, 1926, 1.

————, "Violators of Public Confidence, Two Greats Pay Penalty," *The Pittsburgh Daily Post*, December 23, 1926, 13.

"We Threw World Series, Cicotte, Jackson Admit," *Chicago Tribune*, September 29, 1920, 1.

"West Clears Cobb, Speaker," *New York Daily News*, December 30, 1926, 124.

"West's Story Sounds to Leonard 'Like A Laugh,'" *Boston Globe*, December 30, 1926, 21.

"What Chick Gandil and Bill James Told Landis," *Chicago Tribune*, January 8, 1927, 20.

White, Paul W., "Yanks Run Riot in Celebration of Triumph," *The Standard Union*, October 9, 1927, 18.

Williams, Joe, "Another Good Man Goes Wrong," *Knoxville News-Sentinel*, December 10, 1927, 7.

————, "Christy Walsh Is Interesting Character," *The Pittsburgh Press*, August 1, 1927, 23.

————, "Dutch Leonard Railroaded Out," *Knoxville News*, September 28, 1925, 3.

————, "The Nut Cracker," *Muncie Evening Press*, December 28, 1926, 7.

Wilson, Bob, "Talk Sport," *Knoxville News Sentinel*, April 6, 1927, 13.

Wilson, J. J., "Psychologists Discover Why Ruth Is 30 Percent More Efficient than Other Baseball Players," *El Paso Herald*, September 19, 1921, 4.

Winkworth, Joe, "Home Run King Insists He'll Rise to Greatest Heights in 1926," *Buffalo Labor Journal*, November 12, 1925, 2.

————, "'I've Been the Sappiest of Saps'—Ruth," *The Sporting News*, November 5, 1926, 2.

Woltz, Larry, "Cobb a Broken Man as He Sobs Denial," *Wisconsin State Journal*, December 22, 1926, 15.

"Wood Keeps Silent," *The Windsor Star*, December 23, 1926, 13.

Woody Wilke, conversation with the author, July 18, 2022.

"Writers Back Players," *Pittsburgh Post-Gazette*, December 24, 1926, 14.

"Yankee Star on Way East," *Los Angeles Times*, February 27, 1927, 1.

"Yankees Buy Babe Ruth for Record Sum of About $150,000," *New York Tribune*, January 6, 1920, 1.

"Yankees to Continue at Polo Grounds," *New York Herald*, May 22, 1920, 11.

"Yanks Buy Babe Ruth for $125,000," *The New York Times*, January 6, 1920, 16.

"Young Babe Ruth Patient's Hitting Homer to Health," *New York Daily News*, October 17, 1926, 44.

Zucco, Tom, "Babe Ruth Put on a Show to Remember," *St. Petersburg Times*, February 6, 1995, 1.

Index

About the Author

Dan Taylor is a former award-winning television sportscaster and the author of six books. In addition to *Baseball at the Abyss*, his works include *Walking Alone* and the acclaimed *Lights, Camera, Fastball*, which was a finalist for the 2021 Casey Award for best baseball book of the year. Mr. Taylor's prior works include *Rise of the Bulldogs*, *A Scout's Report*, and *Fate's Take Out Slide*.

During his thirty-year career as a television sportscaster, Taylor was the recipient of the Associated Press Award for best California sportscast. He is currently the television broadcaster for the Fresno Grizzlies.